best of the

best

Editor in Chief **Judith Hill**

Art Director **Perri DeFino**

Managing Editor **Terri Mauro**

Project Manager **Dana Speers**

Designer **Leslie Andersen**

Editorial Associate **Colleen McKinney**

Production Coordinator **Stuart Handelman**

Vice President, Publisher **Mark V. Stanich**

Vice President, Marketing **Bruce Rosner**

Director, Retail Sales **Marshall Corey**

Operations Manager **Catherine A. Bussey**

Business Manager **Joanne Ragazzo**

ISBN: 0-916103-61-7   ISSN: 1524-2862

best of the best

FOOD & WINE presents

best

the best recipes from the year's
25 best cookbooks

American Express Publishing Corporation
New York FOOD & WINE BOOKS

contents

introduction

We've never seen a year so dominated by chefs. Two of our categories—half the book—are devoted to them, whether TV or restaurant or both. Additionally, in a third category, Dessert Books, more than three-quarters of the winners were written by chefs, too. Why such an interest in professionals? The impact of cooking shows can't be denied. The public's heightened awareness of chefs has apparently fostered a huge market for their books. Whatever the reason, we can all enjoy the outpouring of great recipes; we think this is the most luscious group of dishes we've presented in our three years of annual Best of the Best awards.

That said, we didn't plan to make such chef-heavy selections. Whereas many awards choose their categories first and then find books to fill them, we simply pick the best 25 books published over the course of the year and let them dictate the categories. First we read the cookbooks; that's round one, in which we reduce the hundreds of hardbacks published in America each year to about 50. Then we test and test and test, and taste and taste and taste (generally gaining five to ten pounds apiece in the process) to determine the best books and their best recipes—the best of the best. This year, many chef's collections rose to the top of the crop.

In presenting their recipes, we've made only those changes necessary to make our book convenient to use. What you see here is what you'll read in the cookbooks themselves, with the language, recipe style, and idiosyncracies intact insofar as possible. Photos and illustrations are included to give you a taste of the books as well as a preview of the delicious dishes.

Once again this year, the very cream of the crop, the best of the best of the best, is honored with our Editor's Choice Awards. But every book in this collection is a winner.

Judith Hill

Judith Hill, Editor in Chief
FOOD & WINE Books

editor's choice awards

best cookbook of the year

Spago Chocolate by Mary Bergin and Judy Gethers, p. 124

published by Random House, Inc.

Carefully written, always accurate recipes for easy, delectable desserts—and they're all chocolate. Who could ask for anything more?

best recipe of the year

Potato Gratin Forestier Café Boulud Cookbook by Daniel Boulud, p. 59

published by Scribner

And you thought *pommes dauphinoise* couldn't get any better. Leave it to the great Chef Boulud to make this traditional dish more luscious than ever.

best-written cookbook of the year

The Cook and the Gardener by Amanda Hesser, p. 194

published by W. W. Norton & Company, Inc.

At last, another exquisite food writer to take up where M. F. K. Fisher left off. Read together, the chapter introductions constitute a compelling novella.

best photography of the year

The French Laundry Cookbook by Thomas Keller, p. 10

photographs by Deborah Jones
published by Artisan

The oversize pages give plenty of play to the photographs, and they surely deserve it. They're luscious, informative, and inventive. An outrageously gorgeous book.

recipes by course

Restaurant chefs rule the saucepans of the nation. Americans are eating out more than ever before, and if the number of chefs' cookbooks being published is any indication, we want to make the same kind of food at home (or at least read about it). The look and feel of each book in this category matches its restaurant's cuisine and ambience—from the simple, friendly Rose Pistola to the tradition-rooted, yet offbeat Chez Panisse to the refined, *trés sérieuse* hauteness of the French Laundry. Clearly restaurant-style cooking, whatever the ilk, is the hot topic, just like low-fat/no-fat was a few years ago. But, happily, *this* trend is giving us a feast of spectacular recipes.

restaurant cookbooks

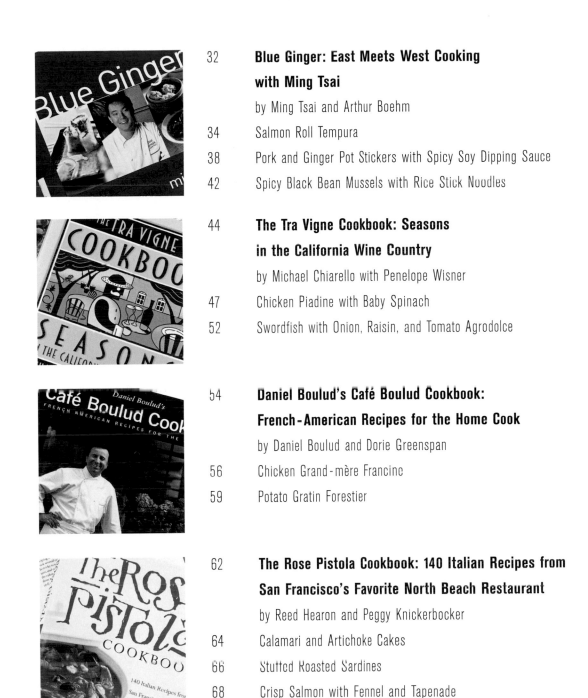

category one

the french laundry cookbook

author

Thomas Keller, chef-owner of the celebrated French Laundry restaurant, located in the town of Yountville in California's Napa Valley.

why he wrote it

To make us slow down and enjoy cooking. "Cooking is not about convenience and it's not about shortcuts. The recipes in this book are about wanting to take the time to do something that I think is priceless. Our hunger for the twenty-minute gourmet meal, for one-pot ease and prewashed, precut ingredients has severed our lifeline to the satisfactions of cooking. Take your time. Take a long time. Move slowly and deliberately and with great attention."

why it made our list

Many restaurant cookbooks take pride in translating their elaborate recipes into simpler dishes, but Keller takes the opposite tack. The recipes in this stunning book are presented in all their complexity, tricky techniques and legions of sub-recipes intact. Though the directions are carefully written and thus accessible to the home cook, these are dishes you will have to set aside a significant portion of the day to prepare. Will the results be as good as you'd get at the restaurant? "You're not going to duplicate the dish that I made," concedes Keller. "You may create something that in composition resembles what I made, but more important—and this is my greatest hope—you're going to create something that you have deep respect and feelings and passions for."

from the book

"Get a few heavy-bottomed pots and pans—you don't need dozens. Buy two good baking sheets that don't buckle in the heat. And look for a great butcher and a good fishmonger with whom you can develop relationships. Use common sense when following a recipe. If it calls for a pan on high heat, but the food is burning, it's probably too hot. If a piece of meat looks as if it's overcooking, it probably is, so take it out even if it hasn't been in as long as the recipe says."

specifics

326 pages, 150 recipes, 212 color photographs.
chapters Canapés › First Course › Fish › Meat › Cheese › Dessert
$50. Published by Artisan.

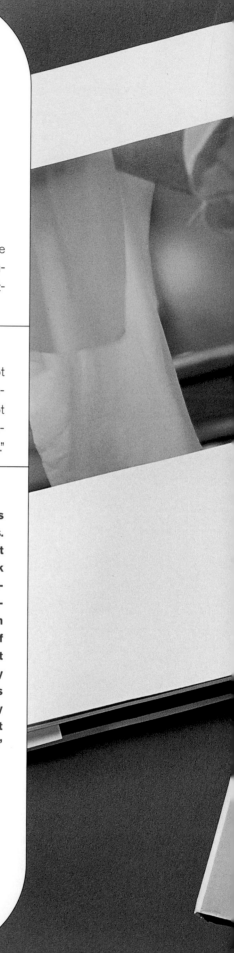

THE FRENCH LAUNDRY COOKBOOK
THOMAS KELLER

sweet potato agnolotti with sage cream, brown butter, and prosciutto

MAKES 6 SERVINGS

For a fall agnolotti, I like a sweet potato filling; it's denser than the traditional version made from the more watery pumpkin. With the cream, butter, and prosciutto, this is a very rich and delicious dish.

SWEET POTATO FILLING

1½ **pounds sweet potatoes**

8 **tablespoons (4 ounces) unsalted butter**

2 **slices bacon, frozen and cut into ¼-inch dice**

Pinch of Squab Spice (page 14) or allspice and nutmeg

Kosher salt and freshly ground black pepper

½ **recipe Pasta Dough (page 14)**

SAGE CREAM

⅓ **cup sage leaves (from about 4 bunches; use the smaller leaves for the fried sage leaf garnish)**

1 **cup crème fraîche**

1 **cup Beurre Monté (page 17)**

Pinch of kosher salt, or to taste

Canola oil for deep-frying

48 **tiny sage leaves (reserved from above)**

2 **tablespoons (1 ounce) unsalted butter**

4 **thin slices prosciutto, cut crosswise into fine julienne**

FOR THE SWEET POTATO FILLING Preheat the oven to 350°F.

Cut the ends off the potatoes and wrap the potatoes individually in aluminum foil, dividing 4 tablespoons of the butter evenly among them. Bake until they are soft, 1 to 2 hours (the time will vary, depending on the size of the potatoes).

Unwrap the cooked potatoes and cut a slit lengthwise in the skin of each. Pull the skin away from the potato and discard. Push the potatoes through a potato ricer while they are hot and place in a saucepan.

Place the diced bacon in a skillet. Cook until it is lightly browned and the fat has been rendered. Transfer the bacon pieces to paper towels to drain briefly, then add them to the potatoes.

Stir the potatoes over low heat, seasoning to taste with the squab spice and salt and pepper. Mix in the remaining 4 tablespoons butter. You will have about 1⅔ cups filling (enough to fill 48 agnolotti). Refrigerate the filling until chilled, or for up to 2 days, before filling the agnolotti.

Roll out the dough and fill the agnolotti according to the instructions on pages 15 and 16. You should have approximately 48 agnolotti.

TO COMPLETE For the sage cream, blanch the sage leaves in boiling water for 2 minutes. Drain, cool in cold water, and drain again. Squeeze the leaves dry.

Heat the crème fraîche, beurre monté, and salt over low heat until hot: do not boil. Place the sage in a blender and process to chop it. With the motor running, pour the hot cream mixture through the top and blend thoroughly. Strain the cream into a large skillet. Check the seasoning and set aside.

In a small pot, heat oil for deep-frying to 275°F. Fry the small sage leaves briefly, just until they are crisp (their color should not change), and drain on paper towels.

Place the butter in a skillet over medium heat and cook to a nutty brown color; reduce the heat and keep warm.

Meanwhile, cook the agnolotti in a large pot of lightly salted boiling water until cooked through, 4 to 5 minutes.

Drain the cooked agnolotti and mix them gently with the sage cream sauce over low heat. Divide the agnolotti among six serving dishes and drizzle with the browned butter. Scatter some prosciutto over each serving and garnish with the fried sage leaves.

squab spice

MAKES ABOUT ⅓ CUP

¼   **stick cinnamon, broken into small pieces**

1   **tablespoon coriander seeds**

1½ **teaspoons cloves**

2   **tablespoons quatre-épices (four-spice powder)**

2   **tablespoons black peppercorns**

Toast the cinnamon, coriander, cloves, and quatre-épices in a small skillet over low heat until fragrant.

Finely grind the toasted spices with the black pepper in a spice or coffee grinder. Sift through a fine-mesh strainer, stirring with a spoon. Store in a sealed container at room temperature or in the freezer. (The squab spice begins to lose some of its intensity after a few days; freeze for longer storage and use directly from the freezer.)

pasta dough

MAKES ABOUT 14 OUNCES DOUGH

1¾ **cups (8 ounces) all-purpose flour**

6   **large egg yolks**

1   **large egg**

1½ **teaspoons olive oil**

1   **tablespoon milk**

Mound the flour on a board or other surface and create a well in the center, pushing the flour to all sides to make a ring with sides about 1 inch wide. Make sure that the well is wide enough to hold all the eggs without spilling.

Pour the egg yolks, egg, oil, and milk into the well. Use your fingers to break the eggs up. Still using your fingers, begin turning the eggs in a circular motion, keeping them within the well and not allowing them to spill over the sides. This circular motion allows the eggs to gradually pull in flour from the sides of the well; it is important that the flour not be incorporated too rapidly, or your dough will be lumpy. Keep moving the eggs while slowly incorporating the flour. Using a pastry scraper, occasionally push the flour toward the eggs; the flour should be moved only enough to maintain the gradual incorporation of the flour, and the eggs should continue to be contained within the well. The mixture will thicken and eventually get too tight to keep turning with your fingers.

When the dough begins thickening and starts lifting itself from the board, begin incorporating the remaining flour with the pastry scraper by lifting the flour up and over the dough that's beginning to form and cutting it into the dough. When the remaining flour from the sides of the well has been cut into the dough, the dough will still look shaggy. Bring the dough together with the palms of your hands and form it into a ball. It will look flaky but will hold together.

Knead the dough by pressing it, bit by bit, in a forward motion with the heels of your hands rather than folding it over on itself as you would with a bread dough. Re-form the dough into a ball and repeat the process several times. The dough should feel moist but not sticky. Let the dough rest for a few minutes while you clean the work surface.

Dust the clean work surface with a little flour. Knead the dough by pushing against it in a forward motion with the heels of your hands. Form the dough into a ball again and knead it again. Keep kneading in this forward motion until the dough becomes silky-smooth. The dough is ready when you can pull your finger through it and the dough wants to snap back into place. The kneading process can take anywhere from 10 to 15 minutes. Even if you think you are finished kneading, knead it for an extra 10 minutes; you cannot overknead this dough. It is important to work the dough long enough to pass the pull test; otherwise, when it rests, it will collapse.

Double-wrap the dough in plastic wrap to ensure that it does not dry out. Let the dough rest for at least 30 minutes and up to 1 hour before rolling it through a pasta machine. The dough can be made a day ahead, wrapped, and refrigerated; bring to room temperature before proceeding.

TO FORM SHEETS FOR AGNOLOTTI Use ½ recipe pasta dough, divided into two or three pieces. Set the rollers of the pasta machine at the widest setting. Run one piece of the pasta dough through the machine and keep the others wrapped in plastic wrap. Fold the dough in half, end to end, turn it a quarter turn, and run it through the same setting again. Repeat this procedure two more times.

Set the openings of the rollers down one notch and run the pasta through. Do not fold it over. Decrease the opening another notch and run the dough through again. Continue the process until the sheet of pasta is quite thin (there may be a recommended setting for your machine: if not, the next-to-the-thinnest setting is usually best). Repeat with the next piece of pasta.

The size will vary according to the pasta machine used, but the sheets should be at least 5 inches wide. It is important that our pasta sheet be thin enough so that you can see your fingers through it, but not so thin that it's translucent. Keep the pasta sheets covered, as they dry out quickly. and proceed with filling the agnolotti.

TO FILL AGNOLOTTI If you are planning on using the agnolotti immediately, have a large pot of lightly salted boiling water ready. Work with one sheet of pasta at a time, keeping the remaining sheets covered. Work quickly, as fresh pasta will dry out.

Lay the pasta sheet on a lightly floured work surface with a long side facing you. Trim the edges so they are straight. Place the agnolotti filling in a pastry bag fitted with a ½-inch plain tip. Pipe a "tube" of filling across the bottom of the pasta sheet, leaving a ¾-inch border of pasta along the left, right, and bottom edges.

Pull the bottom edge of the pasta up and over the filling. Seal the agnolotti by carefully molding the pasta over the filling and pressing lightly with your index finger to seal the edge of the dough to the pasta sheet: don't drag your finger along the dough to seal, or you risk ripping the dough. When it is sealed, there should be about ½ inch of excess dough visible above the tube of filling (where you sealed it). Be certain that you are sealing tightly while pressing out any pockets of air. Seal the left and right ends of the dough.

TO SHAPE AGNOLOTTI Starting at one end, place the thumb and forefinger of each hand together as if you were going to pinch something and, leaving about 1 inch of space between your hands and holding your fingers vertically, pinch the filling in 1-inch increments, making about ¾ inch of "pinched" area between each pocket of filling. It is important to leave this much "pinched" area between the agnolotti, or when the agnolotti are separated, they may come unsealed.

Run a crimped pastry wheel along the top edge of the folded-over dough, separating the strip of filled pockets from the remainder of the pasta sheet. Don't cut too close to the filling, or you risk breaking the seal. Separate the individual agnolotti by cutting through the center of each pinched area, rolling the pastry wheel away from you. Working quickly, place the agnolotti on a baking sheet dusted with a thin layer of cornmeal, which will help prevent sticking. Don't let the agnolotti touch each other, or they may stick together.

Repeat the same procedure on the remainder of your pasta sheets. Either cook the agnolotti immediately in the boiling water, or place the baking sheet in the freezer. Once the agnolotti are frozen, place them in airtight freezer bags and keep them frozen for up to several weeks. Cook the agnolotti while still frozen.

beurre monté:
the workhorse sauce

At the French Laundry, we use an awful lot of butter without actually serving a lot of butter, because of our reliance on the substance called beurre monté. We cook in it, rest meats in it, make sauces with it. It's an extraordinary vehicle for both heat and flavor. Butter in its solid state is an emulsification of butter fat, milk solids, and water. If you melt butter, these three components separate, but beurre monté—a few drops of water and chunks of butter whisked over moderate heat—is a method of melting butter while maintaining the emulsification.

We use beurre monté in many different ways and for different reasons. Poaching lobster in it is one of its primary uses. Its flesh impregnated with the flavor of butter, this lobster reminds me of Maine lobster that you eat with drawn butter, and for me that's what lobster is all about.

Poaching lobster in beurre monté is also an easy way to cook it. Beurre monté stays between 180° and 190°F in our kitchen (it will break, or separate, if you boil it) and therefore it's always at a perfect poaching temperature. Butter-poached lobster is meltingly tender, moist, and flavorful. And because of the gentle temperature, it's harder to overcook it; once the lobster hits the right point of doneness, it stays there for a while. Butter-poached lobster is easy to do at home: Make your beurre monté, bring it to 160° to 190°F, pop your cleaned room-temperature tails and claws into it, and let them poach for 5 to 6 minutes.

We also use beurre monté to baste meats, and this has several purposes. When we sauté beef or venison or a saddle of lamb, we typically finish cooking it in the oven. But before we do, we drain the fat out of the pan and ladle a little beurre monté over the meat. This helps to keep the meat moist, enhances the flavor, and also improves the cooking, because the even layer of fat—the beurre monté—is a heat conductor. (We always let the pan cool down a little, though; if the pan's too hot, the beurre monté will separate and the solids will burn.)

When the meats are done, they come out of the oven and are submerged in beurre monté—it's the perfect resting medium. It actually lowers the temperature of the meat, reducing what is called carryover cooking, then maintains it at a great serving temperature. But most important, the weight of the fat surrounding the meat keeps the meat juices from leaking out—they stay in the meat. So here, we use beurre monté as environmental control, and it enhances the flavor.

And finally, what we don't use, we simply clarify the next day and then use this clear butter for hollandaise or for sautéing scallops, for cooking soft-shelled crabs, crêpes, potato chips. You can do that too, or simply refrigerate it and use it the same way you'd use whole butter for cooking.

PREPARING BEURRE MONTÉ A little bit of water helps the emulsion process: Whether you emulsify 4 tablespoons (2 ounces) or 1 pound of butter, just a tablespoon of water will do. Any amount of beurre monté can be made using the following method.

Bring the water to a boil in an appropriate-size saucepan. Reduce the heat to low and begin whisking the chunks of butter into the water, bit by bit, to emulsify. Once you have established the emulsion, you can continue to add pieces of butter until you have the quantity of beurre monté that you need (we make 20 pounds at a time). It is important to keep the level of heat gentle and consistent in order to maintain the emulsification. Make the beurre monté close to the time it will be used and keep it in a warm place. If you have extra beurre monté, it can be refrigerated and then reheated to use as melted butter or clarified.

black sea bass with sweet parsnips, arrowleaf spinach, and saffron-vanilla sauce

MAKES 6 SERVINGS

Black sea bass is an extremely versatile fish because of its neutral flavor and sturdy texture; it allows you to use your imagination in both cooking method and in the combinations of flavors you want. It's a good fish to cook with the skin on, both for the dramatic visual appeal and for the flavor. This dish is a contrast in textures: the crisp skin on the moist flesh of the fish, and the toasty exterior of the spinach balls surrounding their soft interior. The sauce uses a mussel stock, but not the cooked mussels.

MUSSEL STOCK

18   **mussels, scrubbed and debearded**

2   **large cloves garlic, peeled**

1   **large shallot, peeled**

4   **sprigs thyme**

2   **bay leaves**

1   **cup crisp, dry white wine, preferably Sauvignon Blanc**

SPINACH

Three 2-inch strips orange zest (removed with a vegetable peeler)

¾   **teaspoon olive oil**

6   **ounces spinach, washed and tough stems removed**

Kosher salt

2   **teaspoons unsalted butter**

PARSNIP PURÉE

2   **parsnips (about 5 ounces), peeled**

1   **cup plus 1 tablespoon heavy cream**

½   **cup water**

Pinch of kosher salt

1   **teaspoon unsalted butter**

SAFFRON VANILLA SAUCE

½   vanilla bean, split

Reserved 1 cup mussel stock (from above)

¼   teaspoon saffron threads

1½ teaspoons heavy cream

10   tablespoons (5 ounces) unsalted butter, cut into 8 pieces

BASS

Canola oil

Six 2- by 3-inch pieces black sea bass fillet (about 6 ounces each),

     skin on (see On Crisping Skin, page 22)

Kosher salt and freshly ground white pepper

FOR THE MUSSEL STOCK Place the mussels in a pot with the garlic, shallot, thyme, bay leaves, and wine. Cover the pot and bring to a boil; remove each mussel as soon as it opens. Reserve the mussels for another use. Strain the mussel stock through a chinois (see page 23).

FOR THE SPINACH Place the strips of orange zest in a large skillet with the olive oil. Heat the oil until it is hot and the zest begins to ripple from the heat. Add the spinach and sprinkle with salt (seasoning the spinach before it wilts ensures even seasoning). Cook the spinach until it wilts, then continue to cook for another 2 to 3 minutes to evaporate the moisture. Remove the spinach from the pan and separate it into 6 parts. Take each pile of spinach, place it in a clean tea towel, and twist the towel around the spinach to squeeze out any remaining liquid and form a compact ball. Remove from the towel. Refrigerate the spinach balls until ready to complete the dish.

FOR THE PARSNIP PUREE Slice the parsnips lengthwise in half. Beginning at the narrow end, cut ½-inch pieces. When the parsnip half widens, about one third of the way up, split it lengthwise again and continue to cut. (You want to keep the pieces about the same size.)

Place the cut parsnips in a saucepan with 1 cup of the heavy cream, the water, and salt. Bring to a boil, lower the heat, and simmer gently for 25 to 30 minutes, or until the parsnips are completely soft. Strain the parsnips, reserving the cream, and scrape the parsnips through a tamis (see page 23) with a plastic scraper. Put the purée in a bowl and stir in enough of the strained cream to give them the texture of mashed potatoes. Transfer to a small saucepan and keep in a warm place.

Preheat the oven to 350°F.

FOR THE SAFFRON-VANILLA SAUCE Scrape the seeds from the vanilla bean into a small saucepan and add the vanilla pod, mussel stock, and saffron threads. Bring the stock to a simmer, then simmer until reduced to a glaze (1 to 1½ tablespoons). Add the cream and simmer for a few more seconds. Over medium heat, whisk in the butter bit by bit (as you would for beurre monté). It is critical to maintain the sauce at the correct temperature, as it can break if it becomes too hot or cold. Strain the sauce and mix for several seconds with an immersion blender to emulsify (if you don't have an immersion blender, you can use a regular one, but rinse out the blender container with hot water before adding the sauce, so it stays warm). Keep the sauce in a warm place.

TO COMPLETE Melt the 2 teaspoons butter in a small ovenproof skillet and roll the spinach balls around in it. Place the skillet in the oven to warm while you cook the fish.

Heat ⅛ inch of oil in a large skillet over medium-high heat. Season the fish with salt and white pepper. When the oil is hot, add the fish fillets, skin side down. Press a lid or another pan down on the fish to flatten the fillets and keep the skin in direct contact with the skillet. Cook this way for a minute, or until the fish is "set." Remove the lid and continue to cook for another 2 to 3 minutes, or until the fillets are almost cooked. Turn the fillets and "kiss" (briefly cook) the flesh side of the fish. Remove the fillets from the pan.

While the fish cooks, reheat the parsnips over low heat and stir in remaining 1 tablespoon cream and the butter.

Place a pool of sauce on each serving plate. Spoon some parsnip purée into the center of the sauce and top the purée with a spinach ball. Set the fish fillets, skin side up, on the spinach and serve.

ON CRISPING SKIN

I love the texture and flavor of perfectly crisped fish skin, and there's a key step in preparation that ensures proper crisping: getting as much moisture out of the skin before cooking as possible. Skin will not crisp, obviously, if there's water in it. Skin that is too moist will take a long time to crisp, and you will overcook your fish.

The way we prepare the fish is to take the blade of a knife and drag it over the skin, pressing down gently but firmly to force the water to the surface, then pulling the knife back over the skin to squeegee off the water. Repeat this pressing and scraping until you've gotten as much water out of the fish skin as possible. This will allow you to achieve crisp fish skin without overcooking the flesh.

tools of refinement
the chinois and tamis

Perhaps the most important pieces of equipment in our kitchen are the chinois—also known in French kitchens as a *chinois tamis*, or Chinese sieve—and the *tamis*, sometimes referred to as a drum sieve. The first is a conical fine-mesh sieve that we pass liquids through; the second is a flat fine-mesh sieve that we press puréed solids through.

A tamis prevents lumps and ensures that every particle is the same size. We put a lot of butter (and truffle oil) in mashed potatoes, creating what is in effect an emulsion; potatoes that have been pressed through a tamis will more easily form a stable emulsion. We also press items such as foie gras or anything with veins or skin we don't want through the tamis to remove impurities.

The final clarifying stage of a sauce is passing it through a chinois. French Laundry chefs will pass a sauce through a chinois twenty times or more, till it is perfectly clean and all the particles that can muddy it have been caught in its mesh. We're always "cleaning" sauces with a chinois—no liquid should move from one pot or container into another except through a chinois.

We use a China cap, a coarser conical sieve, to strain bones and vegetables out of stock. For lobster stock, we crush the lobster shells in the China cap to extract as much liquid as possible, then we strain that liquid through a chinois to remove any remaining impurities.

Above all, the tamis and the chinois are tools that create perfect texture. We put our soups in a blender and then pass them through a chinois, tapping the rim rather than plunging with a ladle to move the liquid through. We pass our pea purée for the pea soup through a tamis, then we blend the purée in a blender and pass it through a chinois. The result is texture on your tongue and palate that is almost indescribable. It is the texture of luxury.

chez panisse café cookbook

author

Alice Waters, the visionary chef and owner of Chez Panisse in Berkeley, California. She is the author of four cookbooks, including *Chez Panisse Vegetables* and *Fanny at Chez Panisse*.

why she wrote it

To share the recipes from her restaurant's casual café and to encourage the use of organic ingredients. "We hope our descriptions of some of our suppliers will inspire you to seek out similarly dedicated farmers, foragers, fishermen, and other purveyors who practice and support the sustainable, ecologically sound harvest of nature's bounty."

why it made our list

There's something unique and interesting about so many of these recipes, and the vegetable dishes are particularly inspired. Of course, the specialties you're able to sample will depend on the time of year and what's available in your part of the world. Waters advises, "Go to the market before you decide what you want to cook. Learn to use all your senses and, especially, how to taste — the best skill a cook can cultivate." Recipes this good make tasting a pleasure. In fact, the whole book is a delight, an understated classic — with charming color-block prints throughout as the icing on the cake.

specifics

267 pages, 142 recipes, 98 illustrations.

chapters Vegetables ❯ Eggs & Cheese ❯ Fish & Shellfish ❯ Beef ❯ Pork ❯ Lamb ❯ Poultry ❯ Sweets

$34. Published by HarperCollins Publishers, Inc.

from the book

"It is not an overstatement to say that a restaurant is only as good as its simplest green salad. Our green salad is the important dish on the menu. Judging from the number of salads they order, our customers agree. All our new cooks are taught the nuances of salad making. We stress the importance of handling the greens carefully, choosing an appropriate mixture of lettuces, washing the leaves gently in abundant cold water, drying them and wrapping them in clean linen to await their turn in the salad bowl, dressing them with just the right amount of critically tasted, freshly made vinaigrette."

Tuna Dumplings with Currants and Pine Nuts

These unusual little dumplings sautéed in olive oil make a savory first course in the Sicilian spirit. We serve them for lunch with a little fresh tomato sauce as a main course, or with a salad of rocket leaves and shaved pecorino cheese for a first course. The belly meat and scraps of tuna, which would otherwise go to waste, are perfect for this dish.

Makes 24 dumplings; serves 4 to 6.

1 medium onion, diced fine
1½ tablespoons extra-virgin olive oil
1⅓ tablespoons chopped marjoram
1 small pinch saffron threads, to
¼ teaspoon red pepper fl
Salt
3 tables

Combine the diced tuna with the onion, pine nuts, currants, bread crumbs, pancetta (if using), egg, and cayenne. Add 1 teaspoon salt and a little freshly ground pepper, and mix well. Fry a little of the mixture into taste, and adjust the seasoning. With wet hands, form the mixture into small balls the size of walnuts. Refrigerate the dumplings until ready to cook.

Roll the dumplings lightly in flour. Pour olive oil in a heavy-bottomed pan to a depth of ⅓ inch. Over medium-high heat, fry the dumplings for about 2 minutes per side, until nicely browned and crisp. Drain on absorbent paper and serve.

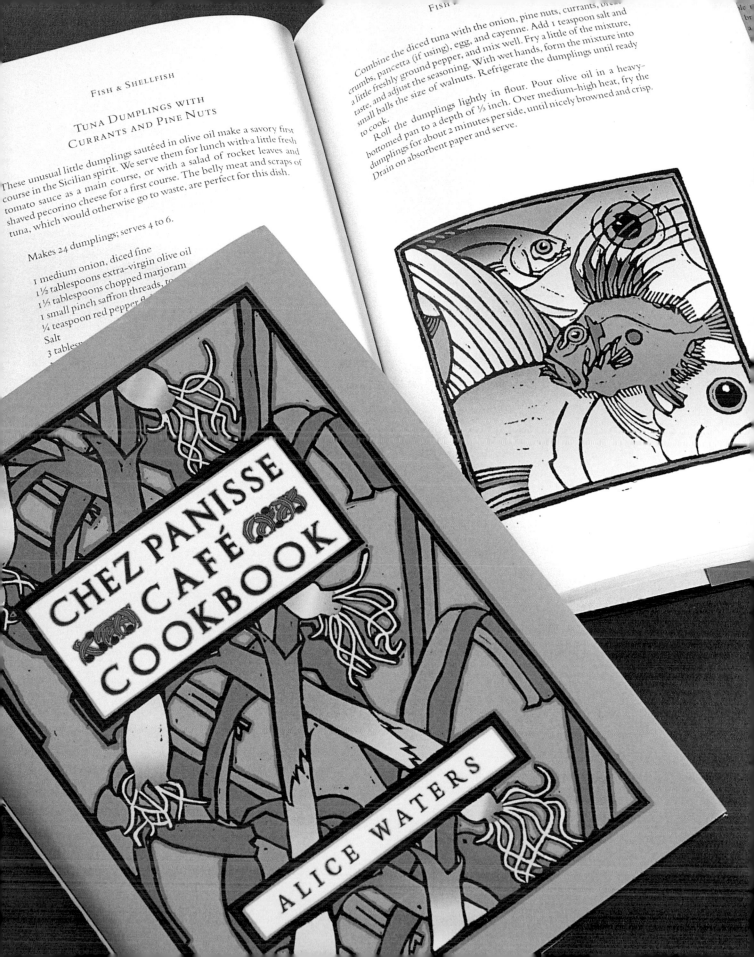

CHEZ PANISSE CAFÉ COOKBOOK

ALICE WATERS

avocado and beet salad
with citrus vinaigrette

SERVES 6

In our temperate climate of Northern California, someone is growing beets all year round, and not just red ones. Golden beets, striped Chioggia beets, rosy pink beets, and ivory beets, lightly pickled, add sparkle to antipasti, grilled fish dishes, or salads like this one.

6   medium red or golden beets

Salt and pepper

1   tablespoon red wine vinegar

Extra-virgin olive oil

1   large shallot, diced fine

2   tablespoons white wine vinegar

1   tablespoon lemon juice

1   tablespoon orange juice

1   tablespoon chopped chervil

¼   teaspoon chopped lemon zest

¼   teaspoon chopped orange zest

2   firm, ripe avocadoes

Chervil sprigs

Preheat the oven to 400°F.

Trim and wash the beets. Put them in a baking dish, add a splash of water, and cover tightly. Roast the beets in the oven for about 45 minutes, until they are cooked through.

When the beets are cooked, allow them to cool uncovered. Peel and cut them into wedges. Put them in a bowl, season generously with salt and pepper, add the red wine vinegar and 1 tablespoon of olive oil, and toss gently.

Put the shallot in a bowl and add the white wine vinegar, lemon juice, orange juice, and a pinch of salt. Let macerate for 15 minutes. Whisk in ¾ cup olive oil and stir in the chopped chervil, lemon zest, and orange zest. Taste for seasoning.

Cut the avocados in half lengthwise and remove the pits. Leaving the skin intact, cut the avocados lengthwise into ¼-inch slices. Scoop out the slices with a large spoon and arrange them on a platter or individual dishes. Season with salt and pepper. Arrange the beets over the avocado slices and drizzle with the vinaigrette. Garnish with a few chervil sprigs.

shaved asparagus
and parmesan salad

SERVES 4

During asparagus season, in April and May, we serve asparagus every day in one form or another. This delightful raw spring salad is best only if the asparagus is very sweet and crisp, like the beautiful purple-tinged asparagus we get at the San Francisco farmer's market. Look for very fresh, large purple or green asparagus with tight buds. (White asparagus is better cooked.) Look at the butt ends of the asparagus where they have been cut: If they're fresh, the flesh will look moist and white.

2 **shallots, diced fine**

2 **tablespoons Champagne vinegar**

2 **tablespoons lemon juice**

Salt

⅓ **cup extra-virgin olive oil**

12 **large asparagus spears**

Pepper

Wedge of Parmigiano-Reggiano cheese, for shaving

To make the vinaigrette, macerate the shallots for 15 minutes in the vinegar, lemon juice, and a little salt. Whisk in the olive oil.

Snap off the tough bottom ends of the asparagus spears. With a Japanese mandolin, very carefully shave each asparagus spear into long, paper-thin ribbons. Put the shaved asparagus in a salad bowl; season with salt and pepper, and dress lightly with the vinaigrette.

Divide the salad among 4 plates. With a sharp vegetable peeler or paring knife, shave large curls of Parmesan over each serving.

tuna dumplings
with currants and pine nuts

MAKES 24 DUMPLINGS; SERVES 4 TO 6

These unusual little dumplings sautéed in olive oil make a savory first course in the Sicilian spirit. We serve them for lunch with a little fresh tomato sauce as a main course, or with a salad of rocket leaves and shaved pecorino cheese for a first course. The belly meat and scraps of tuna, which would otherwise go to waste, are perfect for this dish.

1   **medium onion, diced fine**

1½ **tablespoons extra-virgin olive oil**

1½ **tablespoons chopped marjoram**

1   **small pinch saffron threads, toasted and crumbled**

¼   **teaspoon red pepper flakes**

Salt

3   **tablespoons pine nuts**

3   **tablespoons currants**

1   **ounce pancetta, thinly sliced (optional)**

½   **cup fresh bread crumbs**

¼   **cup milk**

1   **pound fresh tuna, preferably belly meat**

1   **egg, slightly beaten**

¼   **teaspoon cayenne**

Pepper

All-purpose flour

Olive oil for frying

Sauté the onion gently in the 1½ tablespoons extra-virgin olive oil over medium-low heat for 5 minutes. Add the marjoram, saffron, pepper flakes, and a little salt, and continue cooking for about 5 minutes longer, until the onion is translucent and tender, but not colored.

Toast the pine nuts until lightly browned, and chop coarsely. Plump the currants in a little hot water and drain. If using pancetta, render it over medium-low heat. Moisten the bread crumbs with the milk and let them soften.

Cut the tuna into fine dice: cut thin slices, cut the slices into strips, and cut the strips into small cubes.

Combine the diced tuna with the onion, pine nuts, currants, bread crumbs, pancetta (if using), egg, and cayenne. Add 1 teaspoon salt and a little freshly ground pepper, and mix well. Fry a little of the mixture, taste, and adjust the seasoning. With wet hands, form the mixture into small balls the size of walnuts. Refrigerate the dumplings until ready to cook.

Roll the dumplings lightly in flour. Pour olive oil in a heavy-bottomed pan to a depth of ⅓ inch. Over medium-high heat, fry the dumplings for about 2 minutes per side, until nicely browned and crisp. Drain on absorbent paper and serve.

apricot bread pudding

SERVES 6 TO 8

This is a comforting, warm, substantial finish to a meal. In fact, it is often too substantial after a rich meal. However, in this version, the acidity of the apricots tempers the richness.

1 cup dried apricots, sliced, or 8 fresh apricots, cut in small wedges

1¼ cups sugar

PUDDING

7 egg yolks

⅓ cup sugar, plus additional for sprinkling

2 cups half-and-half or whole milk

2 cups cream

Grated zest of 1 orange

¼ teaspoon salt

1 teaspoon vanilla extract

¼ teaspoon almond extract

⅛ teaspoon nutmeg

1 tablespoon kirsch

OPTIONAL

4 ounces good-quality almond paste, cut in pea-size pieces

About 1 pound brioche, pain-de-mie, or good day-old homemade white

bread, cut into ½-inch cubes (about 5 cups)

In a small saucepan, simmer the apricots in 1 cup water and ¼ cup of the sugar. Poach the fruit until tender, about 12 minutes for dried, 5 for fresh. Drain the fruit, saving the liquid, and set the fruit aside to cool. Return the poaching liquid to the saucepan and add the remaining 1 cup sugar and ½ cup water. Boil this mixture, and when it begins to brown, swirl the pan so that it caramelizes evenly. Cook to a medium amber color. Very carefully pour the hot caramel into a 2-quart gratin dish or divide it evenly among 6 small ramekins. Cool.

Whisk the egg yolks in a large bowl. Slowly add ⅓ cup sugar and mix well. Whisk in the half-and-half or milk and the cream. Add the orange zest, salt, vanilla and almond extracts, nutmeg, and kirsch. Gently fold in the poached apricots, the almond paste, if using, and the bread cubes. Transfer the pudding mixture to the gratin dish or ramekins. Let rest at least 1 hour or refrigerate overnight.

Preheat the oven to 375°F. Sprinkle a little sugar over the top of the pudding. Place the gratin dish or ramekins on a baking dish to catch any overflow. Bake until nicely browned, about 55 minutes. Serve warm or at room temperature.

VARIATION Substitute prunes for the apricots and Armagnac for the kirsch.

blue ginger

author

Ming Tsai, chef-proprietor of the restaurant Blue Ginger in Wellesley, Massachusetts, and host of the Food Network show "East Meets West with Ming Tsai," with food writer Arthur Boehm.

why he wrote it

"Cooking is so joyful! As a chef, I get to please people in so many ways. I want to pass my passion on to you in dishes that reflect so much pleasurable eating over time, but which are also excitingly new. When we sat down at table, the Tsais would often say qing-chi— please dine! Let me also add *bon appétit*, peace, and good eating!"

why it made our list

With this collection of recipes, Ming Tsai shows his mastery of the art of blending Eastern and Western influences on one plate. By skillfully combining several cuisines—French, Chinese, Japanese, American—he develops dishes that are as good as, or even better than, the traditional specialties that inspired them, as all fusion cuisine should be but so often isn't. The combinations here are original, the dishes positively yummy. The comprehensive "East Meets West Pantry" section provides a complete rundown on the ingredients found throughout the book. You may have to go to the Asian market to get some of them, but the results are worth the trip.

from the book

"Soup and I go way back. As a chunky little kid, I'd devour two or three bowls at a time, so I wouldn't eat too much of the more fattening stuff to follow. It wasn't a hardship; the steaming noodle soups and wonton-filled broths were deeply satisfying dishes. Later, as an adult and chef, I indulged my love of soup in other ways. Staying close to my Asian culinary roots, but also exploring the joys of the European and American tables, I'd devise richly garnished soups with layers of flavor. And I learned how exciting it could be to contrast ingredient textures and temperatures in a single bowl."

specifics

276 pages, 137 recipes, 39 color photographs, 149 black-and-white photographs.

> **chapters** Soups ❯ Dim Sum ❯ Rice and Noodles ❯ Seafood ❯ Birds ❯ Meat ❯ Over the Top ❯ Sides ❯ Oils, Dips, and Seasonings ❯ Desserts

$32.50. Published by Clarkson N. Potter Publishers.

...th Spicy Soy Dipping Sauce

The recipe for these fried dumplings was passed down to me by my mom, Iris Tsai, and
I wouldn't think of changing it. Some things are perfect as they are.
Like bread, the wrappers used in this are one of those things that are best homemade,
but unlike bread, they're fast to prepare. Filling and pleating the dumplings is easy, too:
after the first couple of dumplings, your fingers will know the way.
Browned and crisped on their bottoms, steamed, and recrisped, these have a great
textural mix. Needless to say, they make perfect hors d'oeuvre.

BEVERAGE TIP: LAGER (TSINGTAO, SHANGHAI, SINGHA) OR JASMINE TEA

MAKES 20 TO 25 POT STICKERS

FILLING

...ups finely chopped napa cabbage
...blespoon salt
...und ground pork (not too lean)
...spoons finely chopped
... ginger
...spoons finely chopped garlic
...oons soy sauce
...ons toasted sesame oil
...y beaten

DOUGH

2 cups water
4 cups all-purpo...
½ teaspoon...

2...

...ling, combine ...
... set as...

Blue Ginger

ming tsai

ARTHUR BOEHM
...RDSON

salmon roll tempura

SERVES 4

To make this tempting riceless sushi I use traditional Japanese maki- and tempura-making techniques and a Westernized filling that includes caramelized leeks.

1   **tablespoon canola oil, plus additional for deep-frying**

4   **large leeks, white parts only, well washed and julienned**

Salt and freshly ground white pepper

1   **cup mirin (Japanese sweet sake)**

4   **toasted nori sheets**

4   **salmon fillets, about 4 ounces each, lightly pounded to ¼ inch thick**

2   **cups rice flour**

4   **cups club soda**

Wasabi Oil and Soy Syrup (page 36)

1. Heat a large skillet or wok over medium heat. Add the 1 tablespoon of oil and swirl to coat the pan. When the oil shimmers, add the leeks and sauté, stirring occasionally, until soft and browned, 6 to 8 minutes. Season with salt and pepper to taste, add the mirin, and cook to evaporate the liquid, about 6 minutes. Cool.

2. Arrange a sheet of the nori, shiny side down, on a rolling mat. Have a small bowl of water handy. Place a salmon fillet on the bottom half of the nori sheet and season with salt and pepper. Arrange a quarter of the leeks on the upper one-third of the salmon. Roll, wet the edge, and press the mat to seal. Repeat with the remaining nori, salmon, and leeks. Allow the maki to rest, seam side down, for 2 minutes.

3. Fill a fryer or heavy medium pot one-third full with the oil and heat over high heat to 375° F. Place the flour in a medium bowl and slowly whisk in the club soda until the mixture resembles a light pancake batter. Dip the rolls in the batter and fry all at once, turning as necessary, until golden, 4 to 6 minutes. Remove the rolls with a mesh spoon and drain them on paper towels. Season to taste with the salt and pepper.

4. With a sharp knife, slice each maki in half. Cut one half straight across into 3 pieces and cut the other half diagonally into 2 pieces. Divide the rolls among 4 plates, garnish with the wasabi oil and soy syrup, and serve.

BEVERAGE TIP Fresh, fruity, slightly sweet Grolleau Blend Rosé (from Anjou)

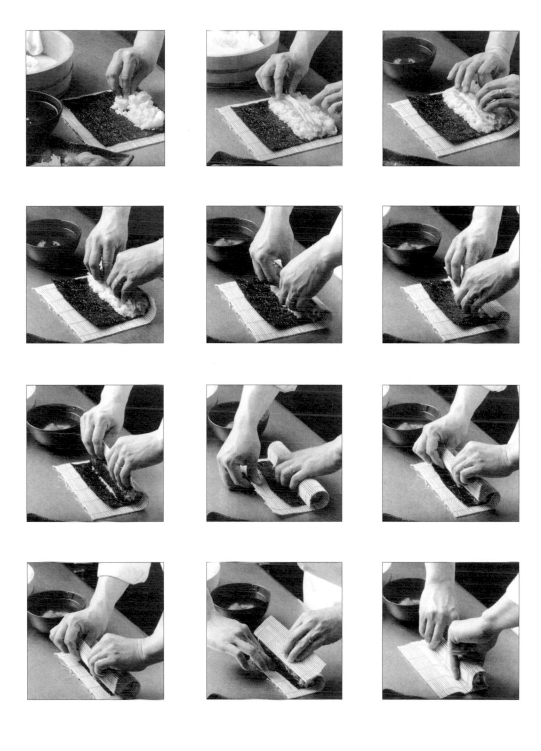

wasabi oil

MAKES ABOUT 1 CUP

This delightfully pungent oil is a wonderful way to enjoy wasabi flavor without what I call "wasabi blast." It's delicious drizzled on grilled fish or added to mayonnaise (in the proportion of 1 part oil to 4 parts mayo) for sandwiches. The oil will keep in an airtight container, refrigerated, for about two weeks, though it loses its zip over time. For extra pungency, reduce the quantity of canola to ⅓ cup oil.

½   **cup wasabi powder**

2   **tablespoons mirin (Japanese sweet sake)**

2   **teaspoons sugar**

½   **cup canola oil**

In a small stainless-steel bowl, combine the wasabi powder, mirin, and sugar and whisk to blend. Add a little less than ½ cup of water gradually, whisking, until a pancake batter–like puree is formed. Whisk in the oil. Let stand for 10 minutes before using.

soy syrup

MAKES 2 CUPS

This thickish flavoring is a perfect seasoning or garnish for fish and all types of sushi. Store it, tightly covered, in the fridge, where it will last for a month. (In a pinch, you can substitute kechap manis, the Indonesian sweet soy sauce, for soy syrup.)

2   **cups soy sauce**

½   **cup brown sugar**

Juice of 1 lime

In a medium saucepan, combine the soy sauce, brown sugar, and lime juice. Bring to a boil slowly over medium heat, turn down the heat, and reduce the mixture by three-fourths or until syrupy, about 30 minutes. Strain, cool, and use or store.

pork and ginger pot stickers with spicy soy dipping sauce

MAKES 20 TO 25 POT STICKERS

The recipe for these fried dumplings was passed down to me by my mom, Iris Tsai, and I wouldn't think of changing it. Some things are perfect as they are.

Like bread, the wrappers used in this are one of those things that are best homemade, but unlike bread, they're fast to prepare. Filling and pleating the dumplings is easy, too; after the first couple of dumplings, your fingers will know the way.

Browned and crisped on their bottoms, steamed, and recrisped, these have a great textural mix. Needless to say, they make perfect hors d'oeuvre.

FILLING

4   **cups finely chopped napa cabbage**

1   **tablespoon salt**

½   **pound ground pork (not too lean)**

2   **tablespoons finely chopped fresh ginger**

1½   **tablespoons finely chopped garlic**

2   **tablespoons soy sauce**

3   **tablespoons toasted sesame oil**

1   **egg, lightly beaten**

DOUGH

2   **cups water**

4   **cups all-purpose flour**

½   **teaspoon salt**

2   **tablespoons canola oil**

Spicy Soy Dipping Sauce (page 41)

1. To make the filling, combine the cabbage and 1½ teaspoons of the salt in a large bowl and toss together; set aside for 30 minutes. Transfer the cabbage to a clean dish towel or cheesecloth, gather the ends of the cloth together, and twist to squeeze as much water as possible

from the cabbage (this will make the filling more cohesive.) In a second large bowl, combine the cabbage with the pork, ginger, garlic, soy sauce, sesame oil, the remaining 1½ teaspoons of salt, and egg and mix.

2. To make the dough, bring the water to a boil. In a large stainless-steel bowl, combine the flour and salt. Slowly add the boiling water in ¼-cup increments, mixing with chopsticks until a ball is formed and the dough is no longer too hot to handle. All the water may not be needed. Knead the dough on a floured work surface until it becomes smooth and elastic, 15 to 20 minutes. Form the dough into a ball, return it to the bowl, and cover it with a damp cloth. Allow the dough to rest for 1 hour.

3. To form the wrappers, add more flour to the work surface. Divide the dough in half. Shape one portion into a log and roll it back and forth under your palms to make a thin sausage shape measuring about 1 inch in diameter. Cut into ½-inch pieces. One by one, stand each piece on end, flatten the piece with your palm, and roll out to form a circular wrapper about 3 inches in diameter and ¹⁄₁₆ of an inch thick. Repeat with the remaining dough.

4. To fill the pot stickers, place about ½ tablespoon of the filling in the center of each wrapper. Avoid getting filling on the edges of the wrapper, which would prevent proper sealing. Fold each wrapper in half to form a half-moon shape. Seal the top center of each dumpling by pressing between the fingers and, starting at the center, make 3 pleats, working toward the bottom right. Repeat, working toward the bottom left corner. Press the dumplings down gently on the work surface to flatten the bottoms.

5. Heat a large nonstick skillet over high heat. Add the oil and swirl to coat. When the oil shimmers, add the pot stickers, flattened bottoms down, in rows of five, and cook in batches without disturbing until brown, about 6 minutes. Add about ½ cup of water and immediately cover to avoid splattering. Lift the cover and make sure about ⅛ inch of water remains in the pan; if not, add a bit more. Steam until the pot stickers are puffy yet firm and the water has evaporated, 8 to 10 minutes. If the water evaporates before the pot stickers are done, add more in ¼-cup increments. If the pot stickers seem done but water remains in the pan, drain it and return the pan to the stove top.

6. Continue to cook over high heat to allow the pot stickers to recrisp on the bottom, 2 to 3 minutes. Transfer the pot stickers to a platter and serve with the dipping sauce.

BEVERAGE TIP Lager (Tsingtao, Shanghai, Singha) or jasmine tea

MING'S TIP When rolling out the wrappers, make the edges a little thinner than the centers. That way, when the edges are folded over themselves to enclose the filling, they'll still be the same thickness as the rest of the wrapper.

spicy soy dipping sauce

MAKES ABOUT 1 CUP

This is my version of the classic vinegar and soy sauce dim sum dip that's a natural accompaniment to Pork and Ginger Pot Stickers (page 38) and other dumplings. I've added sambal oelek for spiciness—a bow to my Hunan roots. Refrigerated, this lasts for two weeks. Try it also with spring rolls and tempura.

⅓   **cup soy sauce**

⅓   **cup rice wine vinegar**

⅓   **cup scallions, green parts only, sliced ⅛ inch thick**

1   **tablespoon toasted sesame oil**

1   **tablespoon sambal oelek**

In a medium bowl combine the soy sauce, vinegar, scallions, sesame oil, and sambal oelek. Stir to blend and use or store.

spicy black bean mussels
with rice stick noodles

SERVES 4

I've always enjoyed dishes that combine mussels and black beans, a traditional Chinese pairing. I've joined the two here, with the addition of Thai basil leaves and a shot of fresh lime—a bow to Thailand. The inclusion of tomatoes—we're traveling West, now—adds freshness and color.

I recommend Prince Edward Island mussels for this dish—they're particularly tender and sweet—but any mussel will work well. To serve, arrange the mussels on top of each portion "to be closer to the gods"—a Chinese practice that also makes the dish look more bountiful.

2   tablespoons canola oil

2   pounds mussels, preferably Prince Edward Island,
     scrubbed, beards removed

1   tablespoon finely chopped garlic

1   tablespoon finely chopped fresh ginger

4   serrano or Thai bird chiles, stemmed and minced

1   tablespoon fermented black beans, rinsed and drained

½   cup dry white wine

2   medium tomatoes, or 4 canned, cut into ¼-inch dice

1   tablespoon Thai fish sauce (*nam pla*)

2   cups chicken stock or low-sodium canned broth

8   ounces rice stick noodles, soaked in warm water to cover until softened,
     about 30 minutes

1   cup fresh Thai or sweet basil leaves

1   bunch chives, cut into ½-inch lengths

2   tablespoons butter

Salt and freshly ground white pepper

2   limes, halved

1. Heat a wok over high heat. Add the oil and swirl to coat the pan. When the oil shimmers, add the mussels and stir-fry until some of the mussels open, about 5 minutes. Add the garlic, ginger, chiles, and black beans and stir-fry until fragrant, about 2 minutes. Add the wine, cover, and cook until all the mussels have opened, 3 to 5 minutes. Add the tomatoes, fish sauce, chicken stock, and drained noodles. Toss and add the basil, chives, and butter. Toss again. Season with the salt and pepper to taste.

2. Transfer the mixture to large pasta bowls, and arrange the mussels on top of each portion. Squeeze lime juice over and serve.

BEVERAGE TIP Fruity Riesling, not bone dry (Australian Grosset, Alsatian Trimbach)

MING'S TIP I sometimes add a bit of butter to a completed dish, as I do in this recipe, to provide light enrichment and to round out flavors. Keep this classic French technique in mind for your own cooking.

the tra vigne cookbook

author

Michael Chiarello, chef-owner of the restaurant Tra Vigne, located in California's Napa Valley. Chiarello's previous books are *Flavored Vinegars* and *Flavored Oils*.

why he wrote it

"My hope is that the recipes in this book will inspire you to cook, and that your increasing confidence and excitement in the kitchen will in turn inspire your family and friends, making the circle around your table grow wider and deeper. I cannot imagine a better way to touch people than through the pleasure of food."

why it made our list

Though it's not devoted to vegetarian cooking—indeed, there's plenty of meat—fresh and flavorful vegetables form the backbone of this lovely-to-look-at cookbook. Bonus chapters include "Tra Vigne Classics" and "Desserts & Cookies," but most of the recipes are divided first into seasons and then into categories celebrating that season's produce. Spring brings asparagus, garlic, fresh peas and shelling beans, and potatoes; summer abounds with corn, tomatoes, bell peppers, and summer squash; autumn features mushrooms, greens, onions, and eggplants; and winter offers broccoli, artichokes, citrus, and winter squashes. With its many color photos, the book is a pleasure to page through, and the Italian-inspired dishes taste as good as they look. All in all, a delightful way to spend a year.

from the book

"Spring doesn't last long. Our rule at the restaurant is never to buy an item until the second week of its season, then as the harvest travels northward, we buy continually until the harvest passes into the Pacific Northwest, and we stop. My advice to home cooks is to wait one or two weeks into a vegetable's season, eat it twice a week during the height of the season, then give it up. Stopping may be hard, but freshly arriving seasonal tastes will distract you soon enough."

specifics

216 pages, more than 100 recipes, 75 color photographs, 16 black-and-white photographs.

chapters Spring › Summer › Autumn › Winter › Tra Vigne Classics › Desserts & Cookies › Pantry

$35.00. Published by Chronicle Books.

Chicken Piadine
with Baby Spinach

Piadine are actually unleavened breads cooked on a stove-top, but I've translated that idea into these addictive sandwiches made with a pizzalike dough. If you have some dough in the freezer, you can assemble them out of any manner of ingredients. This sandwich is a great excuse to make sure you are getting your proper quotient of spinach.

Serves 6

1 recipe Piadine Dough (page 194)
All-purpose flour for dusting work surface
2¼ cups roasted, peeled, and seeded red bell peppers (page 64)
spoons Roasted Garlic Paste (page 197)
freshly ground pepper
grated Parmesan cheese
chopped fresh oregano
sprinkling on baking sheets
spinach
(page 143)

Position the oven racks on the lowest and uppermost rungs of the oven. Place 2 large baking sheets in the oven and preheat to 500°F.

Divide the dough into 6 balls. Working on a surface free of flour, roll each ball under your palm. As it rolls, it will stick slightly to the surface, creating tension that helps form a tight, round ball. Dust the work surface with flour, pat each ball down lightly, dust the tops with flour, cover with a towel, and let rise for about 15 minutes.

Combine 1⅓ cups of the roasted peppers, the garlic paste, and salt and pepper to taste in a blender or food processor and puree until smooth. Cut the remaining ¾ cup peppers into long, narrow strips. Set aside.

With a rolling pin, roll each ball into a circle 8 or 9 inches in diameter and about ⅛ inch thick. Spread each round with about 3 tablespoons of the red pepper puree, then sprinkle with 1 tablespoon Parmesan and 1⅓ teaspoons ...gano.

...ove the baking sheets from the oven, sprinkle ...ornmeal, and transfer the rounds to the ... slightly underdone (they will be lightly ...ges but still pliable), 8 to 12 minutes. ...baking, in a bowl, toss together ...zzarella, reserved pepper ...soning. Let the crusts ...greens when filled. ...salad among ...ne in half.

THE TRA VIGNE
COOKBOOK
SEASONS
IN THE CALIFORNIA WINE COUNTRY
MICHAEL CHIARELLO
WITH PENELOPE
PHOTOGRAPHS

autumn food hugs

Autumn is my time for rejuvenation and new growth. Activity seems to increase throughout the animal world at this time of year. For instance, if you go fishing, the fish are gorging, getting ready for winter. Food tastes best to me in autumn, perhaps this is my body's atavistic attempt to store calories for the coming winter.

Many of my favorite memories and activities are tied to this season. I monitor every rainfall now because twenty-one days after the first cumulative two inches of rain, I begin mushroom hunting. For me, the perfect autumn dish begins with a mushroom hunt in the surrounding hills with a novice hunter from my staff. We pick wild mustard and fennel on the way down and turn our foraged harvest into a pasta dish with stock already on hand. The autumn table is not about long, drawn-out cooking but about quick, big flavor meals.

The flavors of autumn evoke the same feelings as putting on your favorite wool shirt for the first time. They are tastes you can't have other times of the year. Pumpkins don't grow in summer. Peas, tomatoes, and asparagus are available year-round (availability, of course, does not equal quality), but autumn is different. It is persimmons, quinces, nuts picked up off the ground, and fennel, fennel, fennel, and wild fennel seed. (Yes, fennel is my favorite.)

Growing up, life started on the first of September, the opening day of dove season. I haven't missed an opening day since I started shooting when I was about ten years old. I'd hunt from first light until school, dropping any birds off at home and racing my bike as fast as I could so as not to be late. When the second dove season opened at the end of November, I was able to hunt dove, quail, pheasant, duck, and goose and go fishing all in the same day. It was an all-encompassing time, so autumn and I are best friends.

It is the busiest time of year in the kitchen cycle—time to stock the pantry for winter. My family would butcher a pig and make prosciutto and sausage, and the smell of freshly canned tomatoes welcomed me home from school. Great bunches of fennel, oregano, and basil were hung to dry and olives were cured. It was when the family made wine, too.

At the restaurant, we follow these same patterns. We make dried tomatoes and cure olives, and in November, when the weather cools enough, we make our prosciutti, salamis, and sausages. I still find time to hunt and take my staff out to forage for mushrooms, wild mustard, fennel, or the bright orange persimmons that hang so improbably on bare branches.

The reason I love wild fennel is not just because of the flavor. The taste of fennel includes all the times I picked it with my mother and the times I've picked it with my staff and friends. It includes seeing it hanging under the eaves to dry, shaking the bunches gently into a paper bag, and then separating the seeds from the chaff. These events, and the dishes that evoke them, I call food hugs. And autumn has more of them than any other season.

chicken piadine with baby spinach

SERVES 6

Piadine are actually unleavened breads cooked on a stove-top, but I've translated that idea into these addictive sandwiches made with a pizzalike dough. If you have some dough in the freezer, you can assemble them out of any manner of ingredients. This sandwich is a great excuse to make sure you are getting your proper quotient of spinach.

1   recipe Piadine Dough (page 49)

All-purpose flour for dusting work surface

2¼ cups roasted, peeled, and seeded red bell peppers

3   tablespoons Roasted Garlic Paste (page 50)

Salt and freshly ground pepper

⅓   cup freshly grated Parmesan cheese

3   tablespoons finely chopped fresh oregano

Coarse cornmeal for sprinkling on baking sheets

9   cups loosely packed baby spinach

About ½ cup Whole Citrus Vinaigrette (page 51)

1½ cups diced fresh mozzarella cheese (½-inch dice)

3   chicken breast halves, cooked, boned, and torn into shreds (see Chef's Note)

Position the oven racks on the lowest and uppermost rungs of the oven. Place 2 large baking sheets in the oven and preheat to 500°F.

Divide the dough into 6 balls. Working on a surface free of flour, roll each ball under your palm. As it rolls, it will stick slightly to the surface, creating tension that helps form a tight, round ball. Dust the work surface with flour, pat each ball down lightly, dust the tops with flour, cover with a towel, and let rise for about 15 minutes.

Combine 1½ cups of the roasted peppers, the garlic paste, and salt and pepper to taste in a blender or food processor and puree until smooth. Cut the remaining ¾ cup peppers into long, narrow strips. Set aside.

With a rolling pin, roll each ball into a circle 8 or 9 inches in diameter and about ⅛ inch thick. Spread each round with about 3 tablespoons of the red pepper puree, then sprinkle with 1 tablespoon Parmesan and 1½ teaspoons oregano.

Remove the baking sheets from the oven, sprinkle evenly with cornmeal, and transfer the rounds to the sheets. Bake until slightly underdone (they will be lightly browned around the edges but still pliable), 8 to 12 minutes.

While the crusts are baking, in a bowl, toss together the spinach, vinaigrette, mozzarella, reserved pepper strips, and chicken. Taste for seasoning. Let the crusts cool very briefly so they won't cook the greens when filled. Transfer the crusts to plates and divide the salad among them. Serve "open face." Diners fold their piadine in half.

CHEF'S NOTE You can poach, sauté, roast, or grill the chicken. We grill it at the restaurant because that adds the most flavor. You can also save time by using purchased rotisserie chicken.

piadine dough

MAKES ABOUT 2 POUNDS DOUGH, ENOUGH FOR SIX 8- OR 9-INCH PIADINE

Perhaps you think that making dough is a bother. But once you work with this dough, you will want to do it again. It is one of those textures that begs to be touched, caressed. It feels as smooth and silky as a baby's bottom.

1   envelope activo dry yeast

½   cup lukewarm water

About 4 cups all-purpose flour, plus more for dusting work surface

1   cup cool water

2   tablespoons extra-virgin olive oil

2   teaspoons salt

Whisk together the yeast, lukewarm water, and ½ cup of the flour in the bowl of a stand mixer. Dust the top lightly with flour, cover the bowl with a tea towel, and leave the sponge to rise until the flour dusting "cracks," showing the yeast is alive and well, about 20 minutes.

Add 3 cups of the flour, the 1 cup cool water, the olive oil, and the salt. Start kneading at low speed, then increase the speed to medium as the flour is incorporated. Add the remaining ½ cup flour as needed to produce a slightly moist and soft dough. Knead with the dough hook attachment until smooth and silky and the dough adheres to the hook.

Dust the dough lightly with flour and, using a pastry scraper, scrape it out of the bowl onto a lightly floured surface. Knead lightly, folding the dough over on itself. Shape into a ball, flatten slightly, dust lightly with flour, cover with a towel, and leave to rise on a floured surface (or in a bowl) until doubled in bulk, about 1 hour.

Punch the dough down, wrap, and freeze for up to 1 month if not using immediately. Defrost and let rise in a large bowl in the refrigerator.

When ready, continue with the Chicken Piadine recipe.

roasted garlic paste

MAKES ABOUT 1 CUP

For me, this is a kitchen staple. If you like, you can draw off part of the oil remaining in the baking dish after roasting the garlic to use separately as a flavored oil.

1   **pound whole garlic heads**
½   **cup pure olive oil**
Salt and freshly ground pepper

Preheat the oven to 375°F. Peel the outermost layers of skin off the heads of garlic. Cut off the top one-third of the heads to open the cloves. Save the small pieces of garlic for another use (see Chef's Notes). Put the heads, cut sides up, in a small baking dish and pour the olive oil over them. Season with salt and pepper.

Cover tightly, place in the oven, and roast until about three-fourths cooked, about 45 minutes. Uncover and return to the oven until the cloves begin to pop out of their skins and brown, about 15 minutes. Let cool.

When cool enough to handle easily, squeeze the roasted garlic into a small bowl. Press against the skins very well to get out all the sweet roasted garlic you can. Add the oil from the baking dish and mix well until a paste forms. Store, tightly covered, in the refrigerator, for up to 1 week.

CHEF'S NOTES It is hard to have too much roasted garlic around. You can roast the little bits from the tips of the garlic heads. Put them in a separate small baking container, such as an individual custard cup. Season with salt and pepper, douse with olive oil, cover, and place in the oven to bake along with the whole garlic heads. Depending on their size, they will be soft and browned in about half the time needed for the whole heads. The little pieces make a good "cook's snack" while preparing dinner, or can be squeezed into tomato sauce, into pasta, and so on.

whole citrus vinaigrette

SERVES 4

We use citrus vinaigrette regularly at Tra Vigne and in our Cantinetta. In my opinion, citrus vinaigrettes often disappoint. Here, I use the whole fruit, a trick I learned from Alain Ducasse, the three-star French chef of Louis XV in Monte Carlo. It makes a delicious and sunny yellow vinaigrette. When I have it around, I use it on everything. You can spoon it over a piece of cooked fish, use it as a dip, or use it to dress a spinach salad clipped inside piadine (page 47). I prefer to use a juice extractor for this recipe, but I have made it successfully in a blender as well (see variation).

2	**lemons**
½	**navel orange or 1 small orange**
1	**shallot**
1½	**cups pure olive oil**
1	**teaspoon salt**
½	**teaspoon freshly ground pepper**

Juice the lemons, orange, and shallot in a juice extractor. Put the juices in a bowl and whisk in the olive oil in a slow stream to form an emulsion. Season with the salt and pepper. Taste and adjust the seasoning. Whisk again, cover, and refrigerate for up to 3 days. You should have about 2 cups.

Just before serving, place the greens in a salad bowl, add about ½ cup vinaigrette, and toss well. Add more to taste and adjust the seasoning.

VARIATION FOR BLENDER Use 3 lemons, 2 small oranges, 1 shallot, 1 teaspoon salt, ½ teaspoon pepper, and 1½ cups pure olive oil. Cut off and discard the stem ends of 2 lemons and 1 orange. Cut into quarters, cut out the core, and deseed. Place in a blender. Squeeze the juice from the remaining lemon and orange; add to the blender with the shallot, salt, and pepper. Pulse and then blend the fruit until as smooth as possible. With the machine running, add the olive oil in a thin, steady stream. The vinaigrette will be thick like a mayonnaise. If it is too thick, with the machine still on, thin with a little hot water. Taste for seasoning. Cover and refrigerate for up to 3 days. If the vinaigrette separates, return it to the blender and blend until smooth again. Makes about 3 cups.

swordfish with onion, raisin, and tomato agrodolce

SERVES 4

Mariano Orlando has inspired the food of our Cantinetta for the last eight years. He loves hungry people, and it is rare for anyone talking with him to leave the shop without "a little something." Mariano is Sicilian and often makes savory dishes that include raisins and other dried fruits. This agrodolce, a sweet-and-sour sauce, is a classic Sicilian flavoring, a neat package of sun-drenched flavors: caramelized onions, tomatoes, and lemons. Together fish and sauce make a full meal. If the sauce is done ahead, you can have a fabulous dish on the table in fewer than fifteen minutes.

3½ tablespoons extra-virgin olive oil

5 cups thinly sliced onions

Salt

½ cup water

Freshly ground pepper

1 teaspoon finely chopped fresh rosemary

1 can (14½ ounces) chopped tomatoes, or 1½ cups peeled and chopped vine-ripened tomatoes

1 tablespoon sugar

½ cup golden raisins

Freshly grated zest of 1 lemon

Juice of ½ lemon

2 tablespoons finely chopped fresh flat-leaf parsley

4 swordfish steaks, about 7 ounces each, at least 1 inch thick

2 tablespoons *panko* (see Chef's Notes) or other dried bread crumbs

Lemon wedges

Heat 2 tablespoons of the olive oil in a large sauté pan over medium heat until hot. Add the onions and a little salt so the onions release their liquid. Reduce the heat to medium-low and sauté until the onions stop releasing liquid and the pan is nearly dry again, about 4 minutes. Do not allow the onions to brown. Add the water, cover, and cook, stirring occasionally, until the onions are very soft, about 10 minutes.

Uncover, season with pepper, add the rosemary, and increase the heat to medium-high. Sauté until the onions are very lightly browned, about 10 minutes. Remove half of the onions to a plate and set aside.

Add the tomatoes and their juice to the onions remaining in the pan. Bring to a boil over high heat, season with salt and pepper, lower the heat and simmer until thick, about 4 minutes. Add the sugar and the raisins and stir in the lemon zest and lemon juice. Remove from the heat and let cool for a bit. Stir in 1 tablespoon of the parsley. Keep warm. (The recipe may be completed up to this point a day ahead. Cover and refrigerate the reserved onions and sauce separately.)

Preheat the oven to 450°F. Turn on the broiler, if a separate unit. Heat the remaining 1½ tablespoons olive oil in a large, ovenproof sauté pan over medium-high heat until hot. Season the fish steaks with salt and pepper and place in the pan. Lower the heat to medium and cook until the fish is browned on the underside, about 1½ minutes. Turn and top evenly with the reserved onions. Sprinkle each steak with the bread crumbs and place in the oven just until cooked through, about 5 minutes. Run the fish under the broiler to brown the crumbs.

To serve, reheat the sauce, if necessary. It should be warm, not blistering hot. Pour the sauce onto a serving platter or divide among 4 plates. Top with the fish, dust with the remaining 1 tablespoon parsley, and serve immediately with lemon wedges.

CHEF'S NOTES *Panko* are terrific, very crisp, white, unseasoned bread crumbs from Japan. If fresh tomatoes have disappeared from your markets, a good brand of canned tomatoes makes a very successful dish.

daniel boulud's café boulud cookbook

author

Daniel Boulud, chef-owner of the New York City restaurants Daniel and Café Boulud, with cookbook author Dorie Greenspan. Boulud is also the author of *Cooking with Daniel Boulud*.

why he wrote it

"To create this collection, I have chosen the recipes that hold the dearest memories for me, the ones most tied to my culinary life in France and America, and the ones most enjoyed at Café Boulud. All of the recipes have been tested so that they will work as well in your kitchen as they do in mine, and all are offered to you with the hope that when you share this food with your family and friends, it will bring you as much satisfaction, indeed, as much joy, as it has brought me over the years."

why it made our list

Packed with recipes from Café Boulud, this book celebrates the simpler dishes in Chef Boulud's repertoire, his café offerings as opposed to his more complicated Restaurant Daniel cuisine. The book is divided, just like the café menu, into four sections: French classics, seasonal specialties, dishes from countries other than France and America, and vegetarian selections. The recipes are clearly written and easy to follow, and come complete with wine recommendations. We liked the diverse selection of dishes in this book, but, to be honest, we particularly enjoyed those that show Boulud's French roots most clearly.

specifics

400 pages, 167 recipes, 34 color photographs.
chapters La Tradition ❯ La Saison ❯ Le Voyage ❯ Le Potager
$35. Published by Scribner.

from the book

"**Perhaps the most elegant — and certainly the most magical — dough in the pastry chef's repertoire, puff pastry is made by encasing butter, lots of it, in a dough, then rolling the dough out until it is three times longer than it is wide, folding it in thirds, like a business letter, and repeating this process, called a turn, five more times. Done properly, the rolling and folding results in a dough that, when baked, puffs extravagantly, producing almost a thousand layers of pastry, the reason you sometimes hear it referred to as mille-feuilles, literally, a thousand leaves, in French. To be accurate, puff pastry results in 944 layers of pastry separated by 943 layers of butter — and butter is the only thing that should be used in puff pastry.**"

OK: *le potager*

Potato Gratin Forestier

e French region famous for its potato gratins, it wou
ne of these soul-soothing casseroles in my repertoi
y files, but the potato-mushroom gratin—forestier a
—is a favorite and one I've made for many years.
of Beef, the famed restaurant of the Hotel Plaza
r its specialty, a combination of two top rounds of
dish with a potato gratin, most often one like this
ushrooms, drenched with heavy cream, and baked
th the cream. Topped with a dusting of Parmesan
would sit easily next to chicken or beef, or take
side.

MAKES 4 MAIN-COURSE OR 6 T

ild mushrooms, trimmed,
parated by variety
proximately) unsalted butter
round white pepper
eeled, split, germ removed,
opped

¼ teaspoon finely
3 cups heavy crea
Freshly grated nu
4 pounds Idaho
¼ cup finely gr

IN A MEDIUM SAUTÉ PAN or skillet over mediur
nough butter to keep the mushrooms from sticking.
ok, stirring, just until they are tender but not colorec
mushroom is cooked, drain, turn it into a bowl, and
ushrooms separately because each type has a diffe
ooms should be mixed together in the bowl, along
perature until needed. (The mushrooms can be sau
plastic wrap at room temperature.)
ER A RACK in the oven and preheat the oven to
of 10-inch sauté pan or skillet.
R THE CREAM into a large bowl and whisk in s
Add more salt than you might normally, because
otatoes and slice them into ⅛-inch-thick rounds. T

mandoline. Lacking that, use the thinnest slicing blade on the food processor or a sharp knife. Toss the potatoes into the cream as you slice them.

4. USING YOUR HANDS, pull enough potato slices out of the cream to make a single layer on the bottom of the buttered pan, arranging them in even, slightly overlapping concentric circles. Make a second layer of potato slices and then pour some cream over the layers. Press down on the potatoes to compact the layers—when you do this, some of the cream should rise up between the slices. Spread the mushrooms (minus whatever liquid may have accumulated in the bowl) over the potatoes and pour in more cream, again using your hands to press down on the ingredients and bring the cream to the top. Arrange the remaining potato slices in attractive layers over the mushrooms, pouring in cream and pressing down as you finish each layer. Use all of the cream—you'll know you've added enough when, with-out pressing, the cream reaches the edges of the pan. Dust the gratin evenly with the Parmesan cheese.

Daniel Boulud's

Café Boulud Cookbook

FRENCH-AMERICAN RECIPES FOR THE HOME COOK

Daniel Boulud and Dorie Greenspan

FOREWORD BY MARTHA STEWART

chicken grand-mère francine

MAKES 4 SERVINGS

Chicken grand-mère, a savory fricassee, is a classic in French cuisine in general, but it was a classic in my family too. It was a specialty and a favorite of my Grandmother Francine, the grandmother who cooked at the original Café Boulud outside Lyon, and at no time was it better than at mushroom harvest time. Mushrooms are a typical chicken grand-mère ingredient, but there was nothing typical about the dish when my grandmother would add *rose des prés*, pink field mushrooms, newly dug potatoes, and new garlic. Fortunately, this dish always seems to be both satisfying and soothing whether you're making it plain, with cultivated cremini or oyster mushrooms and creamer potatoes, or fancy, dressing it up with exotic mushrooms and any of the small fingerling or banana potatoes that many greenmarkets now offer.

2   tablespoons extra-virgin olive oil

One 3-pound chicken, cut into 8 pieces (see Chicken, page 58)

Salt and freshly ground white pepper

2   tablespoons unsalted butter

12 cipollini onions, peeled and trimmed

4   shallots, peeled and trimmed

2   heads garlic, cloves separated but not peeled

3   sprigs thyme

4   small Yukon Gold potatoes, peeled and cut into 1½-inch chunks

2   small celery roots, peeled and cut into 1½-inch chunks

2   ounces slab bacon, cut into short, thin strips

12 small cremini or oyster mushrooms, trimmed and cleaned

2   cups unsalted chicken stock or store-bought low-sodium chicken broth

1. Center a rack in the oven and preheat the oven to 375°F.

2. Working over medium-high heat, warm the olive oil in a large ovenproof sauté pan or skillet—choose one with high sides and a cover. Season the chicken pieces all over with salt and pepper, slip them into the pan, and cook until they are well browned on all sides, about 10 to 15 minutes. Take your time—you want a nice, deep color and you also want to partially cook the chicken at this point. When the chicken is deeply golden, transfer it to a platter and keep it in a warm place while you work on the vegetables.

3. Pour off all but 2 tablespoons of the cooking fat from the pan. Lower the heat to medium, add the butter, onions, shallots, garlic, and thyme, and cook and stir just until the vegetables start to take on a little color, about 3 minutes. Add the potatoes, celery root, and bacon and cook for 1 to 2 minutes, just to start rendering the bacon fat. Cover the pan and cook for another 10 minutes, stirring every 2 minutes.

4. Add the mushrooms, season with salt and pepper, and return the chicken to the pan. Add the chicken stock, bring to the boil, and slide the pan into the oven. Bake, uncovered, for 20 to 25 minutes, or until the chicken is cooked through. Spoon everything onto a warm serving platter or into an attractive casserole.

TO SERVE Bring the chicken to the table, with plenty of pieces of crusty baguette to sop up the sauce and spread with the soft, sweet, caramely garlic that is easily squeezed out of its skin.

TO DRINK A rustic Bandol Rouge

CHICKEN

Look for chickens that are labeled free-range, or, better still, free-range and organic. Although chicken can be kept for a day or two in the coldest part of your refrigerator, or well wrapped and frozen for a month, I think you should buy the chicken the day you need it and keep it refrigerated until you're ready to use it. When you're ready to prepare it, rinse it inside and out under cold running water and then pat the bird dry with paper towels. If the recipe says that the chicken should be cut into eight parts, here's what you or the butcher should do: First, cut off the legs—this will make it easier for you to handle the rest of the chicken—then cut each leg in two, separating the thigh from the drumstick. Next, using your knife or a pair of poultry shears, detach the backbone all the way to the neck; chop both the backbone and neck into 2 to 3 pieces— keep these aside either for the recipe or for making stock. Finally, split the pair of breasts down the center and then split each breast crosswise in half. Whether or not you want the wings on the breast meat is up to you. If you decide to detach the wings, you can either cook them along with the other eight pieces of chicken, or keep them with the neck and backbone and use them for stock. Of course, this cutting plan works equally well for duck and other poultry.

When it comes to roasting a chicken, we rarely put a metal rack in our roasting pans at the Café. Instead, we make a "rack" from chicken parts. Using poultry shears, clip the chicken wings at the second joint and put the clippings, along with the neck, cut into 2 or 3 pieces, in the center of the roasting pan. Voilà—a rack. Just center the chicken on the bones and carry on.

potato gratin forestier

MAKES 4 MAIN-COURSE OR 6 TO 8 SIDE-DISH SERVINGS

As a son of the Dauphiné, the French region famous for its potato gratins, it would be unthinkable for me not to have at least one of these soul-soothing casseroles in my repertoire. Actually, I have several potato gratins in my files, but the potato-mushroom gratin—*forestier* always means there are mushrooms in the dish—is a favorite and one I've made for many years. Early in my career, I was the chef at the Baron of Beef, the famed restaurant of the Hotel Plaza in Copenhagen. The restaurant was named for its specialty, a combination of two top rounds of beef carved tableside, and I always served the dish with a potato gratin, most often one like this in which the potatoes are layered with wild mushrooms, drenched with heavy cream, and baked until they are soft, custardy, and saturated with the cream. Topped with a dusting of Parmesan that browns as the potatoes bake, this gratin would sit easily next to chicken or beef, or take center plate with a well-dressed salad on the side.

1   pound assorted wild mushrooms, trimmed, cleaned,
    and separated by variety
2   tablespoons (approximately) unsalted butter
Salt and freshly ground white pepper
2   cloves garlic, peeled, split, germ removed, and finely chopped
¼   teaspoon finely chopped thyme leaves
3   cups heavy cream
Freshly grated nutmeg
4   pounds Idaho potatoes
¼   cup finely grated Parmesan cheese

1. Working in a medium sauté pan or skillet over medium heat, sauté each variety of mushroom in just enough butter to keep the mushrooms from sticking. Season the mushrooms with salt and pepper and cook, stirring, just until they are tender but not colored, a few minutes for each batch. When one type of mushroom is cooked, drain, turn it into a bowl, and repeat with the next type. You need to sauté the mushrooms separately because each type has a different cooking time but, once cooked, all the mushrooms should be mixed together in the bowl, along with the garlic and thyme. Set aside at room temperature until needed. *(The mushrooms can be sautéed up to 2 hours ahead and kept covered with plastic wrap at room temperature.)*

2. Center a rack in the oven and preheat the oven to 350°F. Butter the bottom and sides of an ovenproof 10-inch sauté pan or skillet.

3. Pour the cream into a large bowl and whisk in salt and pepper and freshly grated nutmeg to taste. (Add more salt than you might normally, because the potatoes will need it.) One at a time, peel the potatoes and slice them into ⅛-inch-thick rounds. The best way to get rounds this thin is to use a mandoline. Lacking that, use the thinnest slicing blade on the food processor or a sharp knife. Toss the potatoes into the cream as you slice them.

4. Using your hands, pull enough potato slices out of the cream to make a single layer on the bottom of the buttered pan, arranging them in even, slightly overlapping concentric circles. Make a second layer of potato slices and then pour some cream over the layers. Press down on the potatoes to compact the layers—when you do this, some of the cream should rise up between the slices. Spread the mushrooms (minus whatever liquid may have accumulated in the bowl) over the potatoes and pour in more cream, again using your hands to press down on the ingredients and bring the cream to the top. Arrange the remaining potatoes in attractive layers over the mushrooms, pouring in cream and pressing down as you finish each layer. You may not need all of the cream—you'll know you've added enough when, without pressing down, you see cream at the edges of the pan. Dust the gratin evenly with the Parmesan cheese and place the pan on a foil-lined baking sheet that can act as a drip-catcher. (If you'd like your gratin to look like the one in the photograph, don't extend the last layers of potatoes all the way to the edges of the pan. Leave a border of mushrooms visible and give the mushrooms only the lightest dusting of Parmesan.)

5. Bake the gratin for 45 minutes, then check that it's not getting too brown. If necessary, lower the oven temperature to 300°F to keep the gratin from coloring too much. Bake for 15 minutes more, or until you can easily pass a slender sharp knife through all the layers.

6. Remove the gratin from the oven and let it stand in a warm place for about 20 minutes, time enough for the potatoes to soak up more cream. If it's more convenient, you can keep the gratin warm in a 200°F oven.

TO SERVE Bring the gratin to the table and cut it into wedges.

TO DRINK A light, earthy Givry from the Côte Chalonnaise

the rose pistola cookbook

author

Reed Hearon, chef-owner of Rose Pistola and two other San Francisco restaurants, with food writer Peggy Knickerbocker. Hearon is the author of *Bocaditos*, *La Parilla*, and *Salsa*.

why he wrote it

To celebrate the Old World Italian spirit and culinary heritage of the restaurant's North Beach neighborhood. "The cooking techniques in this book are based on home-cooking traditions—nothing fancy, nothing complicated. Some of those traditions—saving pasta water and making homemade ricotta—have long been forgotten and we revive them here, giving careful attention to the description of their execution."

why it made our list

The food at Rose Pistola has been described as a skillful blend of traditional Italian and California cuisines. And the book—an interweaving of restaurant recipes and tales of the character and characters of North Beach, one of the best known Italian quarters in America—is Italian-American to the core. Among the stories here is that of the original Rose Pistola, a 90-year denizen of the neighborhood and legendary bar owner who lent her name to the restaurant in return for her own table, with a meal waiting anytime. Photos of vegetable farmers, merchants, and other locals are sprinkled throughout, along with technique tips and odes to favorite ingredients and dishes like focaccia and garlic. The book, like the recipes it contains, is full of North Beach flavor.

from the book

"Great dishes often involve combinations of only two or perhaps three ingredients, such as bread and cheese, prosciutto and melon, tomatoes and basil, hot fudge and vanilla ice cream, and so on. The flavors create a dialogue as your palate goes back and forth between them, one flavor creating tension of a sort, the other flavor resolving that tension. The dialogue between flavors brings out aspects of each one that might not be apparent when tasted alone."

specifics

278 pages, 140 recipes, 16 color photographs, 51 black-and-white photographs.

chapters Antipasti › Soups › Salads › Pasta › Pizza, Farinata, and Focaccia › Fish and Seafood › Meat and Fowl › Vegetables › Desserts

$35. Published by Broadway Books.

es

from Rose herself, who...
heap and plentiful, frequ...
ted ground calamari for...
of the most appreciated ingre...
calamari in that way in both...
s (page 100) and Gnocchi...
, but this dish is a little differ-
tion of a crab cake and a Chi-

nd tart. Serve this dish as a light
rve with a mixed green salad or
ntrée. A simple, crisp white wine
io would be nice with this.

il in a heavy skillet over
nion until it is translucent, about
arjoram, anchovy paste, and red
sley sizzles and the anchovy paste
utes. Remove from the heat and al-

aves and choke and cut the heart
small pot of water to a boil and drop
ater to a simmer and cook the
million r. Drain.

In a bowl, stir together the calamari, bread crumbs, artichokes, and eggs. Stir in the onion mixture and the salt. Refrigerate while you make the aïoli.

For the Lemon Aïoli

Place the egg yolk, the juice of 2 lemons, garlic, and salt in a
food processor. Process until well blended. With the machine
running, pour in the olive oil in a slow steady stream and process
until the mixture thickens. Scrape into a bowl, squeeze a few
more drops of lemon juice ov—the top, stir, and set aside.

tick sauté
n a

Heat the remaining 2...
pan over medium-...
heaping tablespo...
cook several ca...
be tricky to t...
turn, and c...
the cakes...
them w...
aïoli s...

For the Lemon Aïoli

1 large egg yolk

Juice of 2 lemons, plus a few drops

1 garlic clove

1/2 teaspoon kosher or sea salt

3/4 cup extra virgin olive oil

Serves 6 to 8

The Rose Pistola COOKBOOK

140 Italian Recipes from San Francisco's Favorite North Beach Restaurant

BY REED HEARON AND PEGGY KNICKERBOCKER

calamari and artichoke cakes

SERVES 6 TO 8

The idea to use ground calamari came from Rose herself, who explained that when cala-mari was truly cheap and plentiful, frugal housewives in the neighborhood substituted ground calamari for more expensive ground meat. It is one of the most appreciated ingredients in North Beach. We use ground calamari in that way in both our Spaghetti with Calamari Meatballs and Gnocchi with Calamari Bolognese, but this dish is a little different. It is an Italian take on a combination of a crab cake and a Chinese fish cake.

The aïoli is wonderfully creamy and tart. Serve this dish as a light entrée or a substan-tial antipasto. Serve with a mixed green salad or with polenta if it is the entrée. A simple, crisp white wine such as Vermentino or Pinot Grigio would be nice with this.

¼   **cup extra virgin olive oil**

½   **large white onion, finely chopped**

2   **tablespoons chopped flat-leaf parsley**

1   **teaspoon chopped marjoram**

1   **tablespoon anchovy paste**

Pinch of crushed red pepper flakes

1   **large artichoke**

1   **pound calamari, cleaned, cut into rings and tentacles (see opposite page), and finely chopped in the food processor**

1   **cup fresh Bread Crumbs (page 67)**

5   **large eggs, beaten**

½   **teaspoon kosher or sea salt**

FOR THE LEMON AÏOLI

1   **large egg yolk**

Juice of 2 lemons, plus a few drops

1   **garlic clove**

½   **teaspoon kosher or sea salt**

¾   **cup extra virgin olive oil**

Heat 2 tablespoons of the olive oil in a heavy skillet over medium-high heat. Sauté the onion until it is translucent, about 5 minutes. Add the parsley, marjoram, anchovy paste, and red pepper and sauté until the parsley sizzles and the anchovy paste melts into the oil, about 3 minutes. Remove from the heat and allow to cool.

Trim the artichoke of its leaves and choke and cut the heart into ⅜-inch chunks. Bring a small pot of water to a boil and drop in the chunks. Reduce the water to a simmer and cook the chunks until tender, 10 to 15 minutes. Drain.

In a bowl, stir together the calamari, bread crumbs, artichokes, and eggs. Stir in the onion mixture and the salt. Refrigerate while you make the aïoli.

FOR THE LEMON AÏOLI Place the egg yolk, the juice of 2 lemons, garlic, and salt in a food processor. Process until well blended. With the machine running, pour in the olive oil in a slow steady stream and process until the mixture thickens. Scrape into a bowl, squeeze a few more drops of lemon juice over the top, stir, and set aside.

Heat the remaining 2 tablespoons oil in a large nonstick sauté pan over medium-high heat. For each calamari cake, spoon a heaping tablespoon of the calamari mixture into the oil; you can cook several cakes at a time, but do not crowd them, as they can be tricky to turn. Sauté the cakes until browned on one side, turn, and cook until cooked through, about 4 minutes more. As the cakes are cooked, remove them to a warm platter and keep them warm while you finish the remaining cakes. Serve with the aïoli spooned on top.

CLEANING CALAMARI

1. Cut the tentacles off the calamari just above the eyes and reserve them.
2. Just above the spot where the tentacles were attached is the mouth (it looks like a pea). Squeeze it out between your forefinger and thumb; discard the head and mouth.
3. Pull out the translucent bone from inside the body and discard.
4. Rinse the body inside and out, pulling out and discarding any remaining innards.
5. If the recipe calls for "rings and tentacles," cut the body into rings and leave the tentacles whole, or cut them in half if they are long or too big for your taste.

stuffed roasted sardines

SERVES 4

Monterey Bay used to abound with sardines that were used in North Beach cooking—remember Steinbeck's *Cannery Row*? Today a revival in sardine fishery is occurring. Here is a great recipe with which to celebrate its rebirth. If you have only had canned sardines, please don't think the fresh ones are at all the same. The difference is like the difference between canned and fresh tuna. Fresh sardines look (and taste) a lot like small fresh tuna.

You will need to fillet and butterfly the sardines. You could have your fish dealer do this, but be sure he leaves the tails intact. To accompany them, compose a medley of wild greens such as dandelion, nettles, and milk thistle or domestic greens such as cavolo nero, chard, kale, or even spinach.

A Vermentino di Sardegna, "La Cala" Sela & Mosca, 1997, is recommended.

8   **fresh sardines**

½   **cup extra virgin olive oil**

1   **small white onion, finely chopped**

1   **garlic clove, crushed**

1   **sprig rosemary (3 inches long)**

4   **anchovy fillets, chopped**

1   **cup mixed greens (see headnote)**

Kosher or sea salt and freshly cracked black pepper

½   **cup coarse fresh Bread Crumbs (recipe follows)**

1 tablespoon chopped flat-leaf parsley

To prepare the sardines, cut off the heads. Make a 3-inch slit down the belly of each fish and open the fish out flat. With your fingers, carefully lift the backbone away from the flesh and discard it, along with the innards. Leave the tail on. Rinse and drain on paper towels.

Preheat the oven to 500°F. Oil a baking sheet with 1 tablespoon of the olive oil.

Combine 2 tablespoons of the olive oil and the onion in a medium saucepan over medium heat and sauté until the onion becomes translucent, about 5 minutes. Add the garlic and rosemary. Continue to cook until the rosemary sizzles and the garlic is fragrant, about 3 minutes more. Add the anchovies and sauté, pressing on the anchovies with a fork until they melt into the oil, about 2 minutes. Remove the rosemary and garlic and discard.

Blanch the greens in salted boiling water for 3 to 4 minutes. Drain and, when cool enough to handle, squeeze out as much moisture as possible.

Add the greens and 2 tablespoons of the olive oil and cook in the same pan as the anchovies, stirring often until the greens are tender, about 4 minutes longer. Season with salt and pepper. Remove to a plate and let cool slightly.

Combine the bread crumbs, parsley, 1 tablespoon olive oil, and salt to taste in a small bowl. Mix well.

Arrange the sardines skin side down on the prepared baking sheet. Season each with salt and pepper to taste and drizzle with about 2 tablespoons olive oil. Divide the stuffing among the sardines, sprinkling each fish with a light coating of the mixture and patting it down as you go. (At this point the fish can be refrigerated, covered, for up to 1 hour before baking.)

Bake until the bread crumbs are golden brown and the fish are cooked through, 5 to 8 minutes. Transfer to a platter and serve.

BREAD CRUMBS

Fresh bread crumbs are made from fresh bread. Dried bread crumbs are made from bread that is at least a day old. To make either fresh or dried bread crumbs: Remove the crusts from a few slices of bread. Tear them into pieces, put them in the food processor, and process until the bread is ground to the desired size.

When measuring fresh bread crumbs, do not pack them tightly into the measuring cup, or they will lose their airy texture.

crisp salmon with fennel and tapenade

SERVES 4

This dish combines two of my favorite local products, bridged by the accent of a salty tapenade. A very hot pan is essential for ensuring that the salmon has a nice crispy skin. Use a heavy skillet for even heating, and heat the pan before adding the oil. This allows the skillet to become sizzling hot without burning the oil. Try this same technique with sea bass, mahi mahi, or Arctic char fillets (skin on).

The fennel can be made ahead of time and reheated, although once you put it in the oven, it takes about the same amount of time to cook as does the fish, so preparing the two together is fairly straightforward.

Pour a Chardonnay or a Pinot Gris from Oregon's Eyrie Vineyard.

12 **baby, 4 medium, or 2 large fennel bulbs,**

   trimmed (leafy tops reserved for garnish)

Kosher or sea salt and freshly cracked black pepper

¼ **cup plus 2 tablespoons extra virgin olive oil**

1 **garlic clove, crushed**

1 **sprig rosemary**

1 **cup dry Italian white wine**

1½ **pounds salmon fillet with skin, pin bones removed and cut into 4 pieces**

2 **tablespoons Tuna Tapenade (page 70)**

If using baby fennel bulbs, leave them whole; cut larger bulbs lengthwise into quarters. Season with salt and pepper.

Preheat the oven to 550°F (or the highest setting).

Heat ¼ cup of the olive oil in an ovenproof sauté pan over medium heat. Add the fennel bulbs and brown well on all sides, turning them with tongs to caramelize evenly, 10 to 15 minutes. Add the garlic and rosemary and cook until fragrant. Add the white wine and reduce by half. Add ½ cup water, place the pan in the oven, and cook, turning several times, until the fennel is easily pierced with a fork or wooden skewer, 10 to 15 minutes. You should have about ½ cup liquid remaining in the pan; if you don't, add a little more water.

Meanwhile, preheat a well seasoned griddle or nonstick pan over medium-high heat. Toss the fish fillets with the remaining 2 tablespoons oil and a generous amount of salt and pepper. Add the salmon fillets skin side down to the pan and, regulating the heat as necessary, cook until the skin is crisp, fully rendered of its fat, and browned, about 7 minutes. Turn the fish, increase the heat, and continue cooking until well browned on the other side and cooked medium-rare to medium, about 4 more minutes, or to taste.

Transfer the fennel and its braising liquid to a serving platter. Place the salmon on top of the fennel, skin side up. Top each salmon fillet with a spoonful of tapenade and garnish with the reserved leafy green fennel tops.

tuna tapenade

MAKES ABOUT 1 ½ CUPS

This flavorful, versatile spread can be served on crostini or on flatbread, or as a dip for raw vegetables. Or use it in Crisp Salmon with Fennel and Tapenade (page 68). However you plan on using it, the flavorful spread will keep well under a float of a few tablespoons of olive oil, well covered, in the refrigerator for up to two weeks. Bring it back to room temperature before using.

¾ cup **Niçoise olives, pitted**

¼ **cup green olives, pitted**

1   **garlic clove**

3   **tablespoons capers, drained**

1   **teaspoon thyme leaves**

¼ **teaspoon rosemary leaves, chopped**

One 6½-ounce can Italian olive-oil-packed tuna, drained

Grated zest and juice of 1 lemon

1   **tablespoon Cognac**

About ½ cup extra virgin olive oil

Pulse the olives, garlic, capers, and herbs together in a food processor. Then pulse in the tuna until it is combined. Place the ingredients in a bowl and add the lemon zest, lemon juice, and Cognac. Slowly mix in the olive oil, a little at a time, until the tapenade has a coarse texture. It should not be smooth. Cover and refrigerate until needed; serve at room temperature

PITTING OLIVES

Lay a clean kitchen towel on a flat surface and place about five olives on top. With the flat side of a heavy knife, whack each of the olives so that they split open. Ease the pit out with your fingers, set the pitted olives aside, and proceed until all the olives are pitted.

We just can't get enough of television food shows. At any time, day or night, you can flip through the channels and find at least one or two cooking programs in progress. If it isn't the lively Emeril shouting out to his audience while tossing ingredients into his steaming pot, it's the more subdued Martha making pretty holiday cookies, or Julia and Jacques trading jibes. No matter what the style, we're hooked. And did you notice that we don't have to use last names? It's first-name recognition for cooks today—right up there with Cher and Madonna. Naturally enough, just as the airwaves fill up, so do the bookstore shelves. These are our selects for the best half-dozen of the big batch of program-based cookbooks published this year.

books from tv cooks

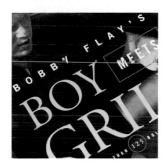

category two

the kitchen sessions with charlie trotter

author

Chicago restaurateur Charlie Trotter, considered to be one of the most innovative chefs in America. His previous cookbooks include last year's *Best of the Best* honoree *Charlie Trotter's Desserts*.

why he wrote it

"In *The Kitchen Sessions*, my intention is to emphasize the notion of interchangeability and the addition or subtraction of foodstuffs in order to best achieve results that will suit your desires. The recipes here, as should always be the case, are meant to be used as guides or as inspiration."

why it made our list

Some chefs seem to pile flavor on top of flavor with no other purpose than to create an architecturally imposing stack. Trotter's creations are no less spectacular-looking, but the best part is that all those assembled elements taste perfectly wonderful together. In this companion book to his PBS television series, Trotter walks us through each component recipe individually and then shows how everything fits together for a dish that's more than the sum of its parts. Even home cooks will be able to make these beautifully balanced dishes. And you'd better believe, friends and family are going to be impressed.

from the book

"**I am greatly inspired by the great jazz musicians of the '40s, '50s, and '60s who routinely went into a studio or club and played live sets. The resulting 'sessions' would represent a given moment. Miles Davis may have played 'Stella by Starlight' or 'My Funny Valentine' hundreds of times, but he played them differently in each session. Cooking is exactly like playing music, and once historical precedence and classical ideas are understood, the possibilities are only as limited as the artist's imagination."**

specifics

240 pages, more than 80 recipes, 39 color photographs, 49 black-and-white photographs.

chapters Soup › Salad › Lobster › Scallop › Catfish › Salmon › Tuna › Pasta › Poultry › Pork › Duck › Beef › Dessert

$29.95. Published by Ten Speed Press.

The Kitchen Sessions

WITH CHARLIE TROTTER

roasted cornish game hen with potato pavé and gingered mustard sauternes sauce

SERVES 4

This preparation allows for the enjoyment of both the plump, moist breast meat and the satisfying, crispy skin of this versatile small bird. The accompanying pavé can be prepared a day or two ahead and reheated just before serving. The Gingered Mustard Sauternes Sauce has a sweet-sour quality to its basic flavor, but its finish is far more complex. This dish can be plated individually or served family-style on a platter with equally fabulous results.

2   Idaho potatoes, peeled and thinly sliced

2   sweet potatoes, peeled and thinly sliced

3   cups heavy cream

5   tablespoons melted butter

Salt and pepper

1   tablespoon canola oil

4   rock Cornish game hens, trussed

8   sprigs thyme

2   cups haricots verts, blanched and cut into 1-inch pieces on the diagonal

Gingered Mustard Sauternes Sauce (see page 78)

2   tablespoons chopped fresh chervil

4   teaspoons Herb Oil, optional (see page 79)

20 strands Preserved Ginger (see page 79)

To prepare the pavé: Place the Idaho and sweet potato slices in a large bowl, pour in the heavy cream, and gently toss to evenly coat the slices. Line an 8 by 8-inch pan with aluminum foil and brush the foil with ½ tablespoon of the melted butter. Arrange a layer of the Idaho potato slices in the bottom of the pan, overlapping them slightly, and season with salt and pepper. Arrange a layer of the sweet potato slices on top of the Idaho potatoes, overlapping them slightly, and season with salt and pepper. Continue alternating layers of Idaho and sweet potatoes until all of the potato slices are used. Tightly cover the pan with a second sheet of aluminum foil brushed

with ½ tablespoon butter. Place another 8 by 8-inch pan over the foil and weight it down with a brick or other heavy, ovenproof object. Bake at 350 degrees for 1½ hours, or until the potatoes are tender. Leaving the weight on the pan, refrigerate the pavé for at least 4 hours.

Remove the pavé from the refrigerator. Remove the weight, the top pan, and the foil, and invert the potato pavé onto a sheet pan. Remove the foil and cut the pavé into 2-inch squares. Place 4 of the pavé squares in a large, nonstick sauté pan with the canola oil and cook over medium-high heat for 3 to 4 minutes, or until golden brown. Carefully turn the pavé and cook for 3 to 4 minutes, or until the pavé is warmed through. (If the pavé is still not warm in the middle, it can be heated in a 375-degree oven for 5 minutes.)

To roast the hens: Season the rock Cornish game hens with salt and pepper and brush the skin with the remaining 4 tablespoons melted butter. Place a whole thyme sprig in the center cavity of each hen. Remove the leaves from the remaining thyme sprigs and sprinkle the leaves on the outside of the hens. Place the hens on a rack in a large roasting pan and roast at 375 degrees for 45 minutes, or until the juices run clear.

Remove the hens from the oven and allow them to rest for 10 minutes before carving the breasts and legs. (Save the carcasses for making a flavorful stock.)

ASSEMBLY Place a piece of the pavé in the center of each plate. Arrange some of the meat from the hens at 4 points around the pavé. Place some of the haricots verts around the plate and spoon the Gingered Mustard Sauternes Sauce over the meat and around the plate. Sprinkle with the chopped chervil and top with freshly ground black pepper. Drizzle the Herb Oil around the plates and sprinkle with the Preserved Ginger.

WINE NOTES This dish calls for a rich, aromatic white wine to balance with the ginger. Alsace Rieslings such as Meyer-Fonne's "Wineck-Schlossberg," Trimbach, or Domaine Weinbach will mesh beautifully.

gingered mustard sauternes sauce

YIELD: 3 CUPS

You can add a spoonful of honey if a sweeter sauce is desired.

4   **cups sauternes, reduced to 2 cups**
3¾ **ounces whole-grain mustard**
¼   **cup Preserved Ginger, chopped (opposite page)**

½ **cup butter**

2 **tablespoons rice wine vinegar**

Salt and pepper

Whisk together all the ingredients and season to taste with salt and pepper.

preserved ginger

YIELD: ABOUT ¾ CUP

1 **cup finely julienned ginger**

2 **cups simple syrup (1 cup sugar and 1 cup water brought to a boil)**

Blanch the ginger in simmering water for 3 minutes. Strain and repeat the process 2 more times. Simmer the ginger in the simple syrup for 30 minutes. Remove from the heat and cool in the syrup. Refrigerate in the syrup until needed.

herb oil

YIELD: ½ CUP

Herb oils can be made with any type of herb, such as basil, dill, or tarragon.

1 **cup fresh chives**

1 **cup fresh flat-leaf parsley**

1 **cup watercress**

1 **cup canola oil**

Blanch the chives, parsley, and watercress in boiling salted water for 20 seconds and immediately shock in ice water to stop the cooking process. Drain the water, squeeze out any excess liquid, and coarsely chop the herbs. Purée the herbs with the canola oil for 3 to 4 minutes, or until the mixture is bright green, and refrigerate overnight. Strain through a fine-mesh sieve and discard the solids. Refrigerate for 24 hours and then decant the oil. The oil may be stored in the refrigerator for up to 1 month.

dried fruit-stuffed pork tenderloin with roasted new potatoes and bacon-sherry vinaigrette

SERVES 4

Intensely flavored dried fruit really seems to bring out the clean, delicate qualities of pork. Furthermore, the dried fruits provide a sweetness, tartness, and acidity that showcase the meat and provide a balance to the bacon-flavored potatoes and the luscious, slightly bitter endive. The flavors in this dish perform in unison and exquisite harmony. This preparation works as well as part of a formal dinner as it does as a simple everyday meal for the family.

2	pounds new red potatoes, halved
½	cup plus 3 tablespoons olive oil
6	sprigs fresh thyme leaves
	Salt and pepper
⅓	cup dried cranberries
⅓	cup dried golden raisins
⅓	cup chopped dried apricots
⅓	cup dried currants
4	tablespoons julienned fresh sage leaves
½	cup water
1	20-ounce pork tenderloin, cleaned and halved
3	tablespoons canola oil
1	large head radicchio, quartered
1	tablespoon butter
2	teaspoons sugar
½	cup Chicken Stock (see page 83)
½	cup uncooked bacon batons
½	cup minced red onion
1	teaspoon minced garlic
2½	tablespoons sherry wine vinegar

To prepare the potatoes: Toss the potatoes with 3 tablespoons of the olive oil and the thyme leaves and season with salt and pepper. Place on a roasting pan or sheet pan and roast at 375 degrees for 45 to 60 minutes, or until the potatoes are golden brown and crispy, turning them once to ensure even browning.

To prepare the filling: Cook the cranberries, raisins, apricots, currants, 2 tablespoons of the sage, and the water in a medium saucepan over low heat for 5 minutes, or until warm. Remove from the heat and let stand for 15 minutes.

To prepare the pork tenderloin: Starting from the end of each half of tenderloin, cut a slit along the center using a sharp boning knife or other thin knife. If the knife is not long enough to reach the far end of the loins, repeat the process starting from the other end. Turn the loins on their sides and cut another slit to create an "X" in the center of the loins. Insert the handle of a long wooden spoon through the incision to help stretch the hole. Using your fingers and the wooden spoon handle, stuff as much filling as possible into each loin. Season the outside of the loins with salt and pepper.

Place the canola oil in a hot sauté pan over high heat. Add the pork loin and sear on all sides. Reduce the heat to medium-high and cook for 5 minutes on each side, or until the pork registers 150 degrees on a meat thermometer. Let rest for 10 minutes before slicing.

To prepare the radicchio: Cook the radicchio and butter in a large sauté pan over medium heat for 3 to 4 minutes, or until it starts to caramelize. Add the sugar and stock, cover, and cook for 5 to 10 minutes, or until the radicchio is tender. Season to taste with salt and pepper.

stuffing a tenderloin

insert thin knife cut slit

rotate and create x

insert spoon to enlarge hole

To prepare the bacon-sherry vinaigrette: Render the bacon in a sauté pan over medium heat. Add the red onion and garlic and cook for 1 minute, or until the red onion is softened. Remove from heat and add the sherry wine vinegar and the remaining 2 tablespoons of sage. Slowly whisk in the remaining ½ cup of olive oil and season to taste with salt and pepper.

ASSEMBLY Place some of the radicchio in the center of each plate and arrange some of the roasted potatoes around the radicchio. Cut the stuffed pork tenderloin into ¼-inch-thick slices and place 3 slices on top of the radicchio on each plate. Spoon the bacon-sherry vinaigrette over the pork and around the plate and top with freshly ground black pepper.

WINE NOTES The dried fruits add acidity to this dish, and the pork and vinaigrette scream out for ripe, spicy flavors in a wine. Zinfandels from producers such as Ravenswood and Ridge are intense styles that will fit the mold for this dish.

chicken stock

YIELD: 2 QUARTS

You can make a large batch of stock, freeze it in ice cube trays, and store it in resealable bags in the freezer.

6	**pounds chicken bones**
3	**cups chopped onions**
2	**cups chopped carrots**
2	**cups chopped celery**
1	**cup chopped leeks**
1	**tablespoon white peppercorns**
1	**bay leaf**

Place all of the ingredients in a large stockpot and cover three-quarters of the way with cold water. Bring to a boil, reduce the heat to low, and slowly simmer uncovered for 4 hours, skimming every 30 minutes to remove impurities that rise to the surface. Strain, discard the solids, and cook over medium heat for 30 to 45 minutes, or until reduced to 2 quarts. Store in the refrigerator for up to 2 days or freeze for up to 2 months.

every day's a party

author

Emeril Lagasse, chef-owner of six restaurants, three of them in New Orleans, and host of the Food Network's *Emeril Live* and *Essence of Emeril*. Among his four other books are two former *Best of the Best* winners, *Emeril's TV Dinners* and *Emeril's Creole Christmas*.

why he wrote it

"I've seen Louisianans get on planes with ice chests filled with crawfish étouffée, various gumbos, and even fresh shrimp to take to the beaches, to the slopes, and anywhere else they're destined. If you can't come to their party, they'll take it to you! Here then, my friends, is my personal invitation to all of you to come to Louisiana, where the fun never stops."

why it made our list

Just reading this book's a party, as Emeril walks us through a Louisiana year full of parades and celebrations, holidays and get-togethers, weddings and christenings, football games and food fairs and festivals of all sorts. Each event has its own special dishes, and collected together they make an irresistible sampler of Louisiana cooking, from jambalaya and gumbo to corn dogs and Frito pie. The book is jammed with photos of revelers and the food that gives them reason to rejoice. Not quite as much fun as being there, perhaps, but a great blueprint for planning your own party.

specifics

338 pages, 130 recipes, 340 color photographs.

chapters January › February › March › April › May › June › July › August › September › October › November › December

$26. Published by William Morrow and Company, Inc.

from the book

"Brunches are quite popular down south and thought to be a very civilized manner in which to work up to another party. Yes, there's nothing like having a party before another party to get everyone in a party mood. Beverages, or eye-openers as they're called here, can run the gamut from Champagne and Bloody Marys to milk punches and the ever-popular Sazerac, perhaps the best known of all New Orleans cocktails. The menu for these affairs usually includes some kind of egg dish but, like everything else here, just about anything goes. All the host must ensure is that whatever is offered is good and that there's plenty of it . . . ."

GARLIC MEATBALL P

THESE GARLIC-STUFFED MEATBALLS
MARCELLE AND HER HUSBAND, ROCK
PARTIES. THEY CAN BE MADE AHEAD
POT ON ONE OF THOSE BUTANE BURN
HERE, OR, YOU CAN HEAT THEM U
INSULATED CONTAINER. ■ PLO
SLATHERED WITH MUSTARD AND
FOR A FEW HOURS. OH, AND JUST S
A POORBOY IN NEW ORLEANS,
"DRESSED" OR "UNDRESSED."
DOLLED UP WITH LETTUCE AND T
TIN' ON IT. NEW ORLEANS HAS
GET THE SEASONING OF THE ME
BALL OF IT, ABOUT THE SIZE OF

In a large mixing bowl, combine th
chopped yellow onion, chopped gar
egg, bread crumbs, Worcestershire,
salt, and ½ teaspoon of the cayenne.
hands and form into 16 meatballs.
in the center of each meatball a
around it.

Combine the flour and Creole s
plate. Roll the meatballs evenly
tapping off any excess. Reserve

In a large skillet, heat the oil o
the meatballs and brown evenl
them. Remove the meatballs fr
With a wooden spoon, scrap
to loosen any brown bits. Stir

ary › J

OYS

OF THE FAVORITES OF
RE IDEAL FOR TAILGATE
E, THEN REHEATED IN A
T ARE SO POPULAR DOWN
E AND TAKE THEM IN AN
N FRENCH BREAD AND
AISE. THEY'LL CARRY YOU
. KNOW. WHEN YOU ORDER
E ASKED IF YOU WANT IT
. MEANS THE SANDWICH IS
. "UNDRESSED" IS WITH NUT-
LANGUAGE SOMETIMES. ■ TO
IGHT, I USUALLY FRY A SMALL
, IN A SKILLET TO TEST IT.

1/4 cup bleached all-purpose
    flour
1 teaspoon Creole Seasoning
    (page 13)
1/4 cup vegetable oil
2 cups thinly sliced yellow onions
One 12-ounce bottle Abita amber
    beer or other amber beer
1 cup water
3 tablespoons chopped fresh
    parsley leaves
1 large (26 to 28 inches long)
    loaf French bread
6 tablespoons Creole or whole-
    grain mustard
6 tablespoons Mayonnaise
    (page 129)
1/2 pound provolone cheese,
    thinly sliced

flour. Stir constantly for 3 to 4 minutes...
brown roux. Add the sliced onions and sea...
remaining 1/2 teaspoon salt and 1/4 teaspoon cayenne.
Cook, stirring constantly, until the onions are slightly
soft, about 2 minutes. Slowly pour in the beer and water
and mix well. Bring to a boil and return the meatballs
to the skillet. Reduce the heat to medium-low and simmer, uncovered, for about 1 hour, until the gravy is
thick, turning and basting the meatballs with the pan
gravy about every 15 minutes.

Remove from the heat and skim off any fat that has
risen to the surface. Add the parsley.

Cut the loaf of bread lengthwise in half. Spread one
half with the mustard and the other half with the mayonnaise. Arrange the provolone on the bottom half of
the bread, overlapping the slices, then arrange the meatballs on top of the cheese. Spoon the gravy over the
meatballs. Top with the remaining bread half, cut into
6 equal portions, and serve immediately.

MAKES 6 SERVINGS

1/2 pound ground veal
1/2 pound ground beef chuck
1/2 pound ground pork
1/2 cup finely chopped yellow
    onion
1/2 teaspoon finely chopped
    garlic
1/4 cup finely chopped
    onions or scallions
    (green part only)
1 large egg
1/4 cup fine dr...
1 tablespoon...
    sauce
1 1/2 teas...
3/4 te...
16 s...

neats,
nions,
of the
h your
c clove
e meat

a shallow
mixture,
ng flour.

n heat. Add
oon to turn
and set aside.
m of the pan
rved seasoned

every day's a party
Louisiana Recipes for Celebrating with Family and Friends

emeril lagasse

with Marcelle Bienvenu and Felicia Willett
photographs by Philip Gould

garlic meatball poorboys

These garlic-stuffed meatballs are one of the favorites of Marcelle and her husband, Rock, and are ideal for tailgate parties. They can be made ahead of time, then reheated in a pot on one of those butane burners that are so popular down here. Or, you can heat them up at home and take them in an insulated container.

Plopped on french bread and slathered with mustard and mayonnaise, they'll carry you for a few hours. Oh, and just so you'll know, when you order a poorboy in New Orleans, you'll be asked if you want it "dressed" or "undressed." "Dressed" means the sandwich is dolled up with lettuce and tomatoes. "Undressed" is with nuttin' on it. New Orleans has its own language sometimes.

To get the seasoning of the meat just right, I usually fry a small ball of it, about the size of a pecan, in a skillet to test it.

½   **pound ground veal**

½   **pound ground beef chuck**

½   **pound ground pork**

½   **cup finely chopped yellow onion**

½   **teaspoon finely chopped garlic**

¼   **cup finely chopped green onions or scallions (green part only)**

1   **large egg**

¼   **cup fine dried bread crumbs**

1   **tablespoon Worcestershire sauce**

1½ **teaspoons salt**

¾   **teaspoon cayenne**

16 **small cloves garlic, peeled**

¼   **cup bleached all-purpose flour**

1   **teaspoon Creole Seasoning (page 88)**

¼   **cup vegetable oil**

2   **cups thinly sliced yellow onions**

One 12-ounce bottle Abita amber beer or other amber beer

1   **cup water**

3	**tablespoons chopped fresh parsley leaves**
1	**large (26 to 28 inches long) loaf French bread**
6	**tablespoons Creole or whole-grain mustard**
6	**tablespoons Mayonnaise (page 88)**
½	**pound provolone cheese, thinly sliced**

In a large mixing bowl, combine the ground meats, chopped yellow onion, chopped garlic, green onions, egg, bread crumbs, Worcestershire, 1 teaspoon of the salt, and ½ teaspoon of the cayenne. Mix well with your hands and form into 16 meatballs. Insert a garlic clove in the center of each meatball and pinch the meat around it.

Combine the flour and Creole seasoning in a shallow plate. Roll the meatballs evenly in the flour mixture, tapping off any excess. Reserve any remaining flour.

In a large skillet, heat the oil over medium heat. Add the meatballs and brown evenly, using a spoon to turn them. Remove the meatballs from the pan and set aside. With a wooden spoon, scrape the bottom of the pan to loosen any brown bits. Stir in the reserved seasoned flour. Stir constantly for 3 to 4 minutes to make a dark brown roux. Add the sliced onions and season with the remaining ½ teaspoon salt and ¼ teaspoon cayenne. Cook, stirring constantly, until the onions are slightly soft, about 2 minutes. Slowly pour in the beer and water and mix well. Bring to a boil and return the meatballs to the skillet. Reduce the heat to medium-low and simmer, uncovered, for about 1 hour, until the gravy is thick, turning and basting the meatballs with the pan gravy about every 15 minutes.

Remove from the heat and skim off any fat that has risen to the surface. Add the parsley.

Cut the loaf of bread lengthwise in half. Spread one half with the mustard and the other half with the mayonnaise. Arrange the provolone on the bottom half of the bread, overlapping the slices, then arrange the meatballs on top of the cheese. Spoon the gravy over the meatballs. Top with the remaining bread half, cut into 6 equal portions, and serve immediately.

creole seasoning

MAKES ABOUT ¾ CUP

2½ tablespoons sweet paprika

2 tablespoons salt

2 tablespoons garlic powder

1 tablespoon freshly ground black pepper

1 tablespoon onion powder

1 tablespoon cayenne

1 tablespoon dried oregano

1 tablespoon dried thyme

Mix all of the ingredients together and store in an airtight container. Can be stored this way for up to 3 months.

mayonnaise

MAKES ABOUT 1 CUP

1 large egg

1 tablespoon Creole or whole-grain mustard

½ teaspoon salt

1 tablespoon fresh lemon juice

1 cup vegetable oil

Combine the egg, mustard, salt, and lemon juice in a food processor or blender and process until smooth, about 15 seconds. With the motor running, pour the vegetable oil through the feed tube in a slow, steady stream. Cover and chill for 1 hour in the refrigerator before serving. Best if used within 24 hours.

jambalaya grits

MAKES 8 APPETIZER SERVINGS OR 4 MAIN-COURSE SERVINGS

Traditional jambalaya is made with rice, but grits work equally well, for a different twist on this Louisiana staple. This is one hearty dish and not for the weak of heart. Sometimes I like to accompany it with a link of warm boudin, the fantastic local sausage made with bits of pork, rice, and, of course, the perfect blend of seasonings.

1	tablespoon olive oil
1	cup chopped yellow onions
½	cup chopped green bell pepper
½	cup chopped celery
1½	teaspoons salt
⅛	teaspoon freshly ground black pepper
½	teaspoon cayenne
¼	pound andouille or other smoked sausage, cut crosswise into ¼-inch-thick slices
¼	pound boiled ham, cut into small dice
1	tablespoon chopped garlic
½	cup peeled, seeded, and chopped vine-ripened tomato
6	cups milk
2	cups quick-cooking white grits
½	pound medium-size shrimp, peeled and deveined
¼	cup chopped green onions or scallions (green part only)
¼	pound sharp white cheddar cheese, grated

In a large, heavy pot, heat the olive oil over medium-high heat. Add the onions, bell pepper, celery, salt, black pepper, and cayenne. Cook, stirring, until the vegetables are soft and lightly golden, about 4 minutes. Add the sausage and ham and continue to cook, stirring occasionally, for 2 minutes. Add the garlic and tomato and cook for 2 minutes. Add the milk and bring to a boil. Reduce the heat to medium and stir in the grits. Stir for 2 minutes, then add the shrimp. Cook, stirring, until the grits are tender and creamy, 7 to 8 minutes. Stir in the green onions, then add the cheese and stir until it is completely melted, about 30 seconds.

Serve hot right from the pot.

julia and jacques cooking at home

authors

World-famous teachers, authors, and TV cooks Julia Child and Jacques Pépin. Child is the author of nine books, most recently *In Julia's Kitchen with Master Chefs*. Pépin's 16 books include *Jacques Pépin's Kitchen: Encore with Claudine*, one of last year's *Best of the Best* honorees.

why they wrote it

As a companion to their Food Network series of the same name.

why it made our list

It may be true that too many cooks spoil the broth, but having a book by these two cooks is more likely to spoil the reader. The recipes are French and American classics, and the detailed steps and tips, accompanied by plenty of color photos, take the mystery out of all the methods. That may be enough if you need to know how to cook artichokes or carve a chicken, but it's not why we love this cookbook; the "conversations" between Julia and Jacques that appear throughout are what make it so delicious. Part mutual-admiration society, part one-upmanship, the give and take between these two masters makes for a collection that's as much fun to read as it is to cook from.

specifics

430 pages, 150 recipes, 328 color photographs.
chapters Appetizers › Soups › Eggs › Salads and Sandwiches › Potatoes and Other Accompaniments › Vegetables › Fish › Poultry › Meats › Desserts
$40. Published by Alfred A. Knopf.

from the book

Julia: "The nation's fear-of-fat phobia has ruined the canned-tuna industry, to my mind. When looking for it on our supermarket shelves, you rarely find anything but tuna canned in 'fresh spring water,' which has far less taste than tuna packed in oil."

Jacques: "I like many cuts of meat rare, but there is an obsession about 'not overcooking' these days that is ridiculous. I go to restaurants and get rare sausage, rare fish, rare chicken, and very rare—really raw—vegetables. I want to tell them, 'Please don't undercook the food!'"

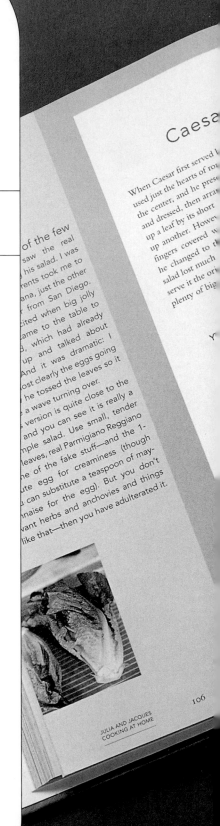

Preparing the salad components
You will probably need 2 large heads of romaine for 3 people—or use a commercially prepared package of "romaine hearts," if they appear fresh and fine. From a large head remove the outside leaves until you get down to the cone where the leaves are 4 to 7 inches in length (see photo on left)—you'll want 6 to 8 of these leaves per serving. Separate the leaves and wash them carefully to keep them ...le, roll them loosely in clean ... and keep refrigerated until ... (Save the remains for ...nately, romaine ...der refrig-

Julia's authentic Ca...
is excellent, but I love Gloria's a...
Caesar salad, the one my wife makes at home. She mixes all the dressing ingredients together first—oil, lemon juice, Worcestershire, seasonings, chopped garlic, egg, and anchovy fillets in little pieces—and then tosses it with the broken-up romaine leaves. And she tosses in some crumbled blue cheese, either Roquefort or Stilton, as well as Parmesan. She made this for me when we first met, and I have never wanted to change it.

...d in the early 1920s, he
...he tender short leaves in
...ole. The salad was tossed
...late so that you could pick
...t down bit by bit, then pick
...omers didn't like to get their
...eese-and-garlic dressing, and
...l torn leaf. Too bad, since the
...ity and drama. You can certainly
...me—just provide your guests with
...nd plan to be extravagant.

s Caesar Salad

...rvings

...risp, narrow leaves from the
...of 2 heads romaine lettuce, or a
...ge of 2 romaine hearts (about 1
...d)
...e Plain Toasted Croutons (page
...08)
...arge clove garlic, peeled
... cup or more excellent olive (il ...
...Salt
1 large egg
Freshly ground black peppe...
1 whole lemon, halved an...
Worcestershire sauce
2 Tbs freshly grated P...
imported Parmig...

Special equipment...
A large mixi...

Julia and Jacques
Cooking at Home

JULIA CHILD and JACQUES PEPIN

caesar salad

When Caesar first served his famous salad in the early 1920s, he used just the hearts of romaine lettuce, the tender short leaves in the center, and he presented them whole. The salad was tossed and dressed, then arranged on each plate so that you could pick up a leaf by its short end and chew it down bit by bit, then pick up another. However, many customers didn't like to get their fingers covered with egg-and-cheese-and-garlic dressing, and he changed to the conventional torn leaf. Too bad, since the salad lost much of its individuality and drama. You can certainly serve it the original way at home—just provide your guests with plenty of big paper napkins. And plan to be extravagant.

JULIA

I am probably one of the few people around who saw the real Caesar Cardini making his salad. I was about 9 when my parents took me to his restaurant in Tijuana, just the other side of the border from San Diego. They were so excited when big jolly Caesar himself came to the table to make the salad, which had already been written up and talked about everywhere. And it was dramatic: I remember most clearly the eggs going in, and how he tossed the leaves so it looked like a wave turning over.

This version is quite close to the original, and you can see it is really a very simple salad. Use small, tender whole leaves, real Parmigiano Reggiano—none of the fake stuff—and the 1-minute egg for creaminess (though you can substitute a teaspoon of mayonnaise for the egg). But you don't want herbs and anchovies and things like that—then you have adulterated it.

JACQUES

Julia's authentic Caesar salad is excellent, but I love Gloria's almost-Caesar salad, the one my wife makes at home. She mixes all the dressing ingredients together first—oil, lemon juice, Worcestershire, seasonings, chopped garlic, egg, and anchovy fillets in little pieces—and then tosses it with the broken-up romaine leaves. And she tosses in some crumbled blue cheese, either Roquefort or Stilton, as well as Parmesan. She made this for me when we first met, and I have never wanted to change it.

julia's caesar salad

YIELD: 2 OR 3 SERVINGS

18 to 24 crisp, narrow leaves from the hearts of 2 heads romaine lettuce,

    or a package of romaine hearts (about 1 pound)

1   cup Plain Toasted Croutons (page 96)

1   large clove garlic, peeled

¼   cup or more excellent olive oil

Salt

1   large egg

Freshly ground black pepper

1   whole lemon, halved and seeded

Worcestershire sauce

2   tablespoons freshly grated Parmesan cheese,

    imported Parmigiano Reggiano only

SPECIAL EQUIPMENT

A large mixing bowl; a small frying pan

PREPARING THE SALAD COMPONENTS You will probably need 2 large heads of romaine for 3 people—or use a commercially prepared package of "romaine hearts," if they appear fresh and fine. From a large head remove the outside leaves until you get down to the cone where the leaves are 4 to 7 inches in length (see photo, below)—you'll want 6 to 8 of these leaves per serving. Separate the leaves and wash them carefully to keep them whole, roll them loosely in clean towels, and keep refrigerated until serving time. (Save the remains for other salads—fortunately, romaine keeps reasonably well under refrigeration.)

To flavor the croutons, crush the garlic clove with the flat of a chef's knife, sprinkle on ¼ teaspoon of salt, and mince well. Pour about a tablespoon of olive oil on the garlic and mash again with the knife, rubbing and pressing to make a soft purée.

Scrape the purée into the frying pan, add another tablespoon of oil, and warm over low-medium heat. Add the croutons and toss for a minute or two to infuse them with the garlic oil, then remove from the heat. (For a milder garlic flavor, you can strain the purée through a small sieve into a pan before adding the extra oil and croutons. Discard the bits of garlic.)

To coddle the egg, bring a small saucepan of water to the simmer. Pierce the large end of the egg with a pushpin to prevent cracking, then simmer it for exactly 1 minute.

MIXING AND SERVING THE CAESAR Dress the salad just before serving. Have ready all the dressing ingredients and a salad fork and spoon for tossing.

Drizzle 2 tablespoons of olive oil over the romaine leaves and toss to coat, lifting the leaves from the bottom and turning them toward you, so they tumble over like a wave. Sprinkle with a generous pinch of salt and several grinds of pepper, toss once or twice, then add the lemon juice and several drops of Worcestershire, and toss again. Taste for seasoning, and add more, if needed.

Crack the egg and drop it right on the romaine leaves, then toss to break it up and coat the leaves. Sprinkle on the cheese, toss briefly, then add the croutons (and the garlicky bits in the pan, if you wish) and toss for the last time, just to mix them into the salad.

Arrange 6 or more leaves in a single layer on individual plates, scatter the croutons all around, and serve.

PLAIN TOASTED CROUTONS (MAKES 4 CUPS) Preheat the oven to 350°F. Remove the crusts from 4 or more thick slices of home-style white bread and slice bread into ½-inch strips and then the strips into ½-inch cubes, to make 4 cups. Spread the cubes in a single layer on a cookie sheet and set in the oven for about 10 minutes, turning once or twice, until lightly toasted on all sides. Spread the cubes on a tray to cool before using or freezing.

pot roast

Nearly five hours of cooking go into Jacques's generous pot roast, but very little of it is work time for the cook. It is the process of braising that produces remarkable tenderness and flavor in the large cut of beef bottom round used here. As the meat cooks slowly in the oven, the lean flesh becomes moist and tender, and exchanges flavors with the liquid and the aromatic vegetables and herbs that surround it.

Here, as with many other braised meat dishes, you'll have most to do at the beginning. The roast is thoroughly browned on the stovetop; then wine, onions, tomatoes, thyme, and bay leaves are added. But aside from putting the big casserole into the oven (twice), the hard work is done. You also have the convenience of cooking all the vegetables for the meal right along with the meat. Open the pot after three or four hours, toss in turnip wedges, small white onions, and baby carrots, and return it to the oven. In an hour or so, they will be perfectly soft and shapely, and will have added even more flavor to the dish. Just before serving, set the pot on the stove and simmer some green peas, to add an extra touch of color to the feast when it is arrayed on your serving platter.

JULIA

The pot roast and vegetables can be cooled and stored in the refrigerator. Reheat on top of the stove or in a low oven. It is particularly easy to slice the meat when cool, and reheat the slices quickly in the sauce. Or serve it cold with vinaigrette *à la Parisienne*.

JACQUES

The piece of beef I prefer for pot roast is cut from the "flat" muscle of the bottom round (part of the animal's hind leg). It is lean and solid and becomes very tender and moist during braising, but still holds its shape and slices easily. You can find this in any market, but may have to ask the butcher to cut the 5-pound piece I use here. I prefer it to the "eye round," a muscle that is attached to the flat, and often suggested for pot roast. It looks nice, but is more fibrous and will not be as tender.

The first step of browning the beef is most important, so be sure to give this plenty of time, about 15 minutes. You want the meat to get a deep-brown crust on all sides and the juices to crystallize in the bottom of the pan as well. The crust and glaze, where the natural sugars have caramelized, are full of flavor. You will see that during the braising all of this crusting will seem to disappear—it literally melts away into the liquid, bringing the flavors to the whole dish.

It's also necessary to use a good pot for pot roast, such as an enameled cast-iron Dutch oven or covered casserole. It must have a heavy bottom and good heat transfer, to form the best crust, and a tight-fitting lid that will lock in the moisture so the meat won't dry out.

It's fine to vary this recipe to suit your taste and what you have on hand. You could use stock or just plain water for the braising liquid, or use canned chopped tomatoes instead of fresh. If you don't like turnips, you can add potatoes instead, or even use both. The flavorful braising liquid reduces slightly in the pot by the end of cooking, and will have a naturally pleasing viscosity for use as a sauce. If you like, though, you can easily thicken it just before serving, using potato starch as described in the recipe. I personally often add a split calf's or pig's foot to the pot at the beginning, as this adds flavor and a gelatinous texture to the juices, but it's fine without. The bits of meat I take from the foot are very nice to serve with the roast too.

jacques's pot roast

YIELD: 10 SERVINGS

One 5-pound piece beef bottom round, from the "flat," trimmed of all fat

1½ teaspoons kosher salt (or 1 teaspoon regular salt), plus more if needed

1 teaspoon freshly ground black pepper, plus more if needed

2 to 3 tablespoons canola or other vegetable oil

2 cups chopped onion, 1-inch pieces (about 8 ounces)

1 large tomato, cored and chopped into 1-inch pieces (about 1½ cups)

2 imported bay leaves

6 sprigs fresh thyme or 1 teaspoon dried thyme leaves

1½ cups white wine, plus more if needed

½ cup water

1½ to 2 pounds large white turnips, peeled, trimmed, and sliced
     into large wedges (10 to 12 pieces)

1 pound small white onions, about 20 the size of Ping-Pong balls,
     blanched and peeled

1 pound baby carrots

1½ to 2 cups green peas, fresh or frozen

Potato starch for thickening (optional)

1 tablespoon chopped fresh parsley, for garnish

SPECIAL EQUIPMENT

A heavy ovenproof casserole, 4- or 5-quart capacity, with a tight-fitting
cover; a large, warm serving platter

BROWNING AND BRAISING THE ROAST Preheat the oven to 300°F.

Season the roast on all sides with 1 to 1½ teaspoons salt and 1 teaspoon black pepper. Set the casserole over high heat with 2 or 3 tablespoons of oil, just enough to film the bottom.

When the oil is hot, lay in the roast and sear for about 3 minutes, until the first side is well browned. Turn the meat onto another side and sear for several minutes, and continue turning and searing, over medium to high heat, until the entire piece is browned and the meat juices have crusted in the pan, about 15 minutes in all. If there is excess oil in the bottom of the pot, pour it out carefully and discard.

Arrange the onion and tomato pieces, the bay leaves, and the thyme sprigs around the meat and pour in the wine and water. Bring the liquid quickly to the boil, cover the casserole, and set it in the oven for 3 to 4 hours, until the meat is tender.

ADDING THE VEGETABLES AND FINAL BRAISING Remove the casserole from the oven. Hold the lid ajar to keep the meat in the pot, and, if you want, pour the braising liquid through a strainer to remove the cooked vegetable pieces and herbs. Press the juices from the vegetables, then return the strained liquid to the pot.

Arrange the turnip wedges, onions, and baby carrots around the roast and season with ½ teaspoon salt. Bring the liquid to the boil, and put the casserole, covered, back in the 300°F oven for 1 to 1½ hours, until the roast is fork-tender and the vegetables are very soft but still holding their shape.

FINISHING AND SERVING THE POT ROAST Set the casserole on the stovetop, over low heat. Add the green peas to the pot, cover, and simmer for 2 to 3 minutes, just until the peas are tender. Lift out the meat and set it on the serving platter.

Taste the sauce and adjust the seasonings. It can be served as is, or, for a thicker consistency, stir together a tablespoon of potato starch with a teaspoon of white wine in a small dish. Stir the dissolved starch, a bit at a time, into the hot liquid. It will thicken immediately on contact with the hot liquid; stir in only as much as needed to reach the proper consistency.

Cut ¼-inch slices from the roast, enough for first servings, and lay them overlapping on the platter—set the rest of the roast on the platter too, if you have room. Spoon the vegetables all around the sliced meat and moisten all with the sauce. Sprinkle the chopped parsley over and bring the platter to the table.

bobby flay's boy meets grill

author

Grill guru and Food Network star Bobby Flay, owner of Mesa Grill and Bolo in New York City, with cookbook author Joan Schwartz. Among the duo's past efforts is last year's *Best of the Best* honoree *Bobby Flay's From My Kitchen to Your Table*.

why he wrote it

"I don't know of any other style of cooking that so easily lends itself to relaxed good times. A meal that's prepared outdoors on the grill invites everyone to loosen up and enjoy the party. People gather around with their drinks, checking on the food and the fire, helping the chef, or just talking and laughing in anticipation of a great meal. . . . This is my kind of entertaining—give it a try."

why it made our list

Grillmeister Flay, one of the country's hottest chefs, has no end of interesting ideas for simple summertime cooking. A companion to his Food Network shows *Grillin' and Chillin'* and *Hot Off the Grill*, this book is spiced with Southwestern sauces and sprinkled with tips on everything from adjusting the fire to planning the menu. The recipes are fairly quick and definitely easy, but a big step beyond simple burgers and hot dogs—duck breasts, lobster, quesadillas, peaches, even radicchio are all grist for the grill.

specifics

274 pages, 125 recipes, 32 color photographs, 72 black-and-white photographs.

chapters A Boy's Introduction to the Grill ›
Burgers, Sausages, and Their Accompaniments ›
Chicken and Other Poultry › Fins and Shells ›
Beef, Lamb, Pork, and Ribs › Vegetables › Sweet
Things › Drinks › Menus

$32.50. Published by Hyperion.

from the book

"The purist considers only charcoal grilling to be the real thing. There is a whole ritual about choosing the best charcoal, laying the fire and lighting it, and moving food around from hotter to cooler cooking areas. Charcoal provides an extremely hot fire, but it can be difficult to get lit, and then it takes about a half hour to reach cooking temperature, when it becomes covered with a film of gray ash. It can be hard to control the heat, to keep it even. True, charcoal does impart a certain distinctive flavor, although I find the real flavor boost comes from marinades and seasonings, and from quick searing directly over a very hot fire—which a good gas grill does as well as charcoal."

tuna burgers with pineapple-mustard glaze and green chile–pickle relish

MAKES 8 SERVINGS

When you don't want to eat red meat, tuna makes a satisfying burger, with its robust flavor and texture. It provides a good canvas for Asian spices, and this recipe is a terrific way to play with Asian ingredients. When you buy a large tuna steak, save the ends to use the next day for burgers.

You have to chop tuna by hand, so it is minced fine. Never chop it in a food processor! Make sure it is very fresh and very cold.

FOR THE PINEAPPLE-MUSTARD GLAZE

3   cups pineapple juice

1   cup white wine vinegar

2   tablespoons soy sauce

1   teaspoon peeled and finely chopped gingerroot

¼   cup light brown sugar, firmly packed

2   tablespoons Dijon mustard

3   tablespoons fresh lime juice

1   teaspoon freshly ground white pepper

In a small saucepan over high heat, combine the pineapple juice, vinegar, soy sauce, gingerroot, and brown sugar, and bring to a boil. Cook until the volume is reduced by half, stirring occasionally, about 30 minutes. Add the mustard and cook an additional 2 minutes. Remove from the heat and add the lime juice and pepper. Let cool at room temperature. May be refrigerated for 1 day; use at room temperature. Makes about 2 cups.

FOR THE GREEN CHILE–PICKLE RELISH

4   poblano peppers, grilled, peeled, seeded, and finely diced (see Note)

3   medium dill pickles, finely diced

¼   cup finely diced red onion

3   tablespoons fresh lime juice

1   tablespoon honey

2   tablespoons finely chopped cilantro

Kosher salt and freshly ground pepper

Combine the poblanos, pickles, onion, lime juice, honey, and cilantro in a medium bowl and season with salt and pepper. Let sit at room temperature 30 minutes before serving. May be refrigerated, covered, for 1 day; serve at room temperature. Makes about 3 cups.

FOR THE TUNA BURGERS

2½ pounds tuna steak, finely chopped by hand

Kosher salt and freshly ground pepper

8   pumpernickel rolls

2   cups watercress

Shape the ground tuna into 8 round patties about 1½ inches thick and refrigerate, covered, 30 minutes or up to overnight. (The burgers must be very cold to hold their shape while cooking.)

Preheat a gas or charcoal grill to high. Season the burgers on both sides with salt and pepper and grill 3 to 4 minutes for medium. Remove and brush on one side with the Pineapple-Mustard Glaze. Split the rolls and toast on the grill. Place each burger in a roll and top with Green Chile–Pickle Relish and watercress. Serve on a large platter.

NOTE To grill poblanos, brush with olive oil and season with salt and pepper. Grill over high heat until charred on all sides. Place in a bowl, cover with plastic wrap, and let sit for 15 minutes. Then peel, halve, and seed.

shrimp skewered on rosemary branches

MAKES 8 SERVINGS

The perfume of rosemary cooking on the grill will give your dinner a delightful Tuscan feeling. Thread the shrimp on long rosemary branches and serve them that way, hot from the fire.

1½ cups olive oil

8   cloves garlic, coarsely chopped

48 large shrimp, peeled and deveined

16 long rosemary branches, soaked in water for 1 hour

Kosher salt and freshly ground pepper

Combine the olive oil and garlic in a large shallow pan or baking dish. Set aside ½ cup and add shrimp to the pan. Let marinate for 2 hours, no longer.

Preheat a gas or charcoal grill to medium high.

Remove 1 inch of leaves from the bottom of each rosemary branch and with a sharp knife, cut the end of the stem on the bias to make a slight point.

Remove the shrimp from the marinade, shaking off any excess (discard the used marinade). Thread 3 shrimp on each rosemary branch. Season with salt and pepper, and grill until just cooked through, 2 to 3 minutes on each side, basting with the reserved marinade every 30 seconds.

To serve, place the shrimp, still on the rosemary branches on a large platter.

martha stewart's hors d'oeuvres handbook

author

Lifestyle authority Martha Stewart, chairman and chief executive officer of Martha Stewart Living Omnimedia and author of 13 books, including *Best of the Best* honoree *Martha Stewart's Healthy Quick Cook*.

why she wrote it

"For me, hors d'oeuvres are a chance for the host or hostess to show off skills in the creation of flavorful bite-sized jewels or other imaginative concoctions that can be served as simple accompaniments for a pre-dinner drink or as elaborately displayed and garnished 'cocktail' food. Hors d'oeuvres must be two things at once: delicious and attractive!"

why it made our list

Just about everything you could ever want to know about hors d'oeuvres, old or new, is in this hefty volume. The first third of the book is devoted to photos of the recipes that follow, and they certainly do whet your appetite, as all good hors d'oeuvres should. The rest of the pages are jam-packed with the recipes themselves, from modern innovations to the hors d'oeuvres your mother used to make. Even the cocktails to sip along with the bites and dips get a chapter. In fact, all the necessities for a fabulous party are here, including advice on drawing up a guest list, determining how many hors d'oeuvres you need, and finding special equipment and ingredients.

from the book

"Whether it's the stock for a soup or the greens for a composed salad, every good dish begins with a good base. For hors d'oeuvres, the bases are just that: the items that you put other ingredients into or on top of. The most interesting hors d'oeuvres are constructed on bases that are somewhat surprising and a bit unusual. This doesn't mean you should search for bizarre edible bases, but you should use your imagination. Not everything has to be placed on a cracker or a square of bread, although there is certainly nothing wrong with either of those when used with a bit of originality."

specifics

496 pages, 300 recipes, more than 100 color photographs.

chapters Building Blocks for the Best Hors d'Oeuvres › Layered and Stacked › Wrapped, Rolled, Filled, Folded, and Stuffed › Tea Sandwiches, Classic Canapés, and Simple Crostini › Skewered and Threaded › Bites and Pieces › Dips, Spreads, Sauces, Relishes, and Salsas › Fondue, Frico, and a Selection of Fine Cheeses › Sips and Drinks › Classics

$35. Published by Clarkson N. Potter Publishers.

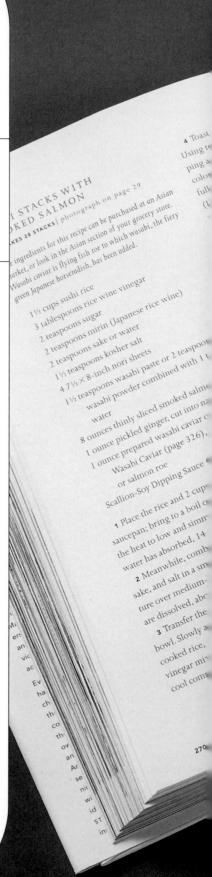

sea scallops with minted pea purée on potato chips

MAKES 2 DOZEN

The purée may be made a day ahead and kept in an airtight container in the refrigerator. Return the purée to room temperature before serving. A thick-cut, good-quality packaged unsalted potato chip, or any other neutral-flavored base, such as toasted brioche rounds, toast points, or pita cups, works fine for these.

2½ tablespoons extra-virgin olive oil

1 garlic clove, minced

1 shallot, finely chopped

1 small leek, white and pale green parts, cut into ¼-inch pieces, well washed

½ teaspoon kosher salt, or more to taste

⅛ teaspoon freshly ground black pepper, or more to taste

1 cup (5 ounces) frozen peas, thawed

2 tablespoons homemade chicken stock or low-sodium canned chicken broth, skimmed of fat, or water

2 tablespoons chopped fresh mint, plus 2½ tablespoons chiffonade for garnish

12 medium sea scallops, sliced in half crosswise

24 Homemade Potato Chips (page 112)

1. In a medium skillet, heat 1 tablespoon of the oil over low heat. Add the garlic, shallots, leeks, salt, and pepper. Cook until very soft but not browned, 8 to 10 minutes. Add the peas, raise the heat to medium, and cook, stirring, until the peas are cooked through, 3 to 5 minutes.

2. Transfer half the pea mixture to the bowl of a food processor. Add the chicken stock and ½ tablespoon of oil. Pulse until the mixture is a coarse purée, about 20 pulses. Transfer the purée to a medium bowl. Process the remaining half of the peas until very smooth, about 30 seconds. Stir into the coarsely puréed peas. Add the chopped mint. Adjust the seasoning with salt and pepper. Set aside.

3. Heat the remaining tablespoon of oil in a medium skillet over medium-high heat. Season the scallops with salt and pepper. Add the scallops to the hot pan, and sear until golden brown, 1 to 2 minutes per side.

4. Place 1 teaspoon of the pea purée on each of the potato chips and top with a scallop. Garnish with the shredded mint. Serve immediately.

homemade potato chips

There are several secrets to making crispy homemade chips. The first is to use plenty of oil; peanut oil works the best for these chips. The second secret is frying in small batches, which prevents the oil temperature from dropping too low, and frying at 340° F—20 degrees lower than usually recommended—which allows the chips to cook through without burning. A third secret is to slice the potatoes on a mandoline. This wonderful tool makes it much easier to create uniform potato slices, which will fry evenly.

2   large (about 1¼ pounds) Idaho baking potatoes, peeled
2   quarts peanut oil, for frying
Kosher salt

1. Slice the potatoes into ¹⁄₁₆-inch-thick slices using a mandoline. Transfer the potato slices to a bowl of cool water to prevent discoloration.

2. Heat the oil in a shallow 10- to 12-inch skillet until a frying thermometer registers 340° F. Place about 16 potato slices on a clean kitchen towel or paper towel and thoroughly pat dry. Carefully slip the potato slices into the oil. (Fry all of the slices in these small batches to ensure the oil temperature remains close to 340° F.) Use tongs or a slotted spoon to move the slices in the oil. Fry until just golden, 2 to 3 minutes. Transfer to paper towels to drain, and sprinkle with salt. Repeat until all the potato slices are fried. Let cool. The chips may be made in advance and kept in an airtight container at room temperature for up to 4 days. In very humid weather, the chips may absorb moisture and soften. To recrisp them, heat in a warm oven. Under these conditions, they are best made just 1 day in advance.

grilled swordfish on ginger-jalapeño rice cakes

MAKES 2 DOZEN

Buy swordfish with firm, glistening, almost translucent flesh. Grill the swordfish just before serving.

¼   **cup homemade (page 115) or prepared mayonnaise**

¼   **cup chopped fresh cilantro, plus extra for garnish**

Kosher salt and freshly ground black pepper

1   **large shallot, finely chopped**

1   **teaspoon prepared chili paste**

1   **tablespoon fresh lime juice**

2   **tablespoons extra-virgin olive oil, plus more for the grill**

13   **ounces fresh swordfish**

1   **recipe Ginger-Jalapeño Rice Cakes (page 114)**

1   **medium jalapeño pepper, thinly sliced crosswise**

1. In a small bowl, combine the mayonnaise, 2 tablespoons of the chopped cilantro, and salt and pepper to taste. Cover and refrigerate until ready to use.

2. In another small bowl, combine the shallot, chili paste, lime juice, and the remaining 2 tablespoons of cilantro. Slowly whisk in the olive oil until incorporated.

3. Place the swordfish in a shallow, nonreactive bowl and cover with the chili-lime marinade. Refrigerate and allow to marinate for 30 minutes, turning once.

4. Heat a lightly oiled grill pan over medium-high heat, or lightly oil a grill rack and prepare a grill. Grill the swordfish for 5 minutes, turn, and cook until the fish is just opaque in the center, 2 to 4 more minutes. When cool enough to touch, cut the swordfish into ¼-inch-thick slices that measure about 1 x 1¼ inches, to fit on the rice cakes. Set aside.

5. Heat the oven to 400° F. Arrange the rice cakes on a baking sheet. Heat until warm, 4 to 6 minutes. Remove and spread lightly with the cilantro mayonnaise. Top with a piece of swordfish and garnish with a thin slice of jalapeño and a leaf of cilantro.

ginger-jalapeño rice cakes

MAKES 2 DOZEN

Make the rice mixture 1 day in advance and refrigerate it so that it is well chilled. These cakes taste delicious topped with Grilled Swordfish (page 113).

½   **cup long-grain white rice**

1   **small jalapeño pepper, seeds and ribs removed, minced**

1   **large egg**

1   **tablespoon freshly grated ginger**

¼   **cup all-purpose flour**

½   **teaspoon baking powder**

1   **teaspoon kosher salt**

3   **tablespoons olive oil**

1. Bring 1 cup of salted water to a boil in a medium saucepan. Stir in the rice, reduce to a simmer over low heat, cover, and cook until the water is absorbed, 15 to 20 minutes. Transfer the cooked rice to a large bowl and allow to cool slightly.

2. In a small bowl, whisk together the jalapeño pepper, egg, and ginger. Set aside. In a separate bowl, combine the flour, baking powder, and salt. Add the egg mixture to the rice. Stir in the flour mixture. The mixture will be sticky.

3. Lightly brush a 12 x 17-inch rimmed baking sheet with olive oil. Transfer the rice mixture to the baking sheet. Moisten your fingers with water and spread the mixture out evenly into a thin, compact layer, about ¼ inch thick and 10 inches square. Brush a piece of parchment or wax paper with olive oil. Cover the rice mixture with the parchment paper, oil-side down, pressing firmly to even out the layer. Cover with plastic wrap and refrigerate for at least 1 hour, or up to 24 hours, until firm.

4. Heat 1 tablespoon of the olive oil in a large skillet over medium heat for 1 to 2 minutes. Working in batches of 10, slip a spatula under the chilled mixture and break off 1½- to 2-inch pieces of the rice mixture; the edges should be rough. Slip them one at a time into the skillet. Cook the rice cakes until golden brown, 3 to 4 minutes on each side. Transfer to paper towels. Repeat until all the rice mixture is used, adding ½ to 1 tablespoon of oil to the pan for each batch. The rice cakes may be stored in an airtight container in the refrigerator for up to 1 day. Reheat refrigerated rice cakes on a baking sheet in a 400° F oven until warm, about 5 minutes.

classic homemade mayonnaise

MAKES 2½ CUPS

Use light olive oil to make the mayonnaise for delicately flavored foods such as tea sandwiches. Use richly flavored extra-virgin olive oils for a more assertive version.

1   **cup light olive oil**

1   **cup vegetable or safflower oil**

2   **large eggs**

¼   **teaspoon dry mustard**

¾   **teaspoon kosher salt, plus more to taste**

2   **tablespoons fresh lemon juice**

Combine the oils in a large glass measuring cup. Place the eggs, mustard, and the ¾ teaspoon of salt in the bowl of a food processor. Process until the mixture is foamy and pale, about 1½ minutes. With the machine running, add the oil, drop by drop, until the mixture starts to thicken (about ½ cup of oil total); do not stop the machine at this point or the mayonnaise may not come together. Add the remaining oil in a slow, steady stream. When all of the oil has been incorporated, slowly add the lemon juice. Taste and adjust the mayonnaise for seasoning. Fresh mayonnaise can be kept, refrigerated, in an airtight container for up to 5 days.

NOTE Because of the slight risk of bacterial poisoning, the USDA advises against the consumption of raw eggs by pregnant women, young children, and anyone with a weakened immune system.

b. smith: rituals & celebrations

author

Barbara Smith, host of the syndicated TV series *B. Smith with Style*, editor-in-chief of the magazine *B. Smith Style*, and owner of B. Smith's restaurants in New York and Washington, D.C.

why she wrote it

"This book combines both my passions: carrying on traditions that keep our pasts alive and creating new ones that celebrate who we are now. It's not so much about Christmases and birthdays as it is about the birth of ideas, ideas for celebrations and rituals whose memories can live with you and take you through the down times."

why it made our list

Making entertaining more fun is what this book's all about, and ideas for favors, decorations, invitations, and gifts are interspersed among the party menus and recipes. The occasions celebrated run from the expected—New Year's, Easter, Thanksgiving, Christmas—to the innovative—a spring hooky day luncheon, a dessert-dance party. Many of the ideas were inspired by the author's family traditions, and the book is designed to help readers start traditions of their own. Whether you follow her blueprints or your own imagination, the book is sure to put you in a party mood.

from the book

"Like any celebration, Valentine's Day gives us an opportunity to do things we don't normally do. Not only do we get to surround ourselves with flowers and Champagne and sensual foods; we also get the chance to make good on promises to a loved one that we didn't keep, or to woo somebody that we've had a crush on for the longest time. It's an occasion for taking liberties you wouldn't normally take, in the name of love."

specifics

242 pages, 101 recipes, 93 color photographs.

chapters January ❯ February ❯ March ❯ April ❯ May ❯ June ❯ July ❯ August ❯ September ❯ October ❯ November ❯ December

$35. Published by Random House, Inc.

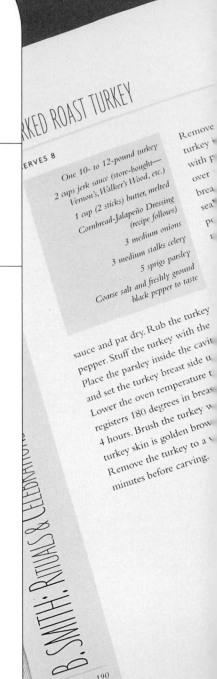

jerked roast turkey

SERVES 8

One 10- to 12-pound turkey

2 cups jerk sauce (store-bought — Vernon's, Walker's Wood, etc.)

1 cup (2 sticks) butter, melted

Cornbread-Jalapeño Dressing (page 120)

3 medium onions

3 medium stalks celery

5 sprigs parsley

Coarse salt and freshly ground black pepper to taste

Remove the giblets from the turkey. Rinse the turkey inside and out with cold water. Blot dry with paper towels. Rub the jerk sauce evenly over and inside of the turkey. Place the turkey breast side down inside a 2-gallon, heavy-duty sealable plastic bag. Squeeze out as much air as possible and seal the bag. Refrigerate and marinate for 48 hours, turning occasionally.

Position the oven rack near the bottom of the oven. Preheat the oven to 350 degrees. Remove the turkey from the plastic bag. Wipe off the jerk sauce and pat dry. Rub the turkey with ¼ cup of the butter and sprinkle with salt and pepper. Stuff the turkey with the dressing or onions and celery cut into large pieces. Place the parsley inside the cavity of the turkey. Tie the legs together with kitchen string and set the turkey breast side up on a rack in a large roasting pan at least 2 inches deep. Lower the oven temperature to 325 degrees. Roast the turkey until a meat thermometer registers 180 degrees in breast meat or 185 degrees in thigh meat, approximately 3½ to 4 hours. Brush the turkey with the remaining butter, basting occasionally. When the turkey skin is golden brown, cover with foil over the breast to prevent overbrowning. Remove the turkey to a warm platter and cover loosely with a towel. Let rest 30 to 40 minutes before carving.

cornbread-jalapeño dressing

YIELDS 9–10 CUPS

6 to 8 cups cornbread cubes (opposite page)

1   cup (2 sticks) butter

2   cups chopped onions

2   cups chopped celery (including some leaves)

½   cup finely chopped jalapeño peppers

2   teaspoons ground sage

2   teaspoons dried thyme leaves

2   teaspoons poultry seasoning

Salt and freshly ground black pepper to taste

2   eggs, slightly beaten

1½ cups turkey or chicken stock

Preheat the oven to 350 degrees. In a large bowl, place the cornbread and set aside. In a large skillet, over medium heat, melt the butter. Add the onions, celery, and jalapeño peppers. Sauté until tender. Do not brown. Remove from heat. Stir in the sage, thyme, poultry seasoning, salt, and pepper. Add to the cornbread. Stir in the eggs. Add the turkey or chicken stock, ½ cup at a time, until the mixture is moist but not wet. Taste and adjust seasoning. Spoon dressing into a large buttered baking dish. Cover and bake 45 to 50 minutes, until the dressing is browned, or stuff the turkey with the dressing and bake as directed.

cornbread

SERVES 8

2   cups cornmeal

1   cup all-purpose flour

3   teaspoons baking powder

1½ teaspoons salt

¼   cup sugar

1¼ cups milk

3   eggs

¾   cup (1½ sticks) melted butter

Preheat the oven to 400 degrees. Grease a 10-inch ovenproof cast-iron skillet. In a large bowl, combine the cornmeal, flour, baking powder, salt, and sugar. Stir in the milk, eggs, and butter, mixing just until the dry ingredients are moistened. Pour the batter into the skillet and bake 20 to 25 minutes, or until a toothpick inserted in the center comes out clean.

pan gravy

YIELDS 3 CUPS

3   cups combined pan drippings and turkey or chicken stock

¼   cup all-purpose flour

½   cup water

Cooked chopped turkey giblets (optional)

Coarse salt and freshly ground black pepper to taste

Using the drippings from the roasting pan, skim off all but 4 tablespoons of the fat in the pan. Place the pan over high heat. Add the turkey or chicken stock and bring to a boil, scraping the bottom to loosen browned bits. Reduce the heat. Mix the flour and water together. Whisk into the gravy. Blend well; add the giblets if desired, and simmer 5 minutes. Season with salt and pepper to taste.

Mom's kitchen is the keynote here. This year, along with books written by esteemed pastry chefs, we were bombarded with collections of homey treats. Among the dessert books published, and there were lots of them, were whole volumes devoted to puddings, to pies, to cookies. The emphasis of the moment is on tasty rather than fancy, and chefs' offerings are not immune. The cookbooks that made it to the final group for this category divide evenly into those that concentrate on familiar American favorites and those that provide more elaborate recipes. Even in the more complex books, though, you're likely to find a recipe for brownies or chocolate-chip cookies.

dessert books

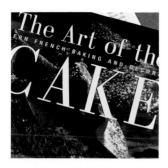

category three

spago chocolate

author

Longtime Spago pastry chef Mary Bergin and cookbook writer Judy Gethers. The two previously collaborated on *Spago Desserts*.

why they wrote it

"Spago customers love our chocolate cakes. Not a day goes by without someone telling us about his or her favorite. These chocolate lovers share one thing in common: They all wish that they could duplicate our desserts at home. Now they can."

why it made our list

Boy, did we have fun testing this one. Every chocolate dessert you could ever hope to try (including Spago's signature desserts, the ones that are so luscious they stay on the menu year after year) is in this beautifully photographed book, and they're all to die for. Bergin and Gethers have perfectly translated the restaurant's scrumptious finales into written recipes that work perfectly and are, for the most part, easy to execute. If it's possible to have dessert down to a science, these two have. We're jaded, picky tasters; yet everything we tested from this book inspired us to indulge with abandon.

specifics

239 pages, 97 recipes, 37 color photographs.
chapters Cakes › Small Cakes, Crêpes, and Pastries › Pies, Tarts, and Cheesecakes › Cookies and Candies › Soufflés, Brûlées, Pots de Crèmes, and Other Creamy Desserts › Frozen Desserts › Fillings and Sauces
$35. Published by Random House, Inc.

from the book

"*Soufflé* **comes from the French verb** *souffler*, **which means "to blow or to breathe," hinting of the delicacy of the perfect soufflé. It consists of two important elements: the foundation, which gives the soufflé its flavor, and the whipped egg whites, which give it its light, airy texture. . . . Making a soufflé is actually quite simple. Though many people are intimidated by them, nothing could be easier, and the result is most impressive. The tricky part is serving — soufflés** *must* **be served as soon as they come out of the oven. They cannot wait for the guests; the guests must wait for the soufflés."**

CHOCOLATE-DATE CAKE

Makes o

kids love this cake, and it's a big hit with the cake that can be cut into small squares for d with confectioners' sugar, and served to gue h can be used instead of the dried dates.

UIPMENT: 8-inch square baking pan, sma
atula

1 CUP PITTED DATES, CUT INTO SMALL PIECES
1 TEASPOON BAKING SODA
1 CUP BOILING WATER
1¾ CUPS ALL-PURPOSE FLOUR
2 TABLESPOONS UNSWEETENED COCOA POWDER
¼ TEASPOON SALT

1. Position the rack in the center of ter or coat with vegetable spra ping out any excess flour

2. Place the cut dates in a sm ing water over. Let sit fo processor fitted with a stee lowing the machine to ru bowl and set aside. (Wo

3. Sift together the flour,

4. Using the food proce ing down the sides vanilla, and proce with on/off turns.

54
SPAGO CHOCOLATE

5. Distribute the flour mixture evenly around the wo[rk]
turns until combined. Add half the chocolate chips (3 ounce[s]
with on/off turns just until combined.

6. Using a rubber spatula, scrape the batter into the prepared pan and level by running the spatula over the top of the cake. Sprinkle the remaining chocolate chips
over the surface of the cake. Bake 40 to 45 minutes, turning the cake front to back
after 20 minutes. The center will not be firm but will become firm while cooling. Cool
on a rack.

7. To serve, with a long sharp knife, cut around the inside of the baking pan, separating the cake from the p[an] [...] onto a clean flat surface and cut away any hard
edges. Turn rig[ht...] [...] [som]ewhat of a company dessert, place a slice of
conf[...] [...]llop of whipped cream or ice cream next to it,
[...] cake can be made 1 day ahead and will
[...] wrap.

× 4-inch pieces
[...]en 2-inch squares

"kids" as well. It is a very
[...]ly or into larger portions,
[...]he markets sell date nuggets,

food processor, sifter, rubber

[...]ES (1½ STICKS) UNSALTED BUTTER,
[...]HILLED, CUT INTO SMALL PIECES
[...] GRANULATED SUGAR
[...]GS
[...]EASPOON VANILLA EXTRACT
[...]OUNCES (ABOUT 1 CUP) BITTERSWEET OR
[...]SEMISWEET CHOCOLATE CHIPS

and [...]

[...]d wi[...]
[...]rkbow[...]
[...]il combi[...]

Spago

CHOCOLATE

MARY BERGIN
AND JUDY GETHERS

PHOTOGRAPHS BY
ALAN RICHARDSON

chocolate-almond toffee

MAKES A 2-POUND BLOCK, 10 X 13 INCHES

When you crave a sweet, this is perfect. It can be broken into larger pieces, wrapped, and stored in a cool spot.

10 ounces whole unblanched almonds

1¼ cups granulated sugar

⅓ cup light corn syrup

⅓ cup water or rum

8 ounces (2 sticks) unsalted butter, cut into small pieces

1 teaspoon salt

½ teaspoon baking soda

8 ounces bittersweet chocolate, cut into small pieces

EQUIPMENT

1 or 2 baking trays, 11 x 15 inches, offset spatula, small deep saucepan, candy thermometer, long-handled wooden spoon, medium heatproof bowl

1. Position the rack in the center of the oven and preheat the oven to 375 degrees.

2. Spread the nuts on a baking tray and bake until toasted, 10 to 15 minutes, turning the nuts after 7 or 8 minutes to ensure even toasting. Cool and then finely chop. You should have about 2 cups. Set aside. Clean the baking tray. Coat the baking tray and both sides of an offset spatula with vegetable spray. Set aside.

3. Make the toffee: Place the sugar in a small deep saucepan. Add the corn syrup and water, and over medium heat, bring to a boil. Let boil until large bubbles form on the surface, 3 to 4 minutes. Cover with foil or a lid and boil 5 minutes longer.

4. Add the pieces of butter and continue cooking, uncovered, over medium heat until the temperature reaches 300 degrees on a candy thermometer, about 30 minutes. (The candy thermometer has a clip on the side that can be slid up or down. If desired, you can fit it on the side of the pan, making sure that the thermometer rests *in* the mixture, not on the bottom of the pan, so that the reading is accurate.) Remove from the heat and immediately add the salt, baking soda, and 1 cup of the chopped nuts. Stir with a wooden spoon until well combined.

5. Pour the toffee mixture on the prepared baking tray and, using the offset spatula, spread the mixture out, making a block about 10 x 13 inches. The toffee will thicken very quickly, so work as fast as you can. When it's cool, blot some of the excess vegetable spray with a clean towel.

6. While the toffee mixture is cooling, in a medium heatproof bowl set over a pan of simmering water, melt the chocolate. When almost melted, turn off the heat and let the chocolate continue to melt, stirring occasionally. Keep warm.

7. When you can pick up the block of toffee in one piece, transfer it to a flat work surface or to a clean baking tray. Pour the melted chocolate over the toffee, spreading to cover the entire block of toffee. Before the chocolate cools, sprinkle the remaining chopped nuts over the chocolate. Refrigerate for about 10 minutes to set the chocolate.

8. Return the block of toffee to the work surface and break it up into pieces, approximately 1 to 1½ inches wide. Then cut into smaller pieces, as desired. Use as needed.

TO PREPARE AHEAD Through step 8, store the toffee in a covered container. Keep in a cool spot.

peanut butter cups

MAKES ABOUT 28 CUPS

These creamy chocolate peanut butter cups literally melt in your mouth. You may want to cover half the peanut butter balls with semisweet chocolate and half with milk chocolate. When spooning out the chocolate, you can fill the cups to the very top or just to cover the peanut butter. The recipe can also be doubled, if desired.

PEANUT BUTTER MIXTURE

1   cup creamy peanut butter

1   cup confectioners' sugar, sifted

1½ ounces (3 tablespoons) very soft unsalted butter, cut into small pieces

1   tablespoon milk

1   tablespoon vanilla extract

½   teaspoon salt

12 ounces semisweet or milk chocolate, cut into small pieces*

EQUIPMENT

medium bowl, rubber spatula, medium heatproof bowl,

28 paper or foil minicups, baking tray

1. Make the peanut butter mixture: In a medium bowl, combine the peanut butter, sugar, butter, milk, vanilla, and salt. Using a rubber spatula, blend together until very smooth. Cover and refrigerate for at least 1 hour.

2. In a medium heatproof bowl set over a pan of simmering water, melt the chocolate. When almost melted, turn off the heat and let the chocolate continue to melt completely, stirring occasionally. Keep the bowl over the warm water.

3. Make the peanut butter balls: Arrange 28 paper or foil minicups on a baking tray. Roll ½ ounce of the peanut butter mixture into a smooth ball and set into one of the cups. Repeat with the remaining mixture and cups.

4. Using a small spoon, carefully spoon the melted chocolate into each cup, covering each peanut butter ball, filling the cup as desired. Refrigerate until set, about 1 hour.

TO PREPARE AHEAD Through step 4, the cups can be prepared and will keep at least 2 weeks, refrigerated in a covered container.

* If using milk chocolate, add 1 tablespoon of vegetable oil while melting.

oatmeal-chocolate chunk cookies

MAKES ABOUT 5½ DOZEN COOKIES

These cookies are rich and chewy, with chunks of chocolate. We use bittersweet choco-late, but you can substitute milk or white chocolate. Just be sure that you use quick-cooking oats (which have been crushed further to speed up the cooking process). The cookies keep best in an air-tight container or cookie jar.

1½ **cups all-purpose flour**

1   **teaspoon baking soda**

1   **teaspoon salt**

8   **ounces (2 sticks) unsalted butter, at room temperature,
    cut into small pieces**

1   **cup dark brown sugar, firmly packed**

1   **cup granulated sugar**

2   **eggs**

1   **teaspoon vanilla extract**

1   **pound coarsely chopped bittersweet chocolate
    (pieces about the size of large chocolate chips)**

2   **cups quick-cooking oats**

1½ **cups (about 5 ounces) pecans, toasted and chopped**

EQUIPMENT

sifter, electric mixer with large bowl, 1 or 2 baking trays, wide metal spatula

1. Sift together the flour, baking soda, and salt. Set aside.

2. In the large bowl of an electric mixer fitted with a paddle or beaters, on medium speed soften the butter. Add the brown and granulated sugars, raising the speed to high when the sugar is incorporated, and continue to mix until fluffy, scraping down the sides of the bowl and under the beaters as necessary. Lower the speed to medium and add the eggs, one at a time, and the vanilla, again scraping down the sides of the bowl as necessary. Turn the speed to low, gradually pour in the flour mixture, and beat just until combined. Stop the machine. Add the chocolate, oats, and pecans, and again beat just until combined.

3. Scrape the dough out of the bowl and wrap in plastic wrap. Refrigerate until firm, 2 to 3 hours.

4. Position the rack in the center of the oven and preheat the oven to 350 degrees. Line one or two baking trays with parchment paper.

5. Remove the dough from the refrigerator and divide it into mounds, about 1 ounce each (about the size of an unshelled walnut). Roll between the palms of your hands, forming about 65 cookies. Arrange the balls on the prepared trays about 2 inches apart. Bake until slightly firm to the touch, 13 to 15 minutes, reversing the trays back to front after 7 minutes to ensure even baking. Place the trays on racks to cool. After a few minutes, remove the cookies with a wide metal spatula and transfer to the rack to cool completely. If reusing the baking tray, cool slightly before arranging balls of dough on it.

TO PREPARE AHEAD In step 5, the balls of dough can be rolled, placed on trays, wrapped well in plastic wrap, and refrigerated until needed, up to 1 week. They can be frozen for up to 2 months.

judy's chocolate-date cake

MAKES EIGHT 2 X 4-INCH PIECES OR SIXTEEN 2-INCH SQUARES

Judy's kids love this cake, and it's a big hit with the Spago "kids" as well. It is a very moist cake that can be cut into small squares for the family or into larger portions, dusted with confectioners' sugar, and served to guests. Some markets sell date nuggets, which can be used instead of the dried dates.

1   cup *pitted* dates, cut into small pieces

1   teaspoon baking soda

1   cup boiling water

1¾ cups all-purpose flour

2   tablespoons unsweetened cocoa powder

¼   teaspoon salt

6   ounces (1½ sticks) unsalted butter, chilled, cut into small pieces

1   cup granulated sugar

2   eggs

1   teaspoon vanilla extract

6   ounces (about 1 cup) bittersweet or semisweet chocolate chips

EQUIPMENT

8-inch square baking pan, small bowl, food processor, sifter, rubber spatula

1. Position the rack in the center of the oven and preheat the oven to 350 degrees. Butter or coat with vegetable spray an 8-inch square baking pan. Dust with flour, tapping out any excess flour.

2. Place the cut dates in a small bowl, sprinkle with the baking soda, and pour the boiling water over. Let sit for about 10 minutes, pour into the workbowl of a food processor fitted with a steel blade, and puree, starting with on/off turns and then allowing the machine to run until the dates are pureed. Scrape back into the small bowl and set aside. (Workbowl does not need to be cleaned at this point.)

3. Sift together the flour, cocoa, and salt. Set aside.

4. Using the food processor fitted with a steel blade, cream the butter and sugar, scraping down the sides of the workbowl as necessary. Add the eggs, one at a time, and vanilla, and process just until combined. Add the reserved date mixture and process with on/off turns.

5. Distribute the flour mixture evenly around the workbowl and process with on/off turns until combined. Add half the chocolate chips (3 ounces) and again process with on/off turns just until combined.

6. Using a rubber spatula, scrape the batter into the prepared pan and level by running the spatula over the top of the cake. Sprinkle the remaining chocolate chips over the surface of the cake. Bake 40 to 45 minutes, turning the cake front to back after 20 minutes. The center will not be firm but will become firm while cooling. Cool on a rack.

7. To serve, with a long sharp knife, cut around the inside of the baking pan, separating the cake from the pan. Invert onto a clean flat surface and cut away any hard edges. Turn right side up and cut into the desired number of pieces. Dust with sifted confectioners' sugar. To make it somewhat of a company dessert, place a slice of cake on individual plates, spoon a dollop of whipped cream or ice cream next to it, and garnish with a few berries.

TO PREPARE AHEAD Through step 6, the cake can be made 1 day ahead and will keep up to 3 days wrapped well in plastic wrap.

alice medrich's cookies and brownies

author

Dessert expert Alice Medrich, who's been called America's "First Lady of Chocolate." Medrich has previously catered to our sweet tooth with *Cocolat: Extraordinary Chocolate Desserts* and *Chocolate and the Art of Low-Fat Desserts*.

why she wrote it

To fill a gap by giving readers all the little steps that lead to perfect cookies. "There is a myriad of uncommunicated details in the simplest cookie recipe — nothing tricky or hard to understand or execute mind you, but hidden details that can make a difference between fabulous cookies and miniature doorstops."

why it made our list

Medrich brings the same greed for perfection to the humble cookie as other chefs do to fancy pastries and elaborate desserts. Though cookies are simple, it's easy to mess them up — to make them too bland, too sweet, too hard, too dry. The recipes in this wonderful little book benefit from Medrich's zeal. God is in the details, and she provides them all. The cookies and bars include perfect versions of old favorites, plus some that will no doubt become favorites due to their out-and-out scrumptiousness.

specifics

120 pages, 46 recipes, 25 color photographs, 10 black-and-white photographs.

chapters   Shortbread › Butter Cookies › Chocolate Cookies › Cookie Classics › Biscotti › Brownies and Bars

$23.95. Published by Warner Books, Inc.

from the book

"Biscotti have become as American as apple pie and infinitely more ubiquitous. Café-goers who invest regularly in single biscotti will be astonished at how easy they are to make. How did a twice-baked, dry-as-bones, anise-flavored Italian cookie — so crunchy that it begs to be splashed in sweet wine or strong coffee — acquire American citizenship? Probably by losing its anise-flavored accent and welcoming a myriad of flavorful chunks and chips, from chocolate to cherries in addition to any nut in the universe or no nuts at all."

Snicker Doodles

Preheat the oven to 400°F. Position the racks in the upper and lower thirds of the oven.

Combine the flour, cream of tartar, baking soda, and salt together in a bowl and mix thoroughly with a whisk or fork. Set aside.

With a large spoon in a medium mixing bowl or with a mixer, beat the butter with 1½ cups of the sugar and the eggs just until smooth and well blended but not f... the dry ingredients and stir just until incorporated. Gather... natty and wrap in plastic wrap. Refrigerate until fi...

Mix the rema...
Form the d...
place 2 i...
lightly...
and ...

Ingredients

2⅔ cups all-purpose flour
2 teaspoons cream of tartar
1 teaspoon baking soda
½ teaspoon salt
16 tablespoons unsalted butter, softened
1½ cups plus 2 tablespoons sugar
2 large eggs
2 teaspoons ground cinnamon

Equipment

2 cookie sheets, ungreased or lined with foil

Classic snicker...
crunchy rounds of cinnamon...
toast. Sometimes I add a cup of rais...

...OKIES **43**

ALICE MEDRICH'S

Cookies and Brownies

By the author of Cocolat and
Chocolate and the Art of Low-Fat Desserts

apricot-lemon bars

MAKES 16 2-INCH BARS

The name says it. Lemon bar lovers will add these to the repertoire. I like them best with a toasted hazelnut crust.

CRUST

8	tablespoons unsalted butter, softened
¼	cup granulated sugar
¾	teaspoon vanilla extract
⅛	teaspoon salt
1	cup all-purpose flour

TOPPING

¼	cup sugar
2	tablespoons all-purpose flour
2	large eggs
½	cup apricot preserves
⅓	cup strained fresh lemon juice

2 to 3 tablespoons powdered sugar, for dusting

EQUIPMENT

8-inch square pan, lined on the bottom and all 4 sides with foil

Preheat the oven to 350°F. Position a rack in the lower third of the oven.

To make the crust: Cut butter into chunks and melt it in a medium saucepan over medium heat. Remove from the heat and stir in the sugar, vanilla, and salt. Add the flour and mix just until incorporated. Press the dough evenly over the bottom of the pan. Bake for 25 to 30 minutes, or until the crust is well browned at the edges and lightly browned in the center.

To make the topping: While the crust is baking, stir together the sugar and flour in a medium bowl until well mixed. Whisk in the eggs. Stir in the preserves, breaking up any extra large pieces. Mix in the lemon juice. When the crust is ready, turn the oven down to 300°F and slide the rack out without removing the pan. Pour the filling over the hot crust.

Bake for 20 to 25 minutes, or until the topping is puffed at the edges and no longer jiggles in the center when the pan is tapped. Set on a rack to cool completely in the pan. Lift the foil liner and transfer to a cutting board. Use a long sharp knife to cut sixteen 2-inch bars. *May be stored, airtight, in the refrigerator.* Apricot-Lemon Bars keep perfectly for about 3 days; after 3 days the crust softens but the bars still taste quite good for the remainder of a week. Do not freeze. Sieve powdered sugar over the bars just before serving.

VARIATION Nut Crust for Apricot-Lemon Bars: Decrease the flour by 3 tablespoons. Put the flour with the sugar, salt, and ¼ cup almonds or toasted and skinned hazelnuts in a food processor fitted with a steel blade. Pulse until the nuts are finely ground. Add the melted butter and pulse just until the dry ingredients look damp and the mixture begins to clump around the blade. Remove the dough from the processor and knead it a few times until smooth. Proceed with the recipe.

chocolate-hazelnut meringue kisses

MAKES ABOUT 60 COOKIES

INGREDIENTS

3   **large egg whites, at room temperature**

⅛   **teaspoon cream of tartar**

½   **teaspoon vanilla extract**

⅔   **cup sugar, preferably superfine**

½   **cup semisweet chocolate chips**

½   **cup hazelnuts, toasted and skinned, coarsely chopped**

EQUIPMENT

2   **cookie sheets, lined with parchment paper**

Preheat the oven to 200°F. Position racks in the upper and lower thirds of the oven.

Beat the egg whites with the cream of tartar and vanilla with a mixer at high speed until soft peaks form when the beaters are lifted. Add the sugar gradually, about 1 tablespoon at a time, continuing to beat until the egg whites are stiff and glossy. Use a large rubber spatula to fold the chocolate chips and nuts into the egg whites.

Drop slightly rounded teaspoons of batter 1½ inches apart on the cookie sheets. Bake for about 2 hours, reversing the cookie sheets from top to bottom and front to back after 1 hour. Turn the oven off and let the cookies cool in the oven. Remove the cookies from the oven and set the pans on racks to cool completely before storing the cookies. *May be stored, airtight, for several weeks.*

VARIATIONS Low-Fat Meringue Kisses: Use only ¼ cup each chocolate chips and nuts.

Mocha-Nut Meringue Kisses: Combine 2 teaspoons instant espresso powder with the sugar before adding it.

snicker doodles

MAKES ABOUT 60 2½-INCH COOKIES

Classic snicker doodles taste like delicate, crunchy rounds of cinnamon-topped French toast. Sometimes I add a cup of raisins.

INGREDIENTS

2⅔ cups all-purpose flour

2   teaspoons cream of tartar

1   teaspoon baking soda

½   teaspoon salt

16 tablespoons unsalted butter, softened

1½ cups plus 2 tablespoons sugar

2   large eggs

2   teaspoons ground cinnamon

EQUIPMENT
2 cookie sheets, ungreased or lined with foil

Preheat the oven to 400°F. Position the racks in the upper and lower thirds of the oven.

Combine the flour, cream of tartar, baking soda, and salt together in a bowl and mix thoroughly with a whisk or fork. Set aside.

With a large spoon in a medium mixing bowl or with a mixer, beat the butter with 1½ cups of the sugar and the eggs just until smooth and well blended but not fluffy. Add the dry ingredients and stir just until incorporated. Gather the dough into a patty and wrap in plastic wrap. Refrigerate until firm, at least 30 minutes.

Mix the remaining 2 tablespoons of sugar and cinnamon in a small bowl. Form the dough into 1-inch balls. Roll the balls in cinnamon sugar and place 2 inches apart on cookie sheets. Bake for 10 to 12 minutes, or until lightly browned at the edges. Rotate cookie sheets from top to bottom and front to back halfway through the baking time to ensure even baking.

Use a metal pancake turner to transfer the cookies from the pan to cooling racks or slide the foil onto the racks. Cool the cookies completely before stacking or storing. *May be stored, airtight, for several days.*

the art of the cake

authors

French pastry authorities Bruce Healy and Paul Bugat, who previously collaborated on *Mastering the Art of French Pastry* and *The French Cookie Book*.

why they wrote it

"French pastry chefs have worked very hard over the past few decades to streamline the techniques of cake making, modernizing their methods and making them less dependent on highly skilled labor. The result is that contemporary French cake making is now within reach of the home cook. The purpose of *The Art of the Cake* is to introduce you to this irresistible subject and teach you the techniques that will enable you to master it."

why it made our list

By breaking complex cake recipes down into basic components and techniques, Healy and Bugat make them less mysterious, though no less magical. Learning the building blocks — like sponge cake, buttercream frosting, and royal icing — makes it possible for even a novice baker to turn out an enormous variety of French cakes. Both the building-block view of cooking and the excellent cakes here are classic French, and the restrained, respectful modernization of methods leaves all the flavor intact. The techniques are clearly taught in helpful diagrams, detailed descriptions, and thorough instructions on how to do everything from creaming butter to glazing a cake to piping decorations. This nearly 600-page instructional bible will prove to be an important addition to any cookbook collection.

from the book

"**The original charlotte — an apple compote baked in a mold lined with toast slices — was created at the end of the eighteenth century and named for the wife of King George III of England. In the nineteenth century, the French chef Marie-Antoine Carême adopted the name and radically refined the concept in response to a kitchen disaster. At a banquet to celebrate the return to Paris of Louis XVIII in 1815, the supply of gelatin was insufficient for the bavarian creams Carême was preparing. To solve the problem, the great chef buttressed the sides of his sagging desserts with ladyfingers.**"

specifics

591 pages, 149 recipes, 40 color photographs.

chapters Simple Cakes › Round Sponge Cake Gâteaux › Round Nut Meringue Gâteaux › Meringues › Rectangular Gâteaux › Bavarians, Charlottes, and Mousse Cakes › Logs and Loaves › Fillings and Frostings › Finishing Touches › Basic Preparations

$35. Published by William Morrow and Company, Inc.

1. Coarsely crush the espresso beans in a mortar and p...
processing in small batches so that none of the coffee is crushed finely.
Combine the crushed espresso beans with the milk in a small saucepan
and bring to a simmer. Remove from the heat, cover, and let steep for
10 minutes. Strain through a fine sieve, pressing down on the beans to
extract as much milk as possible. You should have about ¾ cup (1.8 dL)
of espresso-flavored milk. If necessary, add a little milk to get back up
to ¾ cup (1.8 dL). Discard the coffee grounds and rinse out the sieve
so it will be ready to use again for straining the custard.

2. Combine the espresso-flavored milk with ¼ cup (50 g) of the
sugar in a heavy 1-quart (1-L) saucepan and bring to a simmer.

3. Meanwhile, combine the egg yolks with the remaining sugar in
a mixing bowl and beat with a wire whisk until smooth and lemon-colored. Pour in about half of the hot milk, whisking constantly. Pour this
mixture back into the saucepan and stir until thoroughly blended.

4. Place the saucepan over medium heat and, stirring constantly
with a wooden spatula, bring the custard almost ... simmer. Reduce
the heat to low and cook, stirring constantly...
the custard thickens and coats the spatula ...
line across the back of the custard-coated ...
the custard should not flow back over ...
the lowest possible setting (movi...
burner as needed) and keep the ...
for 4 minutes to pasteurize it ...

5. Immediately strain ...
bowl of the mixer. Be...
speed until it is light, ...

6. Gradually ...
the flat beater if ...
added, beat ...

7. U...
tity ...
pa...

e ...
ative.
follow ...
cup

t beater

cups

600 g); 2⅔ cups

moka

FOR 8 SERVINGS

The first coffee beans that became popular in Europe were grown in the hills of what is now Yemen and shipped from the port of Al Mukha on the Red Sea. In France the word "moka" (usually spelled "mocha" in English) became a generic word for coffee. Later, when chocolate beans first arrived in Europe, they were imagined to be similar to coffee and moka also became associated with the combination of coffee and chocolate.

The gâteau called *moka* is one of the most fundamental gâteaux made from génoise and buttercream. It is just a round of génoise, filled and frosted with coffee buttercream, with chopped almonds around the bottom and coffee buttercream piped on top with a fluted pastry tube. Today it is difficult to imagine a time when the *moka* was a novel cake, and we are likely to underestimate its historical significance. A hundred years ago, pastry chef Pierre Lacam wrote in *Mémorial de la Pâtisserie*, "The *moka* is already a little old; but it will go very far. It is, along with the *gâteau d'amandes*, the brioche, and the *savarin*, the base of the edifice [i.e., the art of pastry]; one has created the *pralinés*, the *purée de marrons*, but all that is based on *crème au beurre* [buttercream] or [*crème à*] *moka*. We attribute the *moka* to [the pastry chef] Guignard, [whose shop was located] at the Odéon intersection; it dates to 1857."

Actually, in its most traditional form the sides of the *moka* were covered with large crystal sugar, which the French call "moka sugar." However, even Lacam mentioned the alternative of chopped toasted almonds. Lacam's contemporaries Émile Darenne and Émile Duval, authors of the classic book *Traité de Pâtisserie Moderne*, went so far as to say, "When the sale price permits, this gâteau is better with chopped grilled almonds." Then, as now, almonds were much more expensive than sugar.

Do not underestimate the *moka*. Well made, it is a beautiful and delicious gâteau, one of the great classics.

CAKE

One round génoise (page 144), baked in either a 9-inch (24-cm) cake pan or an 8¾-inch (22-cm) cake ring

FILLING, FROSTING, AND PIPING

2¼ cups (14 ounces; 400 g) coffee buttercream (page 146)

BRUSHING-SYRUP MIXTURE

⅓   **cup (8 cL) heavy syrup (page 157)**

⅓   **cup (8 cL) double-strength brewed espresso (page 158)**

DECORATION FOR BOTTOM EDGE OF GÂTEAU

3   **tablespoons (1 ounce; 30 g) blanched almonds,**
     roasted (page 156) and finely chopped

EQUIPMENT

9-inch (24-cm) foil board or matt board cake-decorating circle
Optional: 8¾-inch (22-cm) cake ring (if the génoise was baked in one)
Small pastry bag fitted with
>   **fluted decorating tube (such as Ateco #17 open star tube)**

1. Assemble the gâteau from the génoise round (cut into two layers), buttercream filling and frosting, and espresso brushing syrup either by the traditional freehand method or by molding it in the same ring in which the génoise was baked. Save at least ¼ cup (45 g) of excess buttercream for piping on top of the gâteau.

2. While the buttercream on the outside of the gâteau is still soft, lift the gâteau with a large icing spatula and support it on the fingertips of one hand. Take the chopped almonds in the palm of your other hand. Decorate the bottom edge of the gâteau with chopped almonds by pressing it against the almonds in your palm, then rotating the gâteau and repeating until you have covered the bottom edge with a band of nuts ⅜ to ½ inch (10 to 12 mm) high. Return the gâteau to the countertop.

3. Scoop the remaining buttercream into the pastry bag. Pipe the buttercream on the top of the gâteau in a decorative pattern. For example, make a lozenge pattern by piping one set of parallel lines separated by about 1 inch (2½ cm) and a second set of parallel lines on the diagonal with respect to the first set. Pipe tiny rosettes of buttercream at the intersections.

4. Refrigerate the gâteau until ready to serve.

VARIATION Use chocolate buttercream instead of coffee but keep the coffee in the brushing syrup. Decorate the bottom edge of the gâteau with arcs of chocolate sprinkles (about ¼ cup = 35 g) instead of chopped almonds. To avoid any confusion, you can call the chocolate version *moka chocolat*.

STORAGE In the refrigerator for up to 2 days.

génoise

FOR TWO 9-INCH (24-CM) ROUNDS BAKED IN CAKE PANS
OR TWO 8¾-INCH (22-CM) ROUNDS BAKED IN CAKE RINGS

A good génoise should be fine-textured and tender, yet firm and of course not too moist. The classic génoise proportions are 9 ounces (250 g) each of sugar and flour for eight large eggs, plus 1 to 2 ounces (25 to 50 g) of butter. Unfortunately, when you prepare this recipe with American all-purpose flour, the resulting cake is rather coarse. Regardless of the flour, it has a tendency to be unnecessarily dry. We have chosen to remedy these shortcomings by replacing 20 percent of the flour with two egg yolks plus a little potato starch. The resulting cake is exquisitely fine, tender and moist, yet sufficiently absorbent.

BATTER

7   large eggs, at room temperature

2   large egg yolks, at room temperature

1   cup + 2 tablespoons (8 ounces; 225 g) granulated sugar

1¼ cups (6¼ ounces; 175 g) all-purpose flour

2   tablespoons (¾ ounce; 20 g) potato starch

2   tablespoons (1 ounce; 30 g) unsalted butter, barely melted

EQUIPMENT

Large, heavy baking sheet

Either two 9-inch (24-cm) round cake pans, 1½ inches (4 cm) deep

> brush with melted butter

> dust with flour

or two 8¾-inch (22-cm) cake rings, 1⅜ inches (3.5 cm) deep

> brush with melted butter

> dust with flour

> brush outlines of two 9-inch (24-cm) squares on baking sheet
  with melted butter

> place a 9-inch (24-cm) square of kitchen parchment
  on each buttered square

> brush each square lightly with melted butter and place a cake ring on it

Electric mixer

Preheat the oven to 375°F (190°C).

1. Combine the whole eggs, yolks, and sugar in a stainless steel mixing bowl, break up the yolks with a wire whisk, and beat until smooth. Set the bowl over a saucepan of simmering water, and stir with the whisk until warm (about 100°F = 40°C), frothy, and pale yellow.

2. Remove the bowl from the simmering water, and whip at medium speed in the mixer until the batter has risen and cooled, becoming light and thick and almost white in color. It should coat your finger very thickly and form very slowly dissolving ribbons when dropped from the whip.

3. Sift the flour with the potato starch onto a sheet of wax paper. A little at a time, dust the mixture over the batter and fold it in very gently but thoroughly. When the flour and potato starch are completely incorporated, slowly pour the melted butter over the batter and continue folding until the butter is uniformly mixed into the batter.

4. **FOR CAKE PANS** Scoop the batter into the prepared cake pans, filling them to between two thirds and three quarters of their height. Smooth the surface of the batter and make a slight depression in the center. Place the cake pans on the baking sheet.

FOR CAKE RINGS Scoop the batter into the prepared rings, filling them to between two thirds and three quarters of their height. Smooth the surface of the batter and make a slight depression in the center.

5. Bake until the top of the génoise is lightly browned and firm to the touch but not crusty, about 17 to 20 minutes. The tip of a paring knife inserted in the center of the cake should come out clean.

6. Remove the cakes from the oven and slide the tip of a paring knife or small icing spatula between the edge of each cake and the pan to loosen the edge. Let the génoise rest in the pans or rings for about 5 minutes.

FOR CAKE PANS Unmold the cakes onto a wire rack, invert them onto another rack, and let cool there.

FOR CAKE RINGS Lift off the rings. Use a metal spatula to slide each round of génoise onto a wire rack. Invert them onto another rack and peel off the parchment. Invert them again onto the first rack and let cool there.

HOWS AND WHYS Adding the butter last, after the flour is completely incorporated, helps prevent the butter from deflating the foam.

STORAGE Covered airtight with plastic wrap, for up to 2 days in the refrigerator.

Or freeze for as long as 2 months. If frozen, defrost overnight in the refrigerator, and unwrap the cake at least 2 hours before using to allow condensation produced by defrosting to evaporate.

coffee buttercream

FOR 2 POUNDS + 6½ OUNCES (1,080 G); ABOUT 6 CUPS

For this buttercream, the buttercream base is a *crème anglaise* (English custard), but prepared with an unusually high proportion of egg yolks and sugar or, equivalently, a very low proportion of milk. The proportions make the preparation more delicate than an ordinary *crème anglaise*, and the result is a hair less elegant than our French buttercream. However, this method makes it possible for you to incorporate coffee flavor in a way that is superior to anything possible with other types of buttercream.

The problem is that to add sufficient coffee flavor to buttercream after the fact requires a very strong coffee extract in order to avoid adding too much water, which would make the buttercream curdle. The only practical way to make such a strong extract is to dissolve instant coffee in the minimum possible amount of boiling water. It should come as no surprise that the resulting buttercream tastes like instant coffee as opposed to real coffee.

With the custard buttercream base, you can incorporate the coffee flavor from the outset by steeping coarsely crushed coffee beans in the milk before straining the milk and using it in the custard. The result is a buttercream with a freshly brewed coffee taste.

The custard buttercream base also has a second advantage. If you feel uncomfortable about working with hot sugar syrups, then this method may be a less threatening alternative. If you prefer to prepare your basic buttercream using the custard base method, simply follow this recipe, eliminating the coffee and step 1 and reducing the quantity of milk to ¾ cup (1.8 dL).

¾   cup (1¾ ounces; 50 g) espresso coffee beans

1   cup (2.4 dL) milk

1½ cups (10½ ounces; 300 g) granulated sugar

8   large egg yolks, at room temperature

2⅔ cups (1 pound + 5 ounces; 600 g) unsalted butter, softened

EQUIPMENT

Mortar and pestle

Electric mixer, preferably a stand mixer equipped with

    both wire whip and flat beater

1. Coarsely crush the espresso beans in a mortar and pestle [1], processing in small batches so that none of the coffee is crushed finely. Combine the crushed espresso beans with the milk in a small saucepan and bring to a simmer. Remove from the heat, cover, and let steep for 10 minutes. Strain through a fine sieve, pressing down on the beans to extract as much milk as possible. You should have about ¾ cup (1.8 dL) of espresso-flavored milk. If necessary, add a little milk to get back up to ¾ cup (1.8 dL). Discard the coffee grounds and rinse out the sieve so it will be ready to use again for straining the custard.

2. Combine the espresso-flavored milk with ¼ cup (50 g) of the sugar in a heavy 1-quart (1-L) saucepan and bring to a simmer.

3. Meanwhile, combine the egg yolks with the remaining sugar in a mixing bowl and beat with a wire whisk until smooth and lemon-colored. Pour in about half of the hot milk, whisking constantly. Pour this mixture back into the saucepan and stir until thoroughly blended.

4. Place the saucepan over medium heat and, stirring constantly with a wooden spatula, bring the custard almost to a simmer. Reduce the heat to low and cook, stirring constantly with the spatula [2], until the custard thickens and coats the spatula heavily. (When you draw a line across the back of the custard-coated spatula with your fingertip, the custard should not flow back over the line [3]). Reduce the heat to the lowest possible setting (moving the saucepan to the side of the burner as needed) and keep the mixture hot, again stirring constantly, for 4 minutes to pasteurize it.

5. Immediately strain the custard through the fine sieve into the bowl of the mixer. Beat the custard with the wire whip at medium speed until it is light and cool. This is the buttercream base.

6. Gradually beat in the softened butter at medium speed, using the flat beater if your mixer has one [4]. When all of the butter has been added, beat the buttercream vigorously to make it as light as possible.

7. Use the buttercream right away, or refrigerate it for later use.

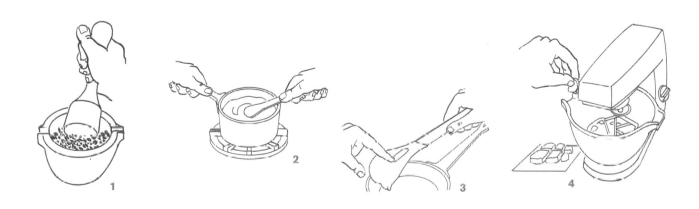

NOTE ON QUANTITY This recipe produces a fairly large quantity of buttercream. Unfortunately, it would be very difficult to prepare a smaller quantity of the custard base. If you do not have a stand mixer with a flat beater, you may want to divide the custard base in half and process each half separately following step 6 with half of the butter.

STORAGE Covered airtight for up to 1 week in the refrigerator. Before using, let the buttercream soften at room temperature. Then beat it vigorously with a wooden spatula or the flat beater of the mixer to make it smooth, spreadable, and light.

Or divide the buttercream into quantities suitable for the desserts you expect to make and freeze for up to 3 months. A typical gâteau requires 1½ to 2½ cups (260 to 425 g) of buttercream for filling and frosting. Defrost overnight in the refrigerator, then proceed as for refrigerated buttercream.

bourbon chocolat

FOR 10 TO 12 SERVINGS

Although this gâteau utilizes two distinctly American ingredients, pecans and Kentucky bourbon, it is clearly French in style. The cake layers are pecan *mousseline*.

FILLING AND FROSTING

1¾ cups (11 ounces; 315 g) coffee buttercream (page 146)

3   tablespoons (1 ounce; 25 g) pecans, finely chopped

CAKE

1   6-cup (1.5-L) loaf pecan *mousseline* (page 152)

BRUSHING-SYRUP MIXTURE

⅓   cup (8 cL) heavy syrup (page 157)

2   tablespoons + 2 teaspoons (4 cL) Kentucky bourbon

2   tablespoons + 2 teaspoons (4 cL) water

GLAZE

12   ounces (340 g) European bittersweet chocolate, melted

3½ tablespoons (1¾ ounces; 50 g) clarified butter (page 159),
    at room temperature

DECORATION FOR TOP OF GÂTEAU

1   pecan half

EQUIPMENT

Rectangle of silver or gold matt board or foil board
   › cut about ¼ inch (6 mm) larger in length and width than the
     génoise loaf
Chocolate thermometer or pocket digital thermometer
Small pastry bag fitted with
   › fluted decorating tube (such as the Ateco #17 open star tube)

1. Set aside about ¼ cup (45 g) of the coffee buttercream for piping on top of the gâteau.

2. Slice off the bottom of the pecan *mousseline* loaf with a wavy-edge bread knife to make it flat. Turn it right side up, and cut the loaf horizontally into three layers. Place the bottom layer on the matt board or foil board rectangle. Brush the top of this layer heavily with the bourbon brushing syrup. Spread ¼ cup (45 g) of the coffee buttercream over it with an icing spatula and scatter half of the chopped pecans over the buttercream. Brush the bottom of the middle cake layer with the bourbon syrup, turn it right side up, and place it on the first layer of buttercream. Brush the top of this layer heavily with the bourbon syrup, spread it with ¼ cup (45 g) of the buttercream, and scatter the remaining chopped pecans over the buttercream. Brush the bottom of the third cake layer heavily with the bourbon syrup, turn it right side up, and place it on the second layer of buttercream. Lightly brush the outside of the loaf with the bourbon syrup.

3. Spread the top and then the sides of the loaf with coffee buttercream, leaving a rim of buttercream around the top edge of the loaf. Sweep the icing spatula across the top to take off the excess buttercream and make it smooth. Slide the loaf to the edge of your countertop and sweep the icing spatula over the side to take off the excess buttercream and make it smooth. Rotate the loaf and repeat with each side in turn until the entire outside of the loaf is coated with a smooth layer of buttercream.

4. Slide the gâteau onto a wire rack and chill it in the refrigerator until the buttercream is firm, at least 1 hour.

5. If you did not melt the chocolate for the glaze in a stainless steel bowl, transfer it to one. Temper the chocolate as follows: Dip the bottom of the bowl of chocolate in a larger bowl of cold water and stir the chocolate until the temperature drops to between 80° and 84°F (26.5° to 29°C) and it begins to thicken. Immediately remove from the cold water and dip the bottom of the bowl of chocolate in a larger bowl of hot water. Stir over the hot water just long enough to warm the chocolate to between 86° and 91°F (30° to 33°C) and make it more fluid again. Then remove from the hot water immediately. Beat the clarified butter with a wooden spatula to make it smooth and creamy, then stir it into the chocolate.

6. Pour the chocolate on top of the gâteau in a rectangle just inside the perimeter so that some of it flows naturally over the edges. Quickly smooth the top surface with an icing spatula to cover the entire top with a thin layer of glaze and make the excess flow evenly down the sides. Pour additional chocolate over any areas that need it, and tilt and tap the wire rack to be sure the chocolate flows evenly over the entire surface. Touch up any uneven areas around the sides with the edge of the icing spatula. Let the chocolate begin to thicken, then clean off any excess chocolate around the bottom edge. Transfer the gâteau to a serving plate and let the glaze set.

7. Scoop the reserved buttercream into the pastry bag, and pipe a row of overlapping teardrops around the rim of the gâteau. Pipe one rosette on the center and four teardrops pointing out from the center. Place a pecan half on the rosette in the center.

8. Refrigerate the gâteau until ready to serve.

STORAGE In the refrigerator for up to 2 days.

Before glazing, freeze for up to 2 weeks. Once frozen, cover airtight with plastic wrap. Remove the plastic wrap and defrost overnight in the refrigerator, then glaze and decorate.

pecan mousseline

FOR ONE 6-CUP (1.5-L) LOAF

We devised this variation on a classic recipe to take advantage of the availability of superb pecans in the United States. Pecan *mousseline* can also be baked in a round cake pan or cake ring and used just like génoise in round gâteaux.

BATTER

4   large eggs, separated, at room temperature

1½   cups (7 ounces; 200 g) nut-and-sugar powder (page 154),
     made with pecans

⅛   teaspoon (a few drops) pure vanilla extract

⅛   teaspoon (a pinch) cream of tartar (optional)

2   tablespoons (1 ounce; 25 g) superfine or extra fine sugar

½   cup (2½ ounces; 70 g) all-purpose flour

EQUIPMENT

Electric mixer

6-cup (1.5-L) loaf pan

   › brush with melted butter

   › dust with flour

Heavy baking sheet

Preheat the oven to 350°F (175°C).

1. Combine the yolks with the pecan-and-sugar powder and beat at medium speed in the mixer until light and cream-colored. Beat in the vanilla extract.

2. Using a clean wire whip and bowl, whip the egg whites in the mixer at low speed until they start to froth. If you are not whipping the whites in a copper bowl, then add the cream of tartar. Gradually increase the whipping speed to medium-high, and continue whipping until the whites form very stiff peaks and just begin to slip and streak around the side of the bowl. Add the sugar and continue whipping at high speed for a few seconds longer to incorporate the sugar and tighten the meringue.

3. Sift the flour over the egg yolk mixture. Scoop about one third of the meringue on top and quickly and thoroughly mix it in with a rubber spatula. Add the remaining meringue and gently fold it into the batter.

4. Scoop the batter from the mixing bowl into the loaf pan, filling it to three fourths of its height. Smooth the surface and make a slight depression down the center. Place the loaf pan on the baking sheet.

5. Bake until the top of the cake is lightly browned and firm to the touch but not crusty, about 35 to 40 minutes. The tip of a paring knife inserted in the center of the cake should come out clean.

6. Remove the cake from the oven and slide the tip of a paring knife or small icing spatula between the edge of the cake and the pan to loosen the edge. Let the cake rest in the pan for about 5 minutes. Unmold the cake onto a wire rack. Turn it upside down and let cool to room temperature.

STORAGE Covered airtight with plastic wrap, for up to 2 days in the refrigerator.

Or freeze for as long as 2 months. If frozen, defrost overnight in the refrigerator, and unwrap the cake at least 2 hours before using to allow condensation produced by defrosting to evaporate.

nut-and-sugar powders

FOR 12 OUNCES (340 G); ABOUT 2½ CUPS

Many of our recipes require a powder made by grinding together equal weights of blanched almonds and confectioners' sugar. Nut-and-sugar powders made with other nuts are prepared by the same method and with the same proportions, but are used less frequently. Since blanched almonds are used much more often than any other nut, we refer to the powder made with blanched almonds simply as almond-and-sugar powder. When raw almonds are required, we specify raw-almond-and-sugar powder. Normally, we use raw hazelnuts for making hazelnut-and-sugar powder, but once in a while we specify a hazelnut-and-sugar powder made from roasted hazelnuts. We have even included a cake made with pecan-and-sugar powder.

If you bake cakes often, we recommend preparing nut-and-sugar powders (particularly almond-and-sugar powder) in large batches to save repeating the same work. Also, if you are using large quantities of nuts, it is much less expensive to purchase them in bulk (for example, at a natural foods market or specialty store) than to buy the small packages sold in supermarkets.

The recipe below can be prepared in a standard 7-cup (1.7-L) food processor. If you have a much larger food processor, you may be able to prepare up to double this recipe in one batch.

6   **ounces (170 g) nuts**
1¼ cups + 3 tablespoons (6 ounces; 170 g) confectioners' sugar

EQUIPMENT

Food processor

1. Combine the nuts with half the confectioners' sugar in the food processor work bowl. Process the nuts and sugar, stopping to scrape down the sides of the bowl and break up any caking as needed, until the nuts are finely ground, but not so long that the mixture becomes oily. (Be especially careful with walnuts, which have a very high oil content.)

2. Sift through a medium sieve—with 1/16- to 3/32-inch (1.5- to 2-mm) mesh. Return the nuts that don't pass through the sieve to the food processor with the remaining confectioners' sugar and process until the nuts have been reduced to a fine powder.

3. Transfer all of the nut-and-sugar powder to a bowl, break up any caking with your fingertips, and mix thoroughly.

HOWS AND WHYS This method is designed to produce the finest possible texture, while extracting the minimum amount of oil from the nuts. The food processor fluffs up the mixture as it grinds the nuts, minimizing compression and heat, which would extract more oil. The sugar in the powder absorbs the oil, helping to keep the powder from caking and turning into a paste.

STORAGE Covered airtight for up to 1 month at room temperature.

roasted nuts

FOR ANY QUANTITY

Roasting nuts enhances their flavor and reduces their moisture content. We frequently call for roasted chopped almonds to decorate the bottom edges of round gâteaux, and roasted chopped almonds or hazelnuts can make a nice addition to some buttercream fillings. You can decorate the top and sides of a gâteau with roasted sliced almonds.

When you are using sliced almonds for decoration, we recommend tossing them with a little heavy syrup before roasting to sweeten them and enhance their browning.

Either almonds (raw, blanched, sliced, or chopped) or hazelnuts (whole)
1   teaspoon (5 mL) heavy syrup (opposite page) for each 1 ounce (60 g)
sliced almonds (optional)

EQUIPMENT
Large, heavy baking sheet

Preheat the oven to 350°F (175°C).

1. If you are roasting sliced almonds, toss them with the heavy syrup to coat them evenly.

2. Spread out the nuts loosely on the baking sheet. Roast them in the preheated oven, stirring occasionally to move the nuts from the edge of the baking sheet to the center and prevent the nuts from browning unevenly. Roast chopped or sliced almonds until lightly browned, about 10 to 12 minutes. Roast whole almonds or hazelnuts until lightly browned in the center, about 15 to 25 minutes, depending on the size and type of nuts; test one by cutting it in half. Be careful not to overcook the nuts or they will burn.

3. FOR HAZELNUTS ONLY Pour the nuts into a large sieve and rub them against the mesh, using a kitchen towel to protect your hands, to remove most of their skins.

4. Pour the nuts out onto your countertop and allow them to cool.

STORAGE Covered airtight for up to 1 week at room temperature.

heavy syrup

This is the standard syrup for cake making. Because it has the ideal density (30° on the Baumé scale), it keeps almost indefinitely. A syrup with a lower concentration of sugar would ferment or become moldy eventually, and one with a higher concentration would crystallize.

In American volume measures the proportions are easy to remember: 2 cups sugar for each 1 cup water. (Or in metric measures, 1,700 g sugar for each 1 L water.) So you can prepare any quantity you like.

2   cups (14 ounces; 400 g) granulated sugar
1   cup (2.4 dL) water

1. Combine the sugar and water in the saucepan and bring to a boil, stirring occasionally to dissolve all the sugar.

2. Cover and allow the syrup to cool.

STORAGE Covered airtight, for up to several months at room temperature. If some sugar crystals form in the syrup (indicating that some water has evaporated), strain them out before using.

double-strength brewed espresso

FOR ANY QUANTITY

Brewing espresso double strength in your espresso maker produces a rich concentrate with an intensely attractive coffee taste. We mix it with heavy syrup to make brushing syrups for the cake layers in coffee-flavored gâteaux. The result has a much nicer coffee flavor than you would get by making a coffee concentrate from instant coffee.

We use a stove-top "moka" espresso brewer of the type first popularized by Bialetti. This is the least expensive, easiest to use, most low-tech machine you can get, and it works fine. If you want to use a fancier espresso machine, by all means do so. Be sure to use freshly roasted espresso coffee beans, finely ground. Resist the temptation to pack in more ground espresso than the machine calls for since that will make the steam take too long to penetrate the coffee and will produce a more bitter rather than stronger brew. The trick is to use only half the water that your machine calls for in relation to the amount of ground beans.

About ¼ cup (16 g) espresso beans, freshly roasted and finely ground,
    for each ⅓ cup (1.2 dL) brewed espresso
Half the quantity cold water specified by your machine for this quantity
    of beans

EQUIPMENT
Espresso machine

1. Place the ground espresso beans and cold water in your espresso machine and brew the coffee according to the manufacturer's instructions.

2. Allow the brewed espresso to cool before using.

STORAGE Covered airtight, for up to 2 days in the refrigerator or 1 month in the freezer.

clarified butter

You clarify butter by removing the residual milk solids. When melted, the clarified butter is clear yellow. In India, clarified butter is boiled to remove any remaining water and to sterilize the butter. The result is called *ghee*, and it can be kept, unrefrigerated (in India!), for a very long time.

Some cakes will stick to the cake pan when baked in a mold brushed with plain melted butter, but will not stick if the pan is brushed with clarified butter. So we recommend brushing cake pans and rings with clarified butter whenever sticking is a problem.

Unsalted butter

1. Place the butter in a butter melter or small saucepan and melt it over low heat, without stirring. When the butter is melted, remove it from the heat and skim off the foam (which contains the whey proteins) that comes to the surface. Let rest for a few minutes to allow all of the milk solids to settle to the bottom.

2. Pour the clear yellow liquid — the clarified butter — through a very fine sieve into a bowl, leaving the milky residue (the protein casein and some salts) at the bottom of the saucepan.

STORAGE Covered airtight for up to several weeks in the refrigerator or indefinitely in the freezer.

simply sensational desserts

author

François Payard, a third-generation pastry chef and the chef-owner of Payard Pâtisserie and Bistro in New York City.

why he wrote it

"To me, it is sad when someone is discouraged from trying baking and pastry making at home. As a pastry chef and a person who loves to communicate what I have learned, I was determined to create a book that would make sophisticated desserts simple to do. I wanted a variety of classic and contemporary creations, some with sleek presentation, others with fun and whimsy, and others with a rustic look. I wanted a spectrum of recipes, from the very simplest to slightly more complex, but all quite doable in a short period of time. Imagine the novelty of a French chef making things easy!"

why it made our list

Payard's brilliance as a pastry chef has been hailed far and wide, and in this, his first book, he shares the recipes that have made his reputation. We expected them to be good, but what surprised us was how manageable many of his signature recipes are. From descriptions of basic ingredients and techniques to storage suggestions for those who like to bake in advance, Payard has put together a book that makes turning out sensational desserts simple and satisfying.

from the book

"Many chefs concentrate too much of their efforts on making their desserts look spectacular, forgetting that flavor is primary. You have had desserts like these in restaurants, I'm sure, and also seen them in pastry books. Towers of mousse, paintings in sauce, sculptures of chocolate — all of them fun to look at, most of them tasting like . . . sculpture. To make the recipes in such books generally requires hours of your time, special skills, and a major investment in new kitchen equipment. The pastry chefs I respect devote their skills, ingenuity, equipment, ingredients, and time to one object alone: flavor."

specifics

236 pages, 140 recipes, 51 color photographs, 12 black-and-white photographs.

    chapters Dessert Soups > Cookies and Petits Fours > Weekend Cakes > Chocolate Cakes > Tarts and Tartlets > Soufflés > Ice Creams, Sorbets, and Granités > Holiday Cakes, Cookies, and Bites > Candies

$35. Published by Broadway Books.

1 cup plus 2 tablespoons (146 grams) cake flour

¼ teaspoon baking powder

3 large eggs

1 cup (200 grams) sugar

⅛ teaspoon salt

Grated zest of 1½ lemons

¼ cup plus 2 tablespoons (87 grams) heavy cream

6 tablespoons (86 grams) unsalted butter, melted and cooled

This is my father's recipe. He would make a big batch of the batter and keep it in the freezer, then take out some of it every Wednesday and bake it up. On Wednesdays, we didn't have school; I would stay home and do homework or go out to play, knowing that the lemon pound cake would be there at day's end.

The batter is not heavy, but it bakes into a dense cake. The more airy a cake, the faster it dries; the more dense, the longer it holds its moisture. You can of these cakes as well in plas-

... 4½ × 2½-inch loaf pan.

... the eggs

1. Preheat the ove...
Dust the pan with fl...
2. Sift togeth...
3. In an el...
at medium...
beat unti...
dry in...
me...

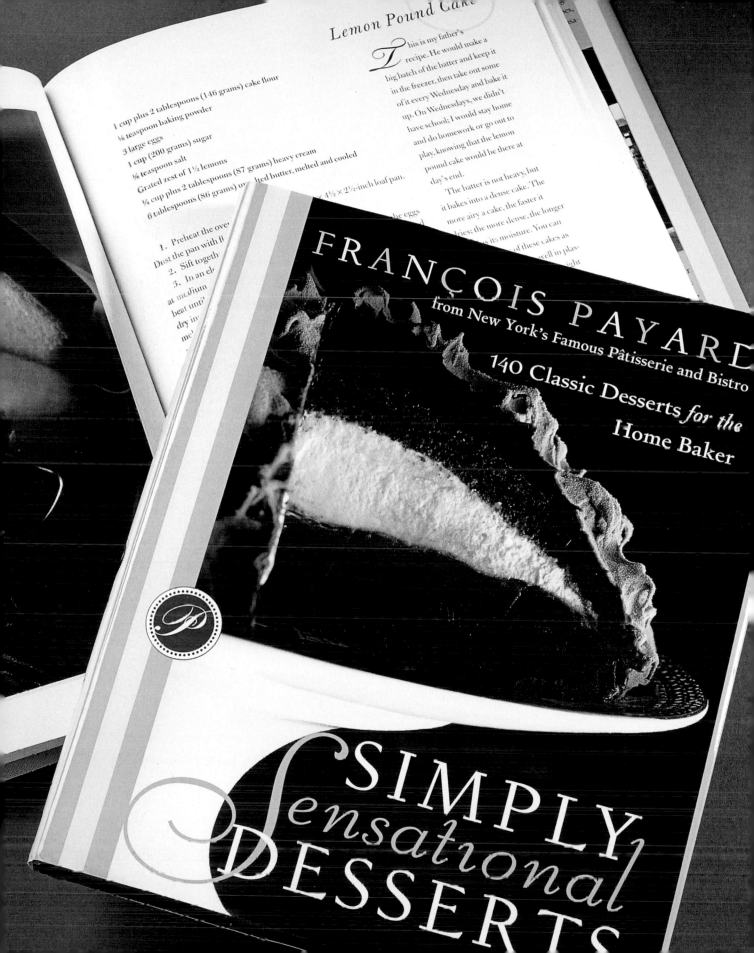

FRANÇOIS PAYARD

from New York's Famous Pâtisserie and Bistro

140 Classic Desserts for the Home Baker

SIMPLY Sensational DESSERTS

lemon pound cake

MAKES 10 TO 12 SERVINGS

This is my father's recipe. He would make a big batch of the batter and keep it in the freezer, then take out some of it every Wednesday and bake it up. On Wednesdays, we didn't have school; I would stay home and do homework or go out to play, knowing that the lemon pound cake would be there at day's end.

The batter is not heavy, but it bakes into a dense cake. The more airy a cake, the faster it dries; the more dense, the longer it retains its moisture. You can make as many of these cakes as you like, wrap them well in plastic, and freeze them. The night before you intend to serve it, take one out and put it in the refrigerator to thaw. This is great for breakfast, sliced and warmed up in the toaster, as well as perfect at afternoon tea.

1	**cup plus 2 tablespoons (146 grams) cake flour**
⅛	**teaspoon baking powder**
3	**large eggs**
1	**cup (200 grams) sugar**
⅛	**teaspoon salt**
	Grated zest of 1½ lemons
¼	**cup plus 2 tablespoons (87 grams) heavy cream**
6	**tablespoons (86 grams) unsalted butter, melted and cooled**

1. Preheat the oven to 325°F. Butter an 8½ x 4½ x 2½-inch loaf pan. Dust the pan with flour, tapping out the excess.

2. Sift together the flour and baking powder.

3. In an electric mixer fitted with the whisk attachment, beat the eggs at medium speed until blended. Gradually add the sugar and salt and beat until thickened and pale, about 2 minutes. At low speed, mix in the dry ingredients and lemon zest alternately with the heavy cream. Add the melted butter and mix until combined. Scrape the batter into the prepared pan, smoothing the top with a spatula.

4. Bake for 1 hour and 5 to 10 minutes, until the top of the cake is golden and a toothpick inserted in the center comes out clean. Cool the cake in the pan on a rack for 15 minutes. Remove the cake from the pan and cool completely on the rack.

warm chocolate tart

MAKES 6 TO 8 SERVINGS

I have made this amazing tart in every restaurant where I've worked and it never fails to sell out. It is very simple to make. The filling is like a ganache, but the egg adds some air. The rich chocolate creaminess of the tart, the chewiness of the dough, and then the temperature and flavor jolt of vanilla ice cream against the warm tart explain why this is so popular. You can serve it warm or cold, but I recommend warm—make it up to a day ahead of time, then just warm it up again in a low oven.

8 ounces (227 grams) bittersweet chocolate, finely chopped

¾ cup (174 grams) heavy cream

½ cup (121 grams) whole milk

1 large egg, lightly beaten

One 9½-inch tart shell made from Sweet Tart Dough (page 168), prebaked

1. Preheat the oven to 325°F.
2. Place the chopped chocolate in a medium bowl and set aside.
3. Combine the cream and milk in a medium saucepan, and bring to a boil over medium-high heat. Pour the hot cream mixture over the chocolate. Allow to stand for 30 seconds to melt the chocolate, then whisk until the chocolate is completely melted and the mixture is smooth. Allow to cool for 10 minutes.
4. Whisk the egg into the chocolate mixture. Pour the filling into the prebaked tart shell.
5. Bake the tart for 8 to 10 minutes, until the edges of the filling are set; the center will still be soft. Cool the tart on a wire rack for 10 minutes and serve warm.

apple cake

MAKES 10 TO 12 SERVINGS

My father created this recipe twenty years ago, and he still sells one hundred of these apple cakes a day from his shop in Nice. The only time he changes the formula is when his preferred apple—*la reine des reinettes*—is not available. Then, because his customers demand some kind of cake, he makes it with apricot. As always, I follow my father's lead. First, when selecting an apple for this cake, find one that is nice and plump. A Rome apple or a Fuji will, like my father's favorite, retain moisture no matter how long it is baked. Second, if you like the idea of this recipe with apricots rather than apples, please try it. (Substitute fifteen to twenty apricot halves for the apples.) When it is baked, an apricot has such wonderful acidity. In fact, I like that even better, but I know that Americans love apples. This will keep in the refrigerator for a week. (The apricot version will last for only two days or so.) This is best served plain.

⅓   **cup (60 grams) raisins**

3   **tablespoons (42 grams) dark rum, such as Meyer's**

1   **scant cup (136 grams) all-purpose flour**

¾   **teaspoon (3 grams) baking powder**

8   **tablespoons (1 stick) (113 grams) unsalted butter, softened**

1   **cup (115 grams) confectioner's sugar**

3   **large eggs**

2   **apples, such as Fuji or Rome, peeled and cored**

¼   **cup (60 grams) Apricot Glaze (page 169)**

1. Preheat the oven to 325°F. Butter an 8½ x 4½ x 2½-inch loaf pan. Dust the pan with flour, tapping out the excess.

2. Bring a small pan of water to a boil, add the raisins, and boil 1 minute. Drain and repeat the process. Drain the raisins well a second time and place in a small bowl with the rum; stir and set aside.

3. Sift together the flour and baking powder.

4. In the bowl of an electric mixer fitted with the paddle attachment, mix together the butter and confectioner's sugar on medium speed. Add the eggs one at a time, beating well after each addition. Scrape down the side of the bowl with a rubber spatula. Mix in the raisins and rum. Add the dry ingredients and mix on low speed until blended. Spoon half of the batter into the pan and smooth into an even layer.

5. Cut one apple into 12 wedges and arrange them over the batter, down the center of the pan, so their sides touch and the domed side of each wedge is on top. Spoon the rest of the batter over and around the apples and smooth the top. Cut the other apple into 8 wedges and then cut each wedge in half crosswise. Arrange the wedges in a single row along each long side of the pan, pressing the center-cut sides of the apples against the sides of the pan. There will be two rows of apple slices, with their points toward the center of the pan and exposed batter in the center. Gently push the apples into the batter, leaving the top of the apples exposed.

6. Bake the cake for 60 to 65 minutes, until the top is golden brown and a toothpick inserted in the center comes out clean. Cool the cake in the pan on a wire rack for 15 minutes. Unmold the cake and turn it right side up. Gently brush the apricot glaze over the the top of the hot cake. Allow the cake to cool completely before cutting into slices.

sweet tart dough

MAKES TWO 9½-INCH TART SHELLS

This recipe for the rich, sweet, short dough known as pâte sucrée is the only one you will need for the tarts in this book. In addition to its use as the pastry shell for tarts and tartlets, pâte sucrée is frequently used in petit fours, for filled cookies, and as a thin sweet crust under mousse desserts. This recipe makes enough pastry for two tart shells. You can freeze half for another time, or you can roll out and shape both shells and freeze one of them, well wrapped, ready to use.

1 cup plus 1 tablespoon (122 grams) confectioners' sugar

1¾ cups (254 grams) all-purpose flour

Pinch of salt

9 tablespoons (127 grams) unsalted butter, softened

1 large egg

1. Sift together the confectioners' sugar, flour, and salt into a bowl.

2. Place the butter in a food processor and process until smooth, about 15 seconds. Scatter the flour mixture over the butter, add the egg, and process just until the dough forms a mass; do not overmix. Turn the dough out onto the counter and divide it in two. Shape each half into a disc, wrap in plastic wrap, and refrigerate for at least 2 hours or up to 24 hours. Half of the dough may be well wrapped and frozen for up to 1 month.

3. Let the dough stand at room temperature for 30 minutes to soften. Lightly butter two 9½-inch fluted tart pans with removable bottoms.

4. Dust a work surface lightly with flour. Dust one of the discs lightly with flour and, using a floured rolling pin, roll it out into a rough 12-inch circle. Lift the dough often, making sure that the work surface and dough are lightly floured at all times. Roll the dough up onto the rolling pin and gently unroll it over one of the prepared tart pans. Press the dough into the pan and roll the pin over the top of the pan to remove the excess dough. Repeat with the remaining dough and tart pan. Prick the bottom of the tart shells all over with a fork. Chill the tart shells for 20 minutes. (The tart shells can be refrigerated for up to 24 hours.)

TO PARTIALLY BAKE THE TART SHELLS Preheat the oven to 325°F. Lightly butter two pieces of aluminum foil large enough to generously line each tart pan. Line the tart shells with the foil, buttered side down, and fill with dried beans, rice, or pie weights.

Bake the tart shells for 15 minutes. Remove the foil and beans and continue baking for 5 minutes, until just set; the tart shells should have little or no color. Cool completely on a wire rack.

TO PREBAKE THE TART SHELLS Preheat the oven to 325°F. Lightly butter two pieces of aluminum foil large enough to generously line each tart pan. Line the tart shells with the foil, buttered side down, and fill with dried beans, rice, or pie weights.

Bake the tart shells for 15 minutes. Remove the foil and beans and continue baking for 8 to 10 minutes longer, until evenly golden brown. Cool completely on a wire rack.

apricot glaze

MAKES ABOUT ¼ CUP

Apricot glaze adds sheen and a subtle flavor to many French tarts and cakes. It also helps keep them moist.

⅓ **cup (95 grams) apricot preserves**

Place the preserves in a small heatproof glass measure and microwave on high power for 30 to 45 seconds, until bubbling. Strain the hot preserves through a fine-mesh sieve into a small bowl. Use the glaze warm.

dessert circus at home

author

Dessert maestro Jacques Torres, executive pastry chef at Le Cirque 2000 in New York City and host of the PBS series *Dessert Circus*. Torres' first book, *Dessert Circus*, was one of last year's *Best of the Best* honorees.

why he wrote it

"I learned that many people bake without understanding why things happen, why cookies turn out differently, or what makes recipes different besides the obvious ingredients. I hope to offer the reasons why things happen and explain how you can adjust your baking so your recipe will turn out the way you want it. Armed with this knowledge, you can take your recipes to the next level."

why it made our list

Torres starts with basics like pastry cream and tart dough and goes on to surefire favorites, from apple crisp to chocolate truffles, as well as his own fanciful creations. The more elaborate of these may be challenging even for an experienced baker, but the majority of the desserts are as delightfully easy as they are delectable. A comprehensive "Getting Started" section sets the tone, describing equipment and ingredients and defining terms. The recipes that follow are clear, thorough, and practically foolproof, granting everyone a taste of sweet success.

from the book

"I get inspiration from the everyday things I see in my life and from the stress of my usual workday. That phrase about necessity being the mother of invention really applies to my job. No matter what, I think it is important to have fun with dessert. Be whimsical. Go out on a limb. You can always say your zany design was the result of ingesting too much sugar!"

specifics

304 pages, 103 recipes, 142 color photographs.

chapters Back to Basics › Tantalizing Tarts › Practically Good for You › Piece of Cake › Kid's Play › The Bread Basket › Signature Desserts › Breakfast and Tea › Homemade and Heavenly › Tiny Temptations › Home for the Holidays

$28. Published by William Morrow and Company, Inc.

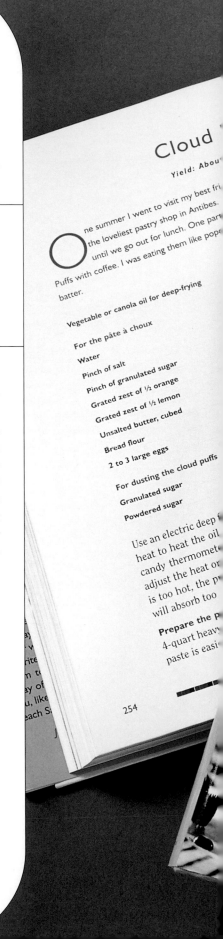

Cloud

Yield: Abou

One summer I went to visit my best fri the loveliest pastry shop in Antibes. until we go out for lunch. One par Puffs with coffee. I was eating them like pope batter.

Vegetable or canola oil for deep-frying

For the pâte à choux

Water

Pinch of salt

Pinch of granulated sugar

Grated zest of ½ orange

Grated zest of ½ lemon

Unsalted butter, cubed

Bread flour

2 to 3 large eggs

For dusting the cloud puffs

Granulated sugar

Powdered sugar

Use an electric deep heat to heat the oil candy thermomet adjust the heat or is too hot, the p will absorb too

Prepare the p 4-quart heavy paste is easi

254

an Cottard. He is a pastry chef and has
time I go to the shop and stay with him
e made our meal and served these Cloud
an old French recipe using cream puff

erous ½ cup   4.5 ounces

3.5 tablespoons

⅓ cup

Dessert Circus at Home
Fun, Fanciful, and Easy-to-Make Desserts
Jacques Torres
with Christina Wright and Kris Kruid • Photography by John Uher
Companion to the National Public Television Series Dessert Circus

francisco's banana walnut tart

YIELD: ONE 10-INCH TART; 8 TO 10 SERVINGS

This recipe was developed by my colleague Francisco Gutierrez. He has worked at Le Cirque for the last eighteen years, making tarts with the best ingredients available during the season. As far as I'm concerned, he makes the best tarts in town. One day we had a lot of extra walnut mix from the soufflé recipes. Francisco added some bananas and some almond cream and created this tart. We feature it at the restaurant and it is always one of the most popular tart specials on the menu.

I like to use a tart pan with a removable bottom for this tart.

FOR THE CRUST
Pâte Brisée (page 176)

FOR THE CARAMEL-WALNUT BASE
Scant 1 cup (7 ounces; 200 grams) granulated sugar
Scant ½ cup (3.5 ounces; 100 grams) heavy cream
Scant ½ cup (3.5 ounces; 100 grams) whole milk
About 1¾ cups (7 ounces; 200 grams) chopped walnuts

FOR THE FILLING
½   recipe Almond Cream (page 178)
4 to 5 large ripe bananas

TO FINISH THE TART
Powdered sugar for dusting or Apricot Glaze (page 179)

PREPARE THE CRUST Make the dough as directed in the recipe. I like to make this well in advance to give it time to rest in the refrigerator. This will allow any gluten that may have developed time to relax.

PREPARE THE CARAMEL-WALNUT BASE Pour the granulated sugar into a 2-quart heavy-bottomed saucepan and place over medium-high heat. Cook, stirring occasionally with a wooden spoon, until the sugar melts and turns a light caramel color. Watch it carefully; once the sugar begins to caramelize, it can burn very quickly. When the sugar has melted and has turned a light golden brown color, slowly and carefully add the heavy cream. The addition of the

cold cream to the hot caramel will cause the mixture to hiss and possibly splatter, so do not lean over the saucepan while you are adding it. When all of the cream has been added, mix thoroughly with a wooden spoon. Remember to mix into the edge of the saucepan where the caramel can stick. Add the milk and mix thoroughly. Add the chopped walnuts and mix until well combined and the walnuts are evenly dispersed. Insert a candy thermometer and cook over medium-high heat until the mixture reaches 225°F (110°C). At this point, the caramel will have thickened and darkened slightly. Remove the saucepan from the heat and pour the filling into a heatproof bowl. Let cool. (This recipe amount yields more than needed for one tart and can be stored in the refrigerator, tightly covered with plastic wrap, for several weeks. I like to eat it on toast for breakfast!)

PREPARE THE FILLING   Make the almond cream as directed in the recipe. Sometimes I like to add a splash of dark rum for extra flavor. You will use the almond cream right away, so there is no need to refrigerate it. If using refrigerated almond cream, allow it to return to room temperature. Beat it with an electric mixer set on medium-high speed until it returns to its original volume and is once again light in color.

Preheat the oven to 375°F (190°C).

ASSEMBLE THE TART   Remove the dough from the refrigerator. Lightly give the dough a few quick raps with the rolling pin to soften it slightly. This will make it easier to roll. Lightly flour the work surface and each side of the dough. Roll the dough into a 12-inch circle about ¼ inch thick. Transfer the dough to a 10-inch tart pan by rolling it around the rolling pin. Unroll the dough over the tart pan. Gently press the dough into the pan, especially where the bottom and the side of the pan meet. Don't forget to press the dough up the side of the pan; this will help the dough hold its shape as it bakes. Remove any excess dough by rolling the rolling pin over the top of the pan to make a nice clean cut. Dock the bottom of the tart shell with a fork.

Spread about a ¼-inch-thick layer of almond cream in the bottom of the tart shell. Peel the bananas and cut them into ¼-inch-thick slices. Arrange the banana slices in concentric circles, starting at the edge of the tart shell and working your way toward the center. Leave about a 2-inch-diameter circle in the center of the tart. Fill this circle with the caramel-walnut mixture. Sometimes I like to sprinkle granulated sugar over the tart just before baking; this gives the bananas a nice crust.

Bake the tart until light golden brown and the filling forms a light crust, about 45 minutes. Remove from the oven and place on a wire rack until the tart has completely cooled.

UNMOLD THE TART Simply push up on the bottom of the tart pan and remove the side. Use a flat metal spatula to slide the tart onto a flat plate or platter. (If you use a plate with slightly raised edges, the tart will break.) If you did not use a tart pan with a removable bottom, you will need to invert the tart to remove the pan. To do this, invert a flat plate over the cooled tart. Place one hand on each side, grasping both plate and tart pan, and flip them both over so that the tart pan is now on top. Gently lift off the tart pan. Invert a second flat plate over the bottom of the tart. Once again, flip both plates so that the tart is upright. Remove the first plate.

You can lightly dust the tart with powdered sugar before serving or top with apricot glaze. If you use apricot glaze, prepare it as directed in the recipe and brush it onto the tart with a pastry brush.

VARIATIONS This tart can also be made with peaches, apples, apricots, or figs. (Peel and core the apples. Pit the peaches or apricots. Slice the apples, peaches, apricots, or figs.) When I have a little more time, I poach some pears (peeled and cored) in 1 quart (32 ounces; 1 liter) of water with 1 cup (7 ounces; 200 grams) of granulated sugar, 2 scraped vanilla beans, the juice of 1 lemon, and the grated zest of 1 lemon. I bring them to a gentle simmer over medium-low heat until tender. Before adding the cooled poached pears to the tart, I drain them on a wire rack placed over a parchment paper–covered baking sheet. Then I slice them and arrange them on the tart.

pâte brisée

YIELD: 15 OUNCES (415 GRAMS); ENOUGH FOR ONE 10- OR 12-INCH TART

Pâte brisée is one of the three classic recipes that form the basis for most tarts. It is similar to a shortbread dough. It is very important to use a good-quality butter, since the taste is very prominent in this recipe.

I learned how to make pâte brisée from my mentor, Louis Franchain. He explains that while the components of the recipe are quite simple, the results depend on the technique for making the dough and understanding how the ingredients interact. Mastery of this very simple recipe is a key to making good tarts.

1⅔ cups (9 ounces; 250 grams) cake flour

Pinch of salt

Pinch of granulated sugar

½ cup + 2 tablespoons (4.5 ounces; 125 grams) cold unsalted butter, diced

Scant ⅓ cup (2.3 ounces; 65 grams) cold water

Combine the flour, salt, and sugar in a large mixing bowl. Add the butter all at once and coat evenly with the flour mixture. Work in the butter with your hands until the mixture resembles coarse meal. The easiest way to do this is to grab a handful of flour mixture and butter, then gently rub the two between your hands to combine them. As you rub, the mixture drops back into the bowl. Keep doing this until most of the butter is combined. If your hands are too warm, the butter will melt. If necessary, wash your hands in ice-cold water every few minutes. Make sure your hands are dry when you return to the mixture. Stop working the mixture while you can still see small chunks of butter. This will make the dough softer and more crumbly.

Add the water all at once and work it in with your hands until the dough holds together. Be careful not to overmix or you risk overdeveloping the gluten, which will cause the dough to be tough and chewy rather than delicate and crumbly. When the dough holds together in a ball, place it on the work surface and knead gently until smooth, about 30 seconds. If the dough is sticky when you begin, very lightly flour the work surface before you knead the dough. If the dough is dry and ropey, just keep kneading it until it becomes smooth and moist. Pat the dough into a disk and place on a parchment paper–covered baking sheet. Cover with plastic wrap and let rest in the refrigerator for at least 30 minutes before using. This will give any gluten strands that have developed a chance to relax. Then proceed with the dough as directed in your particular recipe. The dough will keep well wrapped in the refrigerator for 1 week or in the freezer for 1 month.

almond cream

YIELD: 1¾ CUPS (16 OUNCES; 425 GRAMS)

Almond cream is always baked to a spongy, cakelike texture and can be used by itself or in combination with nuts or fruits. The addition of starch to this recipe ensures that it will not run out of a pastry shell during the cooking process. Its moist and flavorful qualities make it perfect for use as a filling in cookies, tarts, and puff pastries.

The recipe is easy to remember: 1 part butter, 1 part almond flour, 1 part sugar, ⅕ part eggs, ⅐ part all-purpose flour. With that in mind, you can make as much or as little of it as you like.

½ **cup + 1 tablespoon (4.5 ounces; 125 grams) unsalted butter, softened**

Generous ½ cup (4.5 ounces; 125 grams) granulated sugar

Generous 1 cup (4.5 ounces; 125 grams) almond flour (available in specialty gourmet stores and health food stores)

1 **large egg**

Scant ¼ cup (0.75 ounce; 20 grams) all-purpose flour

Place the butter, sugar, and almond flour in a medium-size mixing bowl and beat with an electric mixer set on medium speed until light and fluffy, about 5 minutes. The mixture will be dry and sandy until the butter begins to incorporate. Add the egg and mix well. Use a rubber spatula to scrape down the side of the bowl as needed. The egg is well incorporated when the mixture is light and creamy, about 3 minutes. The batter lightens in color and increases in volume due to the incorporation of air by the mixer. It is important to allow time to beat in air; otherwise the almond cream will be too heavy and will not have as great a rise when baked, causing the texture to be dense.

Add the all-purpose flour and beat on low speed just until it is no longer visible, about 30 seconds. If you overmix, gluten will overdevelop and the almond cream will lose its delicate texture when baked.

Pour the almond cream into an airtight container and store in the refrigerator for up to 5 days until ready to use. While in the refrigerator, the almond cream will darken in color and lose some of its volume. This happens because the butter hardens and the incorporated air escapes. You can also freeze the almond cream for several weeks. In either case, allow it to come to room temperature before using and beat it lightly with an electric mixer set on medium speed until it returns to its initial volume and is once again light in texture and color.

apricot glaze

YIELD: ABOUT ¼ CUP (2.6 OUNCES; 75 GRAMS)

I use glaze to give a professional finish to a tart or cake. You can make almost any kind of fruit glaze you like using any flavor of jam. I use apricot because it is clear and has a neutral flavor. You may have to adjust the amount of water based on the consistency of the jam. Heat the glaze until it is liquid enough to apply with a pastry brush.

¼   **cup (2.6 ounces; 75 grams) apricot jam**
About 1 tablespoon (0.6 ounce; 15 grams) water

Mix the apricot jam with the water in a small microwaveable bowl and heat in the microwave on high power or in a nonreactive 1-quart heavy-bottomed saucepan over medium heat until liquid. Brush it on with a pastry brush. The glaze can be stored in the refrigerator in an airtight container for up to 3 days.

cloud puffs

YIELD: ABOUT 13 DOZEN

One summer I went to visit my best friend, Christian Cottard. He is a pastry chef and has the loveliest pastry shop in Antibes. Most of the time I go to the shop and stay with him until we go out for lunch. One particular day, he made our meal and served these Cloud Puffs with coffee. I was eating them like popcorn. This is an old French recipe using cream puff batter.

Vegetable or canola oil for deep-frying

FOR THE PÂTE À CHOUX
Generous ½ cup (4.5 ounces; 125 grams) water
Pinch of salt
Pinch of granulated sugar
Grated zest of ½ orange
Grated zest of ½ lemon
3.5 tablespoons (1.8 ounces; 50 grams) unsalted butter, cubed
½   cup (2.6 ounces; 75 grams) bread flour
2 to 3 large eggs

FOR DUSTING THE CLOUD PUFFS
1   cup (7.7 ounces; 220 grams) granulated sugar
Generous 1 cup (4.7 ounces; 130 grams) powdered sugar

Use an electric deep fryer or a 4-quart heavy-bottomed saucepan placed over medium-high heat to heat the oil to 330°F (165°C). If using a saucepan, check the temperature with a candy thermometer. It is important to maintain the temperature, so you may need to adjust the heat or remove the pan from the burner to keep it where you want it. If the oil is too hot, the puffs will burn before they are evenly fried. If the oil is too cool, the puffs will absorb too much oil before they finish frying.

PREPARE THE PÂTE À CHOUX Place the water, salt, granulated sugar, zests, and butter in a 4-quart heavy-bottomed saucepan, set it over medium-high heat, and bring to a boil. The paste is easier to mix in a large pan. The butter should be completely melted by the time the mixture boils. Remove the saucepan from the heat. Add the bread flour all at once and incorporate it thoroughly with a wooden spoon.

Return the saucepan to the stove and cook over medium heat for about 3 minutes to dry out the paste. As it cooks, push the paste from side to side with the wooden spoon. Turn it onto itself to allow every side to touch the bottom of the saucepan, which helps it dry. Keep the paste moving, or it will burn. You will know the paste is dry when it begins to leave a thin film on the bottom of the saucepan.

Remove the saucepan from the heat and transfer the paste to a large mixing bowl. Mix with an electric mixer set on low speed or by hand for about 2 minutes to release some of the steam. This will prevent the eggs from cooking and scrambling when mixed together with the paste. Continue to mix and slowly add the eggs one at a time, incorporating well after each addition. (Adding the eggs in this manner ensures they will be evenly distributed throughout the batter.) After each egg is added, the paste will become loose and look separated. Don't worry. Once each egg is well incorporated, the paste will become smooth and homogenous again. The number of eggs used will vary depending on the size of the eggs and how well the *pâte à choux* is dried. The drier it is, the more eggs you will need. After you have added 2 eggs, check the consistency by scooping a large amount of the paste onto a wooden spoon. Hold the spoon horizontally about one foot above the bowl and watch as the batter falls from the spoon back into the bowl. If it is pale yellow, smooth, moist, slightly elastic, sticky, and takes 5 to 7 seconds to fall into the bowl, it is ready. If it appears rough, dry, and falls into the bowl in one big ball, it needs more eggs. Add another egg and check the consistency again after it is well incorporated. If the *pâte à choux* is too dry, it will not pipe well. If it is too wet, it will be loose, runny, and won't hold its shape.

PREPARE THE CLOUD PUFFS Place the *pâte à choux* batter into a pastry bag fitted with a ½-inch opening, no pastry tip. Dip a wooden skewer or chopstick into the hot oil. This will keep the dough from sticking to it. Hold the skewer or chopstick horizontally over the hot oil. Hold the pastry bag over the oil and pipe about ½-inch dollops of batter (about the size of a dime) out of the tip. Use the skewer or chopstick to cut the batter from the tip so the batter drops into the hot oil. Be careful not to splatter the hot oil onto your arms or face. You can also do this with a spoon if you do not have a pastry bag. Simply drop small scoops of the batter into the hot oil. Repeat until the saucepan is full of frying dough without crowding them. Fry the puffs until they are golden brown, 3 to 5 minutes. Turn them over to evenly fry each side. They will increase in size as they cook. Use a large slotted spoon to remove the puffs from the hot oil and set them on a paper towel or a clean towel to drain.

While the puffs are still warm, roll them in a bowl filled with the granulated sugar until evenly coated. Then dust them with the powdered sugar just before serving. They are best served immediately, since they tend to get soggy after a few hours.

If your oil is too hot, add a small amount of cold oil to lower the temperature.

room for dessert

author

David Lebovitz, who for twelve years served as the pastry cook at the legendary Chez Panisse in Berkeley, California.

why he wrote it

To provide recipes that can *really* be done at home. "I left out a lot of recipes because they included steps that belong to the category of Things Nobody Wants to Do at Home: tempering chocolate, for example, or spinning sugar, or decorating anything with more than one pastry bag! I left out others because they had too many steps. I love to eat and I hate to wait too long for an outcome, so I tend to favor recipes that are relatively easy."

why it made our list

These are desserts home cooks will appreciate — simple and delicious, with no overblown garnishes or endless instructions. Like Alice Waters, his employer at Chez Panisse, Lebovitz believes in using fresh, local, seasonal ingredients and feels they don't need a lot of dressing up to make them shine. He wants the main ingredient to come through loud and clear. "A chocolate cake should always have that screaming chocolate intensity. . . . Sauces should complement flavors, not compete with them. I want things to taste good together, not jerk your palate around in different directions — for example, I don't like most desserts that combine fruits and chocolate: The flavors are all over the place." We'll always have room for his straightforward, full-flavored desserts.

from the book

"**Shapes should be clean and interesting. I don't mind decor per se, as long as it's minimal and part of the dessert; but I don't like anything on the plate that I can't devour — and some of these elaborate vertical dessert follies served nowadays have inedible elements: spirals and sharp shards of caramel, for example — ouch! And what's up with those tiny dots of sauce that don't do anything? If a sauce is part of the dessert, I want there to be enough of it, not just a decorative dribble of raspberry sauce purely for show.**"

specifics

221 pages, 110 recipes, 81 color photographs.
chapters Essentials > Cakes > Custards and Soufflés > Fruit Desserts > Sorbets, Sherbets, Ice Creams, and Gelées > Cookies and Candies > Liqueurs and Preserves > Basics
$30. Published by HarperCollins Publishers, Inc.

...UT–PEAR CAKE

ONE 9-INCH CAKE; 10 TO 12 SERVINGS

The glazed pear topping:
¼ cup dark or light brown sugar, firmly packed
⅓ cup maple syrup
½ cup walnuts, toasted
3 ripe Bosc pears

The cake batter:
8 tablespoons (1 stick) butter, at room temperature
½ cup granulated sugar
¼ cup light brown sugar firmly packed

½ teaspoon vanilla extract
2 eggs, at room temperature
1½ cups flour
1 teaspoon baking powder
2 teaspoons ground cinnamon
½ teaspoon salt
½ cup milk, at room temperature

Whipped cream (page 192)

1   Position the oven rack in the center of the... the oven to 350 degrees.

2   To make the glazed... and maple syrup... directly o...

6   Sift together the flour, baking powder, c... into a separate bowl. Gradually mix half the... the butter mixture. Stir in the milk, then add... ingredients, and mix until just combined.

7   Transfer the batter to the cake pan... Smooth it into an even layer, being care... arrangement of the pears.

8   Bake about 50 minutes, until a to... center comes out clean. Let cool for 30... plate over the pan, grasp both the pa... over. Lift off the cake pan. Any waln... the pan can be loosened with a fork. Serve warm, with whipped cream.

...OOM FOR DESSERT

110 RECIPES FOR PIES
CAKES
TARTS
SORBETS
CUSTARDS
SOUFFLES
COOKIES
CANDIES
CORDIALS
SHERBETS
COBBLERS
ICE CREAMS

DAVID LEBOVITZ
...WORD BY ALICE WATERS

chocolate orbit cake

ONE 9-INCH CAKE; 12 TO 14 SERVINGS

Someone told me once that this cake reminded her of the lunar surface, and somebody else added that it launches chocolate lovers into orbit.

½ **pound (2 sticks) butter**

12 **ounces bittersweet chocolate**

6 **eggs**

1 **cup sugar**

OPTIONAL

Crème anglaise (page 190)

1. Position the oven rack in the center of the oven. Preheat the oven to 350 degrees. Butter a 9 by 2-inch round cake pan, and line the inside with a round of parchment paper.

2. Set a large bowl over a pan of simmering water to create a double boiler. Cut the butter and chocolate into small pieces and put them in the bowl to melt, whisking occasionally.

3. Whisk together the eggs and sugar in another bowl. Thoroughly whisk in the melted chocolate.

4. Pour the chocolate batter into the cake pan. Place it in a larger baking pan, and pour in warm water to reach halfway up the sides of the cake pan. Cover tightly with foil and bake for 1 hour and 15 minutes, until the cake appears to have set and when you touch the center, your finger comes away clean.

5. Remove the cake from the water bath and cool completely before serving, plain or with crème anglaise.

NOTE This cake can be refrigerated for several days.

maple walnut-pear cake

ONE 9-INCH CAKE; 10 TO 12 SERVINGS

A little while ago, I received a whole gallon of Grade B maple syrup from some friends in upstate New York. What a gift! This is one of the desserts I invented to help use up my sweet windfall.

Dark maple syrup—Grade B or Grade A "dark amber"—has a more intense maple flavor, which I prefer.

THE GLAZED PEAR TOPPING

¼ **cup dark or light brown sugar, firmly packed**

⅓ **cup maple syrup**

½ **cup walnuts, toasted**

3 **ripe Bosc Pears**

THE CAKE BATTER

8 **tablespoons (1 stick) butter, at room temperature**

½ **cup granulated sugar**

¼ **cup light brown sugar firmly packed**

½ **teaspoon vanilla extract**

2 **eggs, at room temperature**

1½ **cups flour**

1 **teaspoon baking powder**

2 **teaspoons ground cinnamon**

½ **teaspoon salt**

½ **cup milk, at room temperature**

Whipped cream (page 191)

1. Position the oven rack in the center of the oven and preheat the oven to 350 degrees.

2. To make the glazed pear topping: Combine the brown sugar and maple syrup in a 9 by 2-inch round cake pan. Set the pan directly on the stove top and heat until the mixture begins to bubble. Boil gently for 1 minute, stirring frequently. Remove the pan from the heat and set aside.

3. Coarsely chop the walnuts and sprinkle them evenly over the maple glaze in the cake pan. Press them lightly into the glaze. Quarter the pears, then peel and core them carefully, removing not just the seeds, but all the fibrous parts. Cut the quarters into ¼-inch slices, lengthwise. Arrange the pear slices concentrically, overlapping each other, making a circular pattern over the walnuts.

4. To make the cake batter: Beat together the butter, granulated sugar, and brown sugar. If you are using an electric mixer, stop it once and scrape down the sides of the bowl. Continue beating until the mixture is completely smooth and no lumps of butter are visible.

5. Add the vanilla extract and the eggs, one at a time. Stop and scrape down the sides of the bowl, then beat until the eggs are completely incorporated.

6. Sift together the flour, baking powder, cinnamon, and salt into a separate bowl. Gradually mix half the dry ingredients into the butter mixture. Stir in the milk, then add the rest of the dry ingredients, and mix until just combined.

7. Transfer the batter to the cake pan on top of the pears. Smooth it into an even layer, being careful not to disturb the arrangement of the pears.

8. Bake about 50 minutes, until a toothpick inserted into the center comes out clean. Let cool for 30 minutes. Invert a serving plate over the pan, grasp both the pan and the plate, and turn over. Lift off the cake pan. Any walnuts that may have stuck to the pan can be loosened with a fork and reunited with the cake. Serve warm, with whipped cream.

crème anglaise

2½ CUPS

Very early menus at Chez Panisse sometimes offered this classic dessert sauce all by itself — by the glass, as a drink!

Crème anglaise can be flavored by steeping toasted, chopped nuts and spices like cinnamon or cloves in the warm milk — or more easily by adding espresso or Cognac, rum, or any other tasty liquor to the sauce after it has cooled.

½   **vanilla bean, split**

2   **cups milk**

6   **tablespoons sugar**

Pinch of salt

6   **egg yolks**

1. Scrape the vanilla bean seeds into the milk in a heavy saucepan. Add the vanilla bean pod, sugar, and salt and heat until the milk is warm but not simmering. Meanwhile, prepare an ice bath — a bowl partially filled with ice, with another bowl nested inside it.

2. Lightly whisk together the egg yolks in a separate bowl, then gradually add some of the warmed milk, whisking constantly. Pour the mixture back into the saucepan.

3. Cook over low to moderate heat, stirring constantly with a heatproof spatula, always scraping the bottom, until the custard thickens enough to coat the spatula.

4. Immediately strain the cooked custard through a fine sieve into the bowl set in the ice. Stir the crème anglaise with a clean spatula to cool it down. Cover and refrigerate until ready to serve. Crème anglaise will keep in the refrigerator for up to 3 days.

NOTE If you accidentally overcook the crème anglaise and it looks curdled after you've strained it, you can still rescue it. Pour it into a blender while it's still warm, filling the container no more than halfway, and run at low speed until it looks smooth.

whipped cream

2 CUPS

Use the freshest cream available. If possible, avoid using ultrapasteurized cream: It has practically no cream flavor.

1   **cup heavy cream**

1   **tablespoon sugar**

A few drops of vanilla extract

OPTIONAL

¼   **vanilla bean**

1. With an electric mixer or by hand with a whisk, whip the cream until it just begins to hold a shape.

2. Whip in the sugar and add the vanilla extract. If desired, split the vanilla bean and scrape its seeds into the cream.

3. Continue to whip the cream until it is soft and creamy, mounding gently. Do not whip it until it is stiff, or it will be grainy.

NOTE If you make whipped cream in advance, it may be necessary to rewhip it very slightly just before serving, since the cream separates as it sits.

If you overwhip the cream by accident, you can save it by gently folding in small amounts of unwhipped heavy cream until it smooths out.

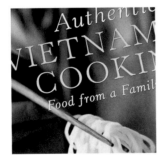
Every year, we find several books that refuse either to slot neatly into an existing category or to accommodate themselves as a group to a specific category title. This year's mixed bag includes a topnotch vegetarian cookbook, two Asian collections, and two gatherings of basic recipes. Also, and not so basic, are a book devoted to foie gras (an ingredient apparently now so familiar to Americans that it gets its own compilation) and one from a new author, Amanda Hesser, that could easily be categorized as literature. Worthy entries, all.

more great books

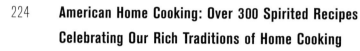

category four

the cook and the gardener

author

Amanda Hesser, a *New York Times* Dining In/Dining Out reporter who trained at the École de Cuisine La-Varenne.

why she wrote it

To relate the story of the year she spent as a cook in a seventeenth-century château in Burgundy, especially her interaction with the gruff gardener, and to record the recipes inspired by the garden's seasons.

why it made our list

This page-turner of a book takes us back to a time when there was a more direct connection between cooking and gardening, a time when a cook made do with what was seasonally available outside in the garden or in the root cellar. A several-page chapter opener for each month and the considerable literary abilities of the "cook" allow us to live vicariously her year at a bucolic Burgundy château. The recipes give us a taste of eating strictly by the seasons, and in each chapter she presents the dishes she came up with to make the most of the parade of just-picked produce that the gardener offered her every day. Not to underestimate the appealing recipes, but we'd buy this book for the evocative, bittersweet prose alone.

from the book

"My first day I began picking early in the morning to beat the noon heat. Monsieur Milbert was out admiring his garden. He did so often, as if it were his Narcissian reflecting pool. First he visited every plant, then doted on his tomato plants, watering them by hand with water warmed by the sun in the shallow well. He dipped his watering cans in the pool, then shuffled over to the rows and tilted the cans so the water just spattered over the plants, slaking them gently, and the clay-thick soil beat down to a smooth round disk under the plants. He bent patiently over each one, seemingly unaffected by the weight of the cans. He did this every day, never faster, never slower."

specifics

632 pages, more than 240 recipes, more than 150 illustrations.

chapters Spring ❯ Summer ❯ Autumn ❯ Winter

$32.50. Published by W. W. Norton & Company, Inc.

g, Montepulciano or Cabernet Sauvignon)

wy-based pan over low heat. Add the onion, sea-
coat with the oil and butter. Add the thyme sprigs
casionally. The trick to this recipe is to cook the
so it releases all its liquid and softens without col-
y and most of the liquid has evaporated, about 30
ace for 35 to 45 minutes over medium heat. Stir
o bind with the sugar and wine, caramelizing to a
yme stems, adjust the seasoning, and serve warm.

d duck confit and Herb-scented Mashed Potatoes
ke the perfect bistro meal. If you have company and
ocolate-Rosemary Soufflé (page 601) would follow
rries or raspberries soaking in eau-de-vie (page 195)
spoonful of them over vanilla ice cream? All of these
be prepared ahead of time, then rewarmed before

eks and Tarragon
on Toast

ason still sit in the ground, thick, and swe
the sun's rays. The starch in leeks con
s get warmer in the spring, the leeks
al bolt toward the sky, when they
ultimately turns to seed. It looks
t of five feet or more.

COOK AND TH

Here I used the sweet old leeks in a way that salvages what
flavor they have left. (If the core of the leek has hardened,
the leeks are too old to use.) The leeks are bound with
cream and soft goat's milk cheese, then scented with
the anise-flavor of tarragon and mounded on toast
rubbed with garlic. Perfect for an appetizer or light
lunch paired with a salad or soup.

SERVES 4

2 medi   trimmed, cut in half
                shed

old as logs in vacuum-packed
and broken into

rigs

THE
COOK
~ AND THE ~
GARDENER

A Year of Recipes and Writings from the French Countryside

AMANDA
HESSER

„

creamy leeks and tarragon on toast

SERVES 4

The leeks of last season still sit in the ground, thick, and sweetened from age and frost, not from the sun's rays. The starch in leeks converts to sugar as it gets old. As the days get warmer in the spring, the leeks begin to harden, bracing themselves for their final bolt toward the sky, when they will produce a pretty topiary ball of flowers, which ultimately turns to seed. It looks like a great overgrown puffball, reaching a final height of five feet or more.

Here I used the sweet old leeks in a way that salvages what flavor they have left. (If the core of the leek has hardened, the leeks are too old to use.) The leeks are bound with cream and soft goat's milk cheese, then scented with the anise-flavor of tarragon and mounded on toast rubbed with garlic. Perfect for an appetizer or light lunch paired with a salad or soup.

2	medium leeks, trimmed, cut in half lengthwise and washed
2	tablespoons butter
	Coarse or kosher salt
⅓	cup heavy cream
¼	cup soft goat's milk cheese (usually sold as logs in vacuum-packed plastic), with rind (if there is one) removed, and broken into small pea-size pieces
2	tablespoons chopped flat-leaf parsley leaves (about 6 sprigs)
1½	tablespoons chopped tarragon leaves (about 4–5 branches)
	Freshly ground black pepper
4	slices crusty bread, toasted in the oven
1	clove garlic

1. Slice the leeks crosswise to make ¼-inch half-moons. Melt the butter in a large sauté pan. Add the leek, season lightly with salt, and cook over low heat so it softens but does not color. Once the leek is meltingly soft (8 to 10 minutes), turn up the heat to high to cook off excess liquid, 1 to 2 minutes. Reduce heat to medium-low and pour in the cream. Reduce to thicken, about 1 minute. Add the goat's milk cheese and stir until it is melted and the mixture is well bound. Add the parsley and tarragon and season to taste with salt and pepper. Remove from the heat and set aside but keep warm.

2. Rub the slices of bread with the garlic clove. Mound the leeks on the toast and serve.

SERVING SUGGESTIONS Have these toasts as a first course, then follow with a roasted chicken and mixed greens for a main course.

soft sorrel-potato galette

SERVES 4-6

The potatoes on top of this *galette* get brown and crispy while the ones in the middle remain soft, sandwiching a thin layer of wilted sorrel and melted Parmigiano-Reggiano and Gruyère. It is warm and filling, the kind of food for a good cold day.

This is probably the most difficult recipe in the book to get right. Like a *tarte Tatin*, you must have the proper ingredients and equipment or it's not worth the effort. You need a heavy iron skillet, good butter, and waxy potatoes.

The potato cake mirrors the *tarte Tatin* on yet another level. It, too, is cooked in its entirety before being inverted and turned out. So why risk it? Because it's magnificent when it's done, and the challenge is refreshing. The recipe itself is quite simple and fast, but it is careful controlling of the heat on the stove that determines its success or failure.

1½ **pounds small, equal-sized waxy potatoes (such as**
yellow fingerlings), peeled

5 **tablespoons butter**

Coarse or kosher salt

Freshly ground black pepper

2 **handfuls sorrel, ribs removed, leaves washed**

¼ **cup freshly grated Gruyère cheese**

¾ **cup freshly grated Parmigiano-Reggiano cheese**

SPECIAL EQUIPMENT

Mandoline (optional)

1. Heat the oven to 350°F. Using a mandoline or a sharp knife, slice the potatoes into ⅛-inch-thick rounds.

2. Heat 3 tablespoons of the butter in an 8-inch iron skillet over medium heat until foaming, then reduce the heat to low while you layer the ingredients in the pan. (The butter will continue to sizzle; this is fine, because you want to color the potatoes. Try not to give in to the temptation to raise the heat — a higher heat will color the potatoes quickly, and they will burn later in cooking. Also, beginning at a low heat allows time for the heat to disperse evenly, and to color the potatoes evenly. Think of this as a soft, soothing dish; in order for the potatoes to get that tender and melting, they must be enticed slowly.) Lay one nice large round slice of potato in the center, then begin layering the potatoes in overlapping concentric circles to fill the base of the pan. Arrange a single overlapping layer on the sides of the pan. Season with salt and pepper.

3. Fill the potato-lined pan with all but one quarter of the remaining potatoes. There is no reason to make concentric circles, but they should be placed evenly so the cake will not be lopsided when it is turned out.

4. Season again with salt and pepper and dot with 1 tablespoon of butter. Lay on the sorrel leaves to cover. They will seem like they are overflowing from the pan, but don't worry — they will soon melt to a thread-thin layer. Cover with the grated cheese and more pepper.

5. Finish with a final layer of potatoes, to cover and weigh down the cheese. Dot with the remaining butter. Increase the heat to medium. If you smell the butter going past the sweet and nutty stage to a burning one, remove from the heat immediately — the bottom is burning. Sauté until the potatoes on the sides of the pan begin to cook, 5 to 7 minutes. You can peek by lifting one edge with a small thin spatula. Cover tightly with a lid or aluminum foil and transfer to the heated oven. Bake in the heated oven for 30 to 35 minutes, until the potatoes are tender all the way through when poked with a fork.

6. Remove from the oven. Run a thin flexible spatula around the sides and outer base of the skillet to loosen any stuck potatoes. Place a round serving plate, large enough to cover the skillet, on top of it. Holding the skillet firmly with a potholder and the plate with your other hand (also covered with a pot holder), quickly invert the two, being aware of dripping butter. Carefully lift off the skillet, gently prodding off any potatoes that have attached themselves to the pan and patching them where possible. The *galette* should be well browned and shiny, like a well-lacquered table. Serve, cutting in wedges at the table. If there are any major flaws, such as a gaping hole, I always remind myself of what Julia Child says: "That's what parsley is for."

SERVING SUGGESTIONS This is a difficult dish and, thankfully, a filling one. Concentrate on the *galette*, sauté veal or chicken sausages or pork chops in another pan and throw together a simple salad.

SHOPPING FOR SORREL

Sorrel is difficult to find in stores because once harvested, it wilts quickly, and unless you are going to cook the sorrel, it's fairly undesirable in this state. The leaves may be flimsy but should still be bright green and solid. If they are peppered with holes or bad patches, this means the sorrel wasn't healthy, even in the garden. In this case, substitute *young* spinach. The best way to buy sorrel is either at a green market or through a friend who grows it.

storing potatoes

From the moment a potato is harvested, germination becomes its key goal in life. If you want to keep potatoes for any period of time, they must be stored in an atmosphere that both staves off rotting and prevents sprouting. A cool, dry, dark cellar that maintains temperatures between 45 and 50°F is ideal. This temperature is low enough for the potatoes to stay sprout-free without the threat of frost. As rugged as tubers look, they have a soft, sensitive side. Frost, moisture, or light will catapult them toward a smelly, moldy end.

In a root cellar, there are three traditional methods for storing potatoes. One form is called a "pie": The potatoes are laid in a trench and piled about three feet high, then mounded with straw. A second way is referred to as the "camp" method: A pit is dug, and the potatoes are piled in it in a pyramidal mound, then covered with soil. Another method is to bury them deep in soil. This way the oxygen that reaches the potatoes is kept at a minimum, therefore preventing sprouting.

Monsieur Milbert practices the pie method in a dirt-floor root cellar. He also takes a preventive measure in the garden by waiting for several consecutive days of hot dry weather before he harvests his potatoes. This keeps them dry for storage.

If you are buying potatoes at a green market or grocery store, you're probably not going to be storing your potatoes in a root cellar. It is still a good idea, though, to store them in a cool, dark place such as a regular home cellar.

madhur jaffrey's world vegetarian

author

The multitalented Madhur Jaffrey, who in addition to writing cookbooks like *Invitation to Indian Cooking* and *Madhur Jaffrey's Taste of the Far East* is also an actress and a film director.

why she wrote it

"I hope my book will open up an international world of new and exciting foods for you to cook and eat. As you turn the pages, you will find old traditional recipes and newly created ones, recipes where new and old ingredients are combined and recipes from one nation that may be made with ingredients from another. That seems to be the kind of world we are living in today."

why it made our list

Vegetarians, rejoice! Madhur Jaffrey dedicates her latest book to appealing and satisfying meat-free dishes. And non-vegetarians, fear not! The recipes are reliable, varied, and interesting, and you won't find yourself wishing for a piece of meat. Of course, Jaffrey is known for her books on Indian cuisine, and there is an impressive selection of recipes here from that part of the world, but all the other major areas are well-represented, too. This is a huge book loaded with a wide variety of recipes. We liked the extensive glossary of terms in the back of the book, as well as the complete list of sources for those ingredients that are difficult to come by. Truly a treasury.

from the book

"Corn belongs to the Americas. However, I have been to parts of the world that believe otherwise. . . . In the Punjab in India, where corn flatbreads and mustard greens might as well be painted on the state flag, I was once scolded by a college professor for suggesting that corn might have come, relatively recently, from another world. No, no, he insisted, corn was always here."

specifics

758 pages, more than 650 recipes, 17 color photographs.

chapters Dried Beans, Dried Peas, Lentils, and Nuts ❯ Vegetables ❯ Grains ❯ Dairy ❯ Soups, Salads, and Drinks ❯ Sauces and Added Flavorings

$40. Published by Clarkson N. Potter Publishers.

polenta with tex-mex chili

SERVES 4 TO 6

This is a meal in itself. I love to serve the polenta in a large, relatively shallow earthen bowl, topped with the chili, which in turn is topped with flecks of chopped fresh cilantro. I stick some corn chips in, even a few slim hot green chiles for those who want them.

The chili can, of course, be made a day ahead. Do not make the chili too thick. It should flow with ease. Add a little extra water if you need to as you are reheating it.

Soft Polenta Mixed with Cheese and Butter, freshly made according
to the recipe below
Tex-Mex Vegetarian Chili (page 207), reheated

FOR THE GARNISH
About 2 tablespoons finely chopped fresh cilantro
A few handfuls of corn chips

Follow the directions above for serving.

soft polenta mixed with cheese and butter

SERVES 4 TO 6

This is one of the simplest ways of serving soft polenta.

A freshly made recipe of soft polenta cooked according to the classical
method or in the oven (pages 206 to 207)
2 to 3 tablespoons unsalted butter, cut into small pats
⅔ cup (2 ounces) grated Parmigiano-Reggiano cheese

As soon as the polenta is made, stir in the butter and cheese. Mix and serve immediately.

polenta cooked in the oven

SERVES 4

2   cups coarse-grained Italian yellow cornmeal (also sold as polenta)
Dab of unsalted butter or vegetable oil
1   tablespoon salt

Put the cornmeal into a bowl. Slowly add 3 cups of water, stirring with a wooden spoon as you do so.

Preheat the oven to 400° F. Butter or oil an 8 x 8 x 4-inch or similar-sized baking dish.

Put 4½ cups of water into a large pan and bring it to a boil over medium-high heat. Add the salt. Stir the cornmeal mixture again and then slowly pour it into the boiling water, stirring with a wooden spoon as you do so. Bring to a boil, stirring all the time. The mixture will thicken very quickly into a homogeneous paste. Quickly pour this paste into the baking dish, smooth over the top with the back of a wooden spoon, cover, and bake for 50 minutes.

Serve as is (with a topping of butter and grated Parmigiano-Reggiano cheese, if desired) or cool, cover, and refrigerate. The polenta is now ready to be used in the same way as the cool, firm, more traditionally cooked polenta. Once cooled, the polenta may be toasted or fried.

the classical method of cooking polenta

SERVES 4

1   tablespoon salt
2   cups coarse-grained Italian yellow cornmeal (also sold as polenta)

Bring 8½ cups of water to a boil in a very large, heavy, preferably nonstick pan. Turn the heat down to medium-high. Add the salt. Using a long-handled wooden spoon, keep stirring with one hand while you pick up a fistful of cornmeal at a time with the other and let it flow through your fingers into the water in a slow but steady stream. You may also empty the cornmeal into a jug and pour it out from the spout in a very slow, steady stream. When all the cornmeal is in, continue the constant stirring for 40 to 45 minutes, breaking up any lumps that might form and scraping away from the bottom and the sides. In the end, you should have a thick, smooth mass that comes away from the sides.

If you want your polenta soft and creamy, serve it immediately.

Polenta sets fast. If you are not going to eat it immediately or if there are leftovers after the first serving, it should be immediately emptied into a flat-at-the-bottom, squarish container or even a bowl that has been rinsed out with cold water. Flatten the top of the polenta with a wet rubber spatula, cover, and refrigerate. It will last in the refrigerator for 4 to 5 days. When cold, the polenta will settle into the shape of the container and may be unmolded and cut into thick slices. To reheat the slices, sprinkle them with water, cover, and heat either in a microwave oven or in a nonstick frying pan. These slices may also be toasted or fried.

tex-mex vegetarian chili

SERVES 4

I love chili and this is about as good as it gets. I do not use any commercially mixed chili powders as they tend to contain too much salt. It is much easier to put in all the spices that go into the making of a chili powder, which is what I have done here.

There are many ways to serve this. My favorite is to ladle the chili into individual bowls and offer baskets of fresh, hot tortillas and some guacamole on the side. If you are not up to all that, you may put a dollop of sour cream over each bowl and serve some tortilla chips and a green salad on the side. Another way is to put all the heated chili into a baking dish, cover the entire top with grated sharp Cheddar or Monterey Jack cheese, and then put the dish briefly under the broiler until the cheese melts and browns in spots. Pita breads or tortillas may be offered on the side as well as a green salad.

This is a great dish for parties, as it can easily be doubled or tripled. If you use a larger pot, all cooking times will remain the same. You may easily make it 24 hours ahead of time and then refrigerate it. If the chili thickens too much as it cools, thin it out with a little water when you reheat it.

I have suggested using anywhere from ¼ to 1 jalapeño pepper. A whole one will make the chili quite hot while ¼ will keep the heat at medium.

For the red kidney beans needed here, you may cook them yourself or use canned ones. Even though there are many ingredients here, the chili is very easy to make.

3   tablespoons canola or olive oil

1   medium onion, peeled and finely chopped

3   garlic cloves, peeled and finely chopped

½   large green pepper, seeds removed and finely chopped

¼ to 1 jalapeño pepper (or ½ to 2 any other fresh hot green chile),
     finely chopped

1½ teaspoons ground cumin seeds

2   teaspoons paprika

½   teaspoon dried thyme

½   teaspoon dried crumbled sage

1   teaspoon dried oregano

¼   teaspoon cayenne

1   cup lentils, picked over and washed

1   cup cooked drained red kidney beans

2 to 3 canned plum tomatoes, drained and finely chopped

3   tablespoons chopped fresh cilantro leaves

1½ teaspoons salt

1   tablespoon yellow cornmeal

Put the oil in a medium pan and set over medium-high heat. When hot, put in the onion, garlic, green pepper, and jalapeño. Stir and fry for about 3 minutes, or until the seasonings just start to brown. Turn down the heat to medium-low and continue to sauté for another 3 minutes. Now put in the cumin, paprika, thyme, sage, oregano, and cayenne. Stir briskly once or twice and put in the lentils, 4½ cups of water, the red kidney beans, plum tomatoes, cilantro leaves, and salt. Bring to a boil. Cover, turn the heat down to low, and cook gently for 50 minutes.

Mix the cornmeal with 3 tablespoons water and then pour the mixture into the chili pot. Stir to mix and bring to a simmer. Cover and simmer gently for 10 minutes, stirring now and then.

eggplants

Eggplants, which are thought to have originated in India, come in many sizes and colors. Tiny little green ones, the size of peas and quite raw, are floated on top of Thai curries, adding a certain in-your-face, wake-up astringency to each morsel. Larger green ones, the size of substantial pomegranates, sometimes with whitish stripes, are hollowed out and stuffed in South and Southeast Asia or else sliced and fried or used in stir-fries. In India, they are cut into small dice and cooked along with other vegetables, such as diced potatoes. White ones, some the shape and size of golf balls, others larger and slightly elongated, have their own pale and creamy taste. They have a fine texture and cook quite fast.

However, the two colors of eggplants most commonly seen in Western markets are purple and pinkish-mauve.

PURPLE EGGPLANTS Most supermarkets tend to carry the large, plump, somewhat oval, purple eggplants that weigh approximately ¾ pound to 1½ pounds. Very small ones, the size and shape of eggs, may be found in Indian and sometimes Chinese markets. Larger long, slim, dark purple ones, often called Italian eggplants, are sold by Italian grocers and sometimes by supermarkets. These vary in length from 4 to 6 inches.

PINKISH-MAUVE EGGPLANTS Sold in America as Japanese eggplants, these can be found in most South and East Asian markets and in many West Coast supermarkets. Slim and long—they range from 6 to 9 inches—these are delicate in both texture and flavor. They are perfect for poaching and steaming. In Japan they are often served with a miso sauce or else dipped in a tempura batter and deep-fried.

Many people believe that eggplants help prevent cancer and that they also inhibit the growth of fatty deposits in the arteries. They are certainly low in calories, with a cupful of the cooked vegetable proudly weighing in with fewer than 40 calories. Unfortunately, oil is their natural partner. They turn slithery, satiny, attractively brown, and positively sensuous when stir-fried or, better still, deep-fried.

But the amount of oil their greedy bodies soak in can be controlled in various ways. One is by cutting the vegetable into segments and either salting it or letting it soak in salty water for at least 30 to 40 minutes. This draws out some of their natural liquid, making them less dry and spongelike. Instead of deep-frying them before cooking with sauces and seasonings, I have also taken to rubbing slices lightly with oil and broiling them until they are lightly browned on both sides. Of course, eggplants may also be steamed, poached, or roasted before they are dressed.

eggplant with minty tomato sauce and yogurt

SERVES 3 TO 4

This is a superb party dish from Afghanistan—rounds of eggplant freshly fried, and topped first with a tomato sauce and then with a dollop of creamy yogurt. Serve rice on the side. You may also serve a single round of eggplant as a first course.

If you wish to use fresh tomatoes, you will need 1½ cups of peeled and chopped tomatoes.

The frying of the eggplant slices should be done at the last minute. It takes 6 to 7 minutes for one batch. You might need to do two batches. Allow yourself another couple of minutes to let the oil heat.

1¼ **pounds eggplant (the large variety)**

1¼ **teaspoons salt**

FOR THE TOMATO SAUCE

¼ **cup peanut or canola oil**

1 **medium onion, very finely chopped**

3 **garlic cloves, peeled and very finely chopped**

8 **plum tomatoes from a can, finely chopped, plus ¼ cup of the can liquid**

1¼ **teaspoons salt**

3 **tablespoons chopped fresh mint leaves**

1 **teaspoon ground cumin**

½ **teaspoon ground coriander**

¼ **teaspoon cayenne**

Freshly ground black pepper

YOU ALSO NEED

½ **cup plain yogurt**

Peanut or canola oil for deep-frying

Extra mint sprigs or leaves for garnishing

Trim the very ends of the eggplant and cut it crosswise into 1-inch-thick slices. Put the slices in a single layer in a large platter or lasagna-type dish. Sprinkle the salt over both sides, rubbing it in well. Set aside for 1 hour.

Meanwhile, make the tomato sauce. Put the oil in a large, nonstick frying pan and set over medium-high heat. When hot, put in the onion. Stir and fry for 2 to 3 minutes, or until the onion pieces begin to brown at the edges. Put in the garlic. Stir for a few seconds. Now put in the tomatoes and their liquid as well as all the remaining ingredients for the tomato sauce. Stir to mix. Cover, turn the heat to low, and cook gently for 10 minutes. Set aside in a warm place.

Make the yogurt sauce. Put the yogurt in a small bowl and beat lightly with a fork.

Just before you sit down to eat, put oil to a depth of 2 to 3 inches for deep-frying in a wok or deep-fryer and set over medium heat. Take the eggplant slices from the platter and dry them off well with paper towels.

When the oil is hot, drop in as many slices as the utensil will hold easily and fry, turning now and then, for 6 to 7 minutes, or until both sides are a medium brown color. Drain well on paper towels. Do a second batch, if needed.

To serve, arrange the eggplant slices in a single layer on a large platter. Top each slice with a dollop of the tomato sauce and then with a tablespoon of the yogurt. Garnish with the mint sprigs or leaves. Serve immediately.

COUSCOUS

Couscous, a food that seems native to the Berbers of North Africa, is really a kind of pasta—little grains formed generally with semolina but sometimes with corn, crushed wheat, or barley as well. It may be eaten very simply with milk (sweetened with sugar and flavored with cinnamon) or with buttermilk, sometimes with the addition of steamed young fava beans and chunks of pumpkin and sometimes the spice mixture Zahtar.

In Algeria, couscous is combined with fennel shoots and young carrot tops and then eaten with a fiery tomato and potato sauce. At a Moroccan breakfast I have had a kind of porridge couscous made with crushed wheat and milk that had been accented delicately with orange flower water. In the Sahara desert, sweet dates might be mixed in with the couscous. Of course, there is also the couscous that we are all more familiar with, which is served with a variety of stews and hot sauces.

In Morocco, the best you can do for favored guests is to offer them couscous that you have made yourself—from scratch. Like any fresh pasta, it requires some practice. First of all, you need two kinds of semolina, a coarse-grained one and a very fine one. Here is how my teacher in Marrakech, a professional chef named Melle Derko Samira, went about it: She spread some coarse semolina in a large, round tray. Then she sprinkled some cold water over it. Next she put the flat of her right hand (palm down) on top of the semolina and began rotating it lightly to form tiny, bread crumb–like pellets. Now the fine semolina was sprinkled on the pellets and some more cold water as well. There was more rotating of the hand to firm up the pellets, which were then passed through a coarse sieve to ensure an even size. There was a final sifting in a fine sieve to get rid of any loose flour. The couscous was now ready to be steamed.

INSTANT OR QUICK-COOKING COUSCOUS This is generally what most of us can manage to buy and to prepare. Sold in many supermarkets and most health food shops, it requires no actual cooking. Water is brought to a boil, 1¼ cups of water to every 1 cup of couscous, then the couscous dropped in along with some salt and oil. The pot is covered, left off the heat, and the couscous, rather like bulgur, is allowed to swell up inside. I like to let the pan sit for a good 15 minutes before I fluff up the couscous very thoroughly with a fork. It is greatly helped by the fluffing, increasing in volume with each stroke.

WHOLE WHEAT COUSCOUS Sold now in most health food stores, this is rather dense and tastes of wheat. I use organic whole wheat couscous. The required ratio of boiling water to couscous, in volume, is 1:1. It cooks for about 5 minutes but does need to sit off the heat for 5 to 15 minutes and requires thorough fluffing with a fork to increase its volume.

I thought I could improve the texture of this couscous by trying to cook it by the long Moroccan method, but after 2 hours of sprinkling water, raking, and double steaming, I found no great improvement. What does improve the texture, and this I discovered almost by accident, was browning the grains in a little bit of oil before cooking them for 5 minutes.

MOROCCAN (SEMOLINA) COUSCOUS   This is available only in specialty stores that carry Middle Eastern and North African ingredients. It is this couscous that deserves to be cooked in a traditional couscoussière, using the traditional Moroccan method. I have tried improvising other utensils for the steaming but find that, for one reason or another, none are really adequate; a couscoussière has just the right shape to do the job properly.

ISRAELI COUSCOUS   This is relatively new on the market and consists of small balls about the size of peppercorns. It is sold by Middle Eastern grocers where it is sometimes labeled Israeli Toasted Pasta, as the balls are very lightly toasted. I like to cook this couscous like most pastas, in lots of boiling, salted water. It cooks in 8 to 10 minutes, but you should check by removing one ball and biting into it.

If you like, you can undercook this couscous slightly (cooking it for just 7 minutes or so) and then add it to other vegetables that are in the process of being sautéed, where it will finish cooking and pick up exciting new flavors. I like this couscous very much.

LEBANESE COUSCOUS   This also consists of small balls that have been toasted, but they are slightly larger in size than Israeli couscous. Lebanese couscous is sold by Middle Eastern grocers, often under the name *maghrebia* or *mograbeyeh*. *Maghreb* means "west" in Arabic, so to the Lebanese this is the pasta of the "western" nations, Algeria, Tunisia, and Morocco. It cooks slowly (taking about 25 minutes) and unevenly and is therefore, in my opinion, best for soups or stews where it turns into pea-sized dumplings.

israeli couscous with asparagus and fresh mushrooms

SERVES 3 TO 4

I make a very elegant dish using a mixture of fresh morel mushrooms (you only need 2 or 3 so this will not break the bank!), fresh shiitake mushrooms, and plain mushrooms. Any combination of mushrooms will do; you may even use all plain ones.

Serve this dish by itself, with a salad on the side. It may also be served as a first course and should feed 5 to 6 people.

Salt

2   **cups Israeli couscous**

3   **tablespoons olive oil**

1   **medium shallot (½ ounce), peeled and finely chopped**

1   **small garlic clove, peeled and finely chopped**

2   **large white mushrooms (2 ounces), sliced thinly lengthwise**

4 to 5 fresh shiitake mushrooms (2 ounces),

  stems removed and the caps thinly sliced

2 or 3 fresh morel mushrooms (1 ounce), halved lengthwise,

  then cut crosswise into ¼-inch slices

½   **pound asparagus (of medium thickness), trimmed, peeled,**

  and cut into 1-inch sections

½   **cup vegetable stock**

¼   **cup dry white vermouth**

Freshly ground black pepper

3   **tablespoons grated Parmigiano-Reggiano cheese**

2   **tablespoons finely chopped fresh parsley**

Bring 4 quarts of water to a rolling boil. Add 1½ tablespoons of salt and stir, then add the couscous. Let it boil rapidly for about 7 minutes, or until it is almost but not quite ready; it should have a hard core in its very center. Drain the couscous quickly and then rinse it thoroughly under cold running water, turning it over several times. Leave in a sieve or colander.

Put the oil in a large sauté pan or large frying pan (preferably nonstick) and set over high heat. When hot, put in the shallot and garlic. Stir for 20 seconds and put in all the mushrooms. Stir rapidly for about 1 minute, or until the mushrooms look satiny. Now put in the asparagus. Stir for 30 seconds, then add the stock, vermouth, and about ⅛ teaspoon salt. Bring to a boil, cover, and keep cooking on high heat for 2½ minutes. Put in the partially cooked couscous and cook, uncovered, for another 2½ minutes on high heat, stirring frequently. Turn off the heat. Check the salt. You will probably need about ¼ teaspoon more. Add the salt, pepper, cheese, and parsley. Stir to mix and serve immediately.

authentic vietnamese cooking

author

Culinary writer and food consultant Corinne Trang, who is half-French and half-Chinese and grew up in Phnom Penh, Paris, and New York. Trang has written articles for several publications, including FOOD & WINE.

why she wrote it

"In Vietnamese cooking, especially, the tricky processes of evolution we so value in our contemporary world have been distilled into magnificent dishes, complex flavors, and unexpected combinations that can delight any palate. And all cooks can learn from the historical Vietnamese process of absorption, adaptation, refinement—of invention and discipline held in the mind simultaneously."

why it made our list

We loved these authentic, easy-to-make recipes. And we were fascinated by the information packed into this slim volume: from sweeping statements like "China and France—the major powers that colonized Vietnam—have also been the most influential in its cooking" to such specific observations as "*Banh gan* is based on the French dessert crème caramel . . . ." The country's three distinct culinary regions, what Trang calls the Simple North, the Sophisticated Center, and the Spicy South, are all well-represented in the recipes, which are delicious. A winning look at a fascinating corner of the food world.

from the book

"**Condiments are an integral part of nearly every Vietnamese dish. The cuisine assumes that they necessarily complete an item rather than optionally enhance it. Complex in flavors and well balanced in terms of sweet and savory as well as texture, they are never used to mask an ingredient. Suffice it to say that a Vietnamese table without its array of condiments is a table that has not yet been fully set.**"

specifics

256 pages, 116 recipes, 53 black-and-white photographs.

chapters Condiments › Stocks & Soups › Rice, Noodles & Bread › Vegetables › Fish & Seafood › Poultry & Meats › Sweets & Drinks $30. Published by Simon & Schuster.

Serves 4 to 6

2 cups long-grain rice, such as jasmine
2¾ cups chicken stock (page 61)
3 shallots or 1 small red onion, peeled and minced
1 cup mint leaves, julienned or finely chopped
1 pound cooked chicken breast meat, skinned and shredded (from chicken stock)
Nuoc cham (page 42)

RAU THOM COM GA
Mint Rice with Shredded Chicken

RAU THOM COM GA is a refreshing dish made with fresh mint leaves. The rice is cooked in chicken stock. Then, just [be]fore serving, finely chopped shallots, julienned mint, and shred[ded] chicken breast are mixed into the rice while it is still hot. [This] dish is served as a full meal with *nuoc cham* drizzled over it.

[...] rice in a bowl with a few [...]ater. Gently swirl your [...] the bowl to allow the [...]eparate from the grains. [...] water becomes white, [...]epeat this process twice [...] each time, the water [...]loudy. The idea is not [...] all the starch, just [...] the rice will not be [...] dry when cooked. [...] as always given me [...]. Put the rice in a [...] until the rice is

[...]d chicken sto[ck]

COM CHIEN
Fried Rice

Serves 6 to 8

- 1 tablespoon vegetable oil
- 2 Chinese sweet pork sausages, quartered lengthwise and diced (or any leftover meat)
- 1 scallion, root end and tough green tops removed, thinly sliced into rounds
- 8 large napa cabbage leaves or any Asian greens, thinly sliced
- 4 cups cooked long-grain rice, refrigerated overnight
- 1 large egg
- 2 tablespoons soy sauce
- Freshly ground bla[ck ...]

FRIED RICE is an excellent way to prepare leftover cooked rice. It is important, however, that the rice be completely dry prior to stir-frying. For this reason, and for the best results, refrigerate it overnight. Rice that is not completely dry will get sticky when stir-fried, whereas chilled rice will separate beautifully. Fried rice can be made with cut-up leftover meats and vegetables or with fresh ingredients. This is one of those dishes for which you should really have fun experimenting.

[...] in a wok or large
[...] over high heat.
[...] scallion, and
[...]fry until the
[...]ir fat, 3 to 5
[...] and contin-
[...] all the in-
[...] egg and
[...] ice dries
[...]inutes.
[...]o taste
[...] a[nd]
[...]he

CHINESE SWEET PORK SAUSAGES

Authentic
VIETNAMESE COOKING
Food from a Family Table

CORINNE TRANG

Foreword by Martin Yan

[...]pher Hirsheimer

cha ca thang long
hanoi fried fish with dill

SERVES 4 TO 6

This dish of fried fish nuggets with fresh herbs is northern. Ever since I picked up the recipe on my last trip to Hanoi, it has become one of my family's favorites. Unlike small whole fish, morsels are dredged in rice flour so they do not fall apart when fried. The fried fish is surprisingly light, and the licorice-like dill—a popular herb used in Vietnamese cooking—uplifts the palate when eaten with the fish. In this dish one can get a sense of how herbs are used in Vietnamese cooking. They are not just garnishes sparingly sprinkled, but are used in great quantities with every bite of fish.

½   **pound dried rice vermicelli**

Vegetable oil for deep-frying, plus one tablespoon for stir-frying

½   **cup rice flour or all-purpose flour**

½   **teaspoon turmeric**

1   **to 1½ pounds white fish fillets, such as flounder or striped bass, skinned and cut into 1-inch squares**

4   **scallions, trimmed, cut into 1-inch-long pieces and halved lengthwise**

¼   **cup roasted unsalted peanuts, split**

½   **cup small holy basil leaves**

½   **bunch cilantro, root ends trimmed**

½   **bunch dill, trimmed**

Nuoc cham **(page 222)**

1. Soak the rice vermicelli in lukewarm water to cover in a bowl until pliable, about 15 minutes. Bring a pot filled with water to a boil over high heat. Drain and divide the vermicelli into 4 equal portions. Place them, one portion at a time, in a sieve and lower it into the boiling water. Untangle the noodles with chopsticks and boil until tender but firm, about 5 seconds. Remove, drain, and place in a bowl. Repeat this step until you have 4 individual servings. For 6 servings simply divide vermicelli into six smaller portions.

2. Heat the oil in a wok over medium heat to about 350° to 375°F. Meanwhile, mix the rice flour and turmeric in a plastic bag. Add the fish to the flour mixture, seal the bag, and shake it to coat each piece evenly. Put the fish pieces, a few at a time, in the palms of your hands and shake off the excess flour. Working in batches, deep-fry the fish until golden crisp, about 2 minutes per side. Drain on paper towels and arrange in the center of a serving platter.

3. Heat 1 tablespoon oil in a wok or nonstick skillet over high heat. Add and stir-fry the scallions for 1 minute. Add the peanuts, holy basil, cilantro, and dill and continue stir-frying for 30 seconds more. Arrange the stir-fried herbs around the fried fish. To eat, place some herbs and fish pieces on top of the vermicelli and drizzle some *nuoc cham* over the ingredients.

One day, during the week prior to Tet, the Vietnamese New Year celebration, I was walking through Hanoi's old French Quarter, also known as 36 Streets. I noticed that each street was named after the business it catered to. On Paper Street, vendors sold paper products, including gift wrapping and ceremonial make-believe money. Leather was sold on Leather Street, flowers on Flower Street, and so forth. Then I stumbled upon Cha Ca Street, where several restaurants offered *cha ca*. I walked into Cha Ca La Vong, which I later found out was the original restaurant offering this specialty. A small hibachi made of sand—much like a sand pot—was filled with red-hot coals and placed on my table. The waiter then set a cured cast-iron pan with sizzling golden pieces of fish over the coals and proceeded to add scallions, peanuts, holy basil, cilantro, and dill. The fragrance of the herbs sizzling with the fish was amazing. Added to a bowl of *bun*, rice vermicelli, and drizzled with the indispensable *nuoc cham*, the dish was refreshing and more delicious with every bite.

rau thom com ga
mint rice with shredded chicken

SERVES 4 TO 6

Rau thom com ga is a refreshing dish made with fresh mint leaves. The rice is cooked in chicken stock. Then, just before serving, finely chopped shallots, julienned mint, and shredded chicken breast are mixed into the rice while it is still hot. This dish is served as a full meal with *nuoc cham* drizzled over it.

2	cups long-grain rice, such as jasmine
2¾	cups chicken stock (opposite page)
3	shallots or 1 small red onion, peeled and minced
1	cup mint leaves, julienned or finely chopped
1	pound cooked chicken breast meat, skinned and shredded (from chicken stock)

Nuoc cham (page 222)

1. Put the rice in a bowl with a few cups of water. Gently swirl your fingers in the bowl to allow the starch to separate from the grains. Once the water becomes white, drain and repeat this process twice more. With each time, the water will get less cloudy. The idea is not to get rid of all the starch, just enough so that the rice will not be too sticky or too dry when cooked. Three times has always given me the best results. Put the rice in a sieve and drain until the rice is fairly dry.

2. Put the rice and chicken stock in a medium clay pot or heavy-bottomed pot and stir to level the rice. Cover the pot and cook the rice over medium heat until it has absorbed all the stock, about 25 minutes. Turn off the heat and with a wooden spoon stir in shallots, mint, and chicken until evenly mixed. Allow to rest covered for 5 to 10 minutes. Drizzle *nuoc cham* over each serving.

nuoc leo ga
chicken stock

MAKES ABOUT 3 QUARTS

There are two basic approaches to creating a successful chicken stock. The first is to use meaty bones such as wings, necks, carcasses, or any other small parts. The second is to use a skinned whole chicken that has adequate fat. The cooked meat is reserved for other recipes such as *rau thom com ga*, mint rice with shredded chicken (opposite page), in which the meat is shredded. Innards can be included in making a stock, but be sure to exclude the liver, as it will cloud your stock.

3 to 3½ pounds meaty chicken bones, including heads, feet, wings,
    necks, backs, and carcasses, or whole chicken, skinned
    (innards such as gizzard and heart are optional)
1   **large yellow onion, peeled**
3   **scallions, trimmed, halved crosswise, and lightly crushed**
4   **ounces fresh ginger, peeled, cut into 4 slices, and lightly crushed**
2   **tablespoons fish sauce**
1   **teaspoon white or black peppercorns**
Coarse sea salt

1. If using meaty bones, put them in a large stockpot. Add the onion, scallions, ginger, fish sauce, and peppercorns, cover with 5 quarts water, and bring to a boil over high heat. Skim off the foam, reduce the heat to low, and season with salt. Simmer, uncovered, occasionally skimming off any foam, until the stock is reduced by 2 quarts, about 3 hours.

2. If using a whole chicken, use a cleaver to carefully separate the legs from the body of the chicken, then the wings. Cutting through the rib cage, separate the back from the breast. Halve the breast lengthwise through the bone. You now have 7 pieces in addition to the optional innards, neck, and head. Proceed with step 1, but after the first hour of simmering, remove the breast halves and legs and debone them. (Reserve the meat for use in another dish.) Return the bones to the stock and continue simmering, uncovered and undisturbed, until the stock reduces further, about 2 hours more. At this time, skim off as much fat as you desire.

3. Strain the stock, discard the solids, and use according to the recipe of your choice. The stock can be kept up to 3 days in the refrigerator or 3 months in the freezer.

nuoc cham
fish dipping sauce

MAKES ABOUT 2 CUPS

A meal without *nuoc cham* is no meal at all. Served as a dipping sauce with many dishes such as *cha gio*, spring rolls; *banh xeo*, sizzling "sound" crêpes; and grilled meats and seafood; it is perhaps the most important sauce you will learn to make. There are several variations on this recipe. If you like your sauce spicier, mince rather than slice the chilies and garlic. Sometimes distilled rice wine vinegar is used to round out the flavor. My aunt Loan likes to slice and add shallots, saying they make the sauce sweeter. Try it different ways, mild or hot, more sweet or sour, with or without shallots. All are interesting. Following is my favorite version, which balances the sweet, sour, and spicy levels. I suggest you make 2 cups, as it goes quickly. Any left over can be refrigerated for up to 2 weeks.

5	tablespoons sugar
3	tablespoons water
⅓	cup fish sauce
½	cup lime or lemon juice (about 3 limes or 2 lemons)
1	large clove garlic, crushed, peeled, and sliced or minced
1	or more bird's eye or Thai chilies, seeded, and sliced or minced
1	shallot, peeled, thinly sliced, rinsed, and drained (optional)

1. Whisk together the sugar, water, fish sauce, and lime or lemon juice in a bowl until the sugar is completely dissolved. Add the garlic, chili, and shallot (if using), and let stand for 30 minutes before serving.

I've been making *nuoc cham* ever since I can remember. In fact, it was perhaps the first Vietnamese recipe I learned to make as a child. Nobody liked chopping the garlic, so I was stuck doing it. I became such an expert at making this sauce that every time we cooked, my mother would ask me to make it. The one difficult thing was to please both my mother and father simultaneously. She liked it sour, while he preferred it sweet. I resolved this quandary by creating a finely balanced version that allowed all of the various flavors to come out, and I continue to use it to this day.

american home cooking

authors

Husband-and-wife cookbook writers Bill Jamison and Cheryl Alters Jamison, whose *Born to Grill* was one of last year's *Best of the Best* honorees.

why they wrote it

"This is a cook's tour of American home cooking, focused on what's flavorful, fun, and practical, not a culinary manual or a scholarly survey of all we ate and eat. It's an invitation to pull up a chair at our national table, to relish the treasures of a delightful cuisine as democratic and spirited as the people."

why it made our list

The Jamisons traveled the country collecting the best traditional American recipes they could find, and compiled them here with generous dashes of culinary background. The dishes, originally from so many cultures, are diverse and delicious. You'll find no shortcuts here—time-honored methods are emphasized instead. By the same token, there are no unnecessary steps or fancy techniques, either; the recipes are as simple as they can be without sacrificing the quality of the end result.

from the book

"Americans plucked down oysters in the nineteenth century as if they were candy. We ate them from the beginning, out of beds far more abundant than in Europe, but after the colonies won independence they came close to an addiction, a kind of badge of American prosperity and democracy. One English visitor remarked that one of the main social distinctions in the United States between the rich and poor was whether they washed down their oysters with champagne or beer."

specifics

470 pages, over 300 recipes, 16 color photographs.

chapters Flapjacks, Grits, Hash, and Other Hearty Ways to Start the Day › Piled High: The American Sandwich › Little Whims to Whet the Appetite › Soup's On › From Sea to Shining Sea, the Catch of the Day › Fryers, Roasters, and Wild Turkeys › We've Always Gone Whole Hog › Beefy Passions › Love Me Tender: Game, Lamb, and Veal › Fresh from the Garden › Potatoes, Dried Beans, and Other Keepers › Sweets and Sours for the Pantry › Amber Waves of Grain › "The More Perfect the Bread, the More Noble the Lady" › Peerless Pies, Crisps, Cobblers, and Creams › Cooking to Excess with Cakes, Cookies, and Candies › Cherry Shrubs to Mint Juleps

$35. Published by Broadway Books.

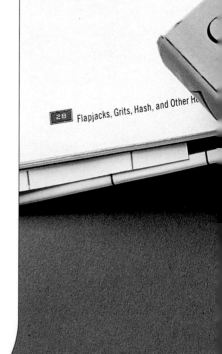

WeatherBerry Scramble

We went to Owensboro, Kentucky, a number of years ago for the so... the local specialty, barbecued mutton. We left in awe of an even bette... scrambled eggs that Susie and Bill Tyler serve at their stately 1840s... bed-and-breakfast. They go great with buttery grits.

Five 4- to 5-ounce red waxy potatoes, scrubbed but unpeeled

¼ cup (½ stick) unsalted butter

2 large onions, halved and sliced very thin

1¼ cups julienned country ham or other well-smoked ham

¼ cup minced scallion greens, optional

5 large eggs, beaten

3¼ cups small-curd ...

½ cup plus 2 tables... seasoned poultry ... crumbs (Susie u ... Farm)

Salt and freshly r...

Orange slices or ... wedges

Cut each potato in half, preferably lengthwise if they're ... have a lengthwise. Then slice the potatoes ⅛ inch thick.

Warm the butter in a large heavy skillet over medium ... in the potatoes and onions and pat down into a thick l... the potatoes are tender with brown edges, 10 to 15 mi... bottom a couple of times and patting the mixture ... the ham and, if you wish, the scallion greens, our o... in the eggs and continue cooking, stirring the eggs t... to set, mix in the cottage cheese and stuffing crumbs ... and remove from the heat when the eggs have cooke...

Serve immediately, garnished with oranges or toma...

28 Flapjacks, Grits, Hash, and Other H...

Tex-Mex Migas

Migas may have evolved from Mexican *chilaquiles*, but it became a scrambled egg dish only north of the border. The name derives from the Spanish word for crumbs, a reference to the tortilla chips that provide a distinctive flavor and texture. Serve the savory concoction with warm flour tortillas.

8 large eggs
Salt and freshly milled black pepper
2 small red-ripe tomatoes, preferably Italian plum
1 fresh jalapeño chile
4 ounces Mexican-style chorizo or other spicy sausage

¼ cup chopped onion
2 to 2½ dozen tostada chips, broken into bite-size pieces
6 to 8 ounces mild Cheddar cheese, grated (1½ to 2 cups)
2 tablespoons minced cilantro

Whisk the eggs lightly in a small bowl with 2 tablespoons of water and sprinklings of salt and pepper. Set aside.

Roast the tomatoes and jalapeño. Either hold them on a fork directly over the ___me of a gas-stove burner, or place them on a baking sheet under the broiler ___ browned all over and blackened in spots. The tomato skins, in particular, will ___ly split a bit. When cool enough to handle, chop the tomato and the ___kin fine, then seed the jalapeño and mince it.

___hinly slice the *chorizo* and fry it in a large heavy skillet over medium ___ around the edges. Add the onion and sauté until limp, then stir ___ jalapeño and heat through. Pour in the eggs and *stir* them up ___ f the skillet as they cook to your desired doneness. About ___gs are done, add the chips. Serve the migas ___ and stir in the cheese and cilantro. Serve the migas

---

To me the quintessential American country breakfast is the strange (to a European) and unforgettable mingling of sweet and meat—of syrup-saturated pancake sausage, waf bacon, h

melted, stir
mixture until
g up from the
again. Stir in
or color. Pour
As they begin
pepper to taste
___ds.

Cheryl Alters Jamison & Bill Jamison

___d-Winning Authors of *The Border Cookbook* and *Smoke and Spice*

American Home Cooking

Over 300 Spirited Recipes
Celebrating Our Rich
Traditions of Home
Cooking

tex-mex migas

SERVES 4

Migas may have evolved from Mexican *chilaquiles*, but it became a scrambled egg dish only north of the border. The name derives from the Spanish word for crumbs, a reference to the tortilla chips that provide a distinctive flavor and texture. Serve the savory concoction with warm flour tortillas.

8   large eggs

Salt and freshly milled black pepper

2   small red-ripe tomatoes, preferably Italian plum

1   fresh jalapeño chile

4   ounces Mexican-style chorizo or other spicy sausage

¾   cup chopped onion

2 to 2½ dozen tostada chips, broken into bite-size pieces

6 to 8 ounces mild Cheddar cheese, grated (1½ to 2 cups)

2   tablespoons minced cilantro

Whisk the eggs lightly in a small bowl with 2 tablespoons of water and sprinklings of salt and pepper. Set aside.

Roast the tomatoes and jalapeño. Either hold them on a fork directly over the flame of a gas-stove burner, or place them on a baking sheet under the broiler until browned all over and blackened in spots. The tomato skins, in particular, will probably split a bit. When cool enough to handle, chop the tomato and the charred skin fine, then seed the jalapeño and mince it.

Crumble or thinly slice the chorizo and fry it in a large heavy skillet over medium heat until brown around the edges. Add the onion and sauté until limp, then stir in the tomato and jalapeño and heat through. Pour in the eggs and stir them up from the bottom of the skillet as they cook to your desired doneness. About a minute before the eggs are done, add the chips, stirring them in well. Remove the eggs from the heat and stir in the cheese and cilantro. Serve the migas immediately.

tidewater peanut soup

SERVES 6

You can trace the lineage of this soup from Africa to the West Indies and the American South, but it never found so hospitable a home as in the peanut farmlands of eastern Virginia. Don't frown at the idea if you've never tried it. This is a velvety rich soup with true tropical spark. It found favor as far away as San Francisco by 1904, when a version appeared in the Telegraph Hill Neighborhood Association cookbook, *High Living*.

2   tablespoons peanut oil

2   tablespoons unsalted butter

1   cup chopped onion

1   cup chopped celery plus 2 tablespoons minced celery leaves

1   garlic clove, minced

2   tablespoons unbleached all-purpose flour

Pinch of curry powder

1   teaspoon minced fresh chervil or thyme,
     or ½ teaspoon dried chervil or thyme

⅛ to ¼ teaspoon crushed dried hot red chiles

4   cups chicken stock, preferably homemade

1   cup creamy peanut butter

½   cup whipping cream

Salt

Chopped roasted peanuts, optional

In a large heavy saucepan, warm the oil and butter together over medium heat. Stir in the onion and celery, and sauté until the onion is soft and translucent, about 5 minutes. Add the garlic and cook 1 minute longer. Sprinkle in the flour, curry powder, chervil, and chiles, and cook an additional minute, stirring constantly. Pour in 2 cups of the stock and stir to combine. Pour the mixture into a blender, add the peanut butter, and purée. Pour the liquid back into the pan, add the remaining 2 cups stock, cream, and salt, and heat through. Ladle into bowls, garnish with peanuts if you wish, and serve.

buttermilk-bathed pan-fried chicken

SERVES 4 TO 6

Fried chicken rules the roost when it comes to American chicken specialties. Nothing is more popular, even in an age that is afraid of frying, and nothing is tastier when it is fried well. Mary Randolph provided the first recipe in *The Virginia Housewife* (1824), but as she knew, it worked well only with tender young chickens, which few people could afford to sacrifice from their egg-producing responsibilities. Fried chicken began its ascent into national prominence in the late nineteenth century, after the introduction of the range improved the control of frying temperatures, and gained icon status a few decades later when commercial chicken raised for meat became cheaper and more plentiful. As Laurie Colwin says about her recipe in *Home Cooking* (1988), everyone knows there is only one right way to fry chicken, but they happen to be wrong in thinking that it's their way. This is our approach, honed over many years of making and munching.

CHICKEN

Approximately 3 cups buttermilk

2 to 3 teaspoons hot pepper sauce, such as Texas Pete or Tabasco

2 to 3 teaspoons salt

3½- to 4-pound chicken, preferably a roaster,
    cut into 8 bone-in serving pieces

1½ teaspoons freshly milled black pepper

1   teaspoon dry mustard

2   cups unbleached all-purpose flour

Approximately 1½ pounds (3 cups) lard or 1½ pounds Crisco or other solid
    vegetable shortening plus 3 tablespoons bacon drippings

CREAM GRAVY

Pan drippings

3   tablespoons seasoned flour

12-ounce can evaporated milk

1   cup chicken stock, preferably homemade

3   tablespoons whipping cream or half-and-half

½   teaspoon freshly milled black pepper or more to taste

Salt

Mix the buttermilk, as much hot pepper sauce as you like, and 1 teaspoon of the salt in a shallow dish. Add the chicken parts, turning to coat them well. Cover and refrigerate for at least 2 hours and up to 12 hours, turning occasionally.

Combine the remaining 1 to 2 teaspoons salt, pepper, dry mustard, and flour in a large plastic bag or in the time-honored brown paper grocery sack. Place a wire rack for draining the chicken near the cooking area.

Melt the lard or shortening in a 12-inch to 14-inch cast-iron skillet over medium-high heat. If using shortening, then add the bacon drippings to the skillet. When the lard or shortening reaches 375°F, reduce the heat to medium and begin to prepare the chicken.

Starting with the dark meat and ending with the breasts, lift the chicken pieces, one by one, out of the marinade, letting excess liquid drain back into the dish. Drop each chicken piece into the seasoned flour and shake to coat it. Place each in the skillet, skin side down. The pieces should fit snugly together in a 12-inch skillet, although they shouldn't stick to each other. Quickly adjust the heat as needed to maintain a temperature of about 300°F (adding all of the chicken to the oil should have dropped the temperature to this degree already). Cover the skillet and fry for 10 minutes, resisting the urge to open the skillet. You should hear a constant ongoing bubbling and sizzling, neither urgent nor lackadaisical. After the allotted time, remove the lid and turn the chicken with tongs, using light pressure to avoid piercing the crust. Fry uncovered for 15 to 17 additional minutes, until the now crackling crust is a rich golden brown and the meat is cooked through but still juicy. Drain the chicken on the rack.

Prepare the gravy, pouring off the pan drippings through a strainer and leaving about ¼ cup of the drippings in the skillet. Return any brown cracklings from the strainer to the skillet and discard the remaining drippings.

Return the skillet to medium heat. Whisk in the flour, stirring to avoid lumps. Slowly add the evaporated milk, stock, and cream, whisking as you pour them in. Bring to a boil, then simmer until the gravy is thickened and the raw flour taste is gone, about 3 minutes. Stir the gravy up from the bottom frequently, scraping up the browned bits. Add pepper and salt to taste, keeping in mind that the pepper should be pronounced but pleasant on your tongue. Transfer the gravy to a gravy boat and the chicken to a platter. Serve immediately.

TECHNIQUE TIP Soaking the chicken in buttermilk adds moisture as well as tang, so don't skimp on the time. Fry in a hefty cast-iron skillet, eschewing anything with an electric cord or a designer color. Never cook the chicken in more than ½ inch of oil or you will be deep-frying rather than pan-frying, and will lose the optimum balance between a crispy exterior and juicy interior. In the unlikely event of leftovers, eat fried chicken cold, which tastes much better than a reheated encore.

foie gras
. . . a passion

author

Foie gras entrepreneur and food columnist Michael A. Ginor, the co-founder, co-owner and president of Hudson Valley Foie Gras and New York State Foie Gras.

why he wrote it

"My objective was to produce an exhaustive manuscript that would reflect the historical significance of foie gras as well as the versatility and sensual pleasures that this extraordinary delicacy affords. *Foie Gras . . . A Passion* is at once a collection of preferences, fabulous recipes provided by renowned chefs, and a historical study of human expression at its culinary finest."

why it made our list

As much a coffee table book as a cookbook, this beautiful celebration of foie gras includes a thorough history of the delicacy and mouthwatering full-page photographs of each of the dishes. Those who get past turning the pretty pages can sample the foie-gras-inspired recipes of Paul Bocuse, Daniel Boulud, Alain Ducasse, Bobby Flay, Emeril Lagasse, Jacques Pépin, and 75 other leading culinary lights, a veritable who's who of contemporary chefs. Though some of their preparations may take time, they're not really difficult—and what exquisite luxury awaits you in the eating.

from the book

"Despite your preconceived notions, or what you may deduce from the media and your dining companions, a passion for foie gras is not synonymous with adverse health. The reality is that most people with a penchant for foie gras do not consume enough of it to have an effect on their health. As most nutritionists agree, moderation is the key to a healthful, balanced diet. But even if one's foie gras consumption were to rise above a moderate level, scientific facts detailing the composition of foie gras fat suggest the potential risk to one's nutritional well-being is negligible. There is growing evidence suggesting that foie gras may aid the heart."

specifics

338 pages, 83 recipes, 118 color photographs.

chapters History › Production › Foie Gras Primer › Recipes

$49.95. Published by John Wiley & Sons, Inc.

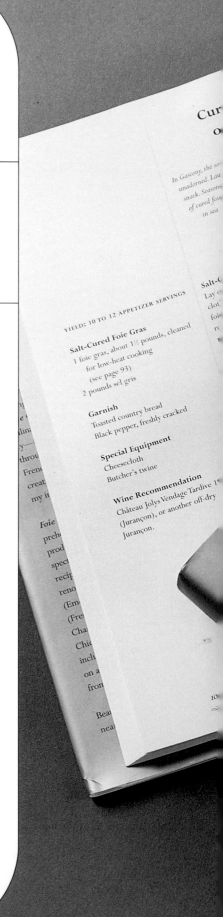

curls of salt-cured foie gras on toasted country bread

YIELD: 10 TO 12 APPETIZER SERVINGS

In Gascony, the southwestern region of France famous for foie gras, the liver is sometimes served raw and unadorned. Laurent Manrique, a Gascon native, prepares this interpretation of his favorite childhood snack. Seasoned with nothing but granules of briny sea salt and cracked black pepper, the thin curls of cured foie gras melt deliciously into warm toasted country bread. Because the foie gras is buried in sea salt, which draws out the moisture, the liver is in effect "cooked" in the same manner in which gravlax is prepared.

SALT-CURED FOIE GRAS

1   foie gras, about 1½ pounds, veins and membranes removed

2   pounds sel gris

GARNISH

Toasted country bread

Black pepper, freshly cracked

SPECIAL EQUIPMENT

Cheesecloth

Butcher's twine

WINE RECOMMENDATION

Château Jolys Vendage Tardive 1995 (Jurançon), or another off-dry Jurançon.

SALT-CURED FOIE GRAS   Lay out a double rectangular layer of cheesecloth on the counter. Arrange the cleaned foie gras along one of the long edges. Tightly roll up the foie gras in the cheesecloth to make a sausage-shaped cylinder about 2 inches in diameter. Be sure to tighten and tuck under the cheesecloth after each turn to make a compact roll. Tie the ends tightly with butcher's twine like a bonbon.

Place half the salt in a baking dish or roasting pan large enough to hold the foie gras "sausage." Position the foie gras on top and cover with the remaining sel gris. Use more sel gris if necessary to ensure the foie gras is completely buried. Refrigerate for 16 hours.

Remove the cured foie gras from the refrigerator and brush off the sel gris. Keep refrigerated until 1 hour before service.

SERVICE AND GARNISH One hour before service, place the cured foie gras in the freezer. To serve, carefully remove the cheesecloth from the foie gras. Using a sharp cheese knife, thinly slice the liver into curls and place the curls directly onto warm toast. The heat of the toast will cause the fat of the liver to melt into the bread. Sprinkle with cracked pepper and serve.

CHEF NOTES The cured foie gras should be used within 24 hours of being prepared. Keep refrigerated until served.

foie gras sauté on polenta cake with country ham and blackberries

YIELD: 8 APPETIZER SERVINGS

At his glorious country inn in Virginia, Patrick O'Connell incorporates Southern ingredients into his French-inspired cooking. The blackberries, cornmeal, and country ham in this dish evoke some of the traditional flavors of the South. Although foie gras is not a Southern staple, the combination of flavors and textures produces a sophisticated appetizer redolent of Southern hospitality.

BLACKBERRY SAUCE

1	tablespoon unsalted butter
1	small shallot, finely chopped
½	bay leaf
1½	pints fresh blackberries
½	cup water
½	cup cassis liqueur
2	tablespoons currant jelly
2	tablespoons chicken stock
½	teaspoon fresh thyme leaves, finely chopped

Black pepper, freshly ground

POLENTA

2	tablespoons unsalted butter
¼	cup olive oil
1	small clove garlic, chopped
1	bay leaf
1	cup water
1	cup milk
1	cup heavy cream
½	cup yellow cornmeal
⅓	cup grated Parmigiano-Reggiano or Asiago cheese

Coarse salt

Cayenne pepper

FOIE GRAS

1½ pounds foie gras, cut into 8 slices, each about 3 ounces and ½-inch thick

Coarse salt

Black pepper, freshly ground

GARNISH

2 cups mixed colorful baby lettuces or greens

¼ cup extra-virgin olive oil

Coarse salt

Black pepper, freshly ground

8 very thin slices country ham, trimmed of fat (see Chef Notes, page 236)

Fresh chives

WINE RECOMMENDATION

Domaine Henri Gouges Nuits-St.-Georges Clos de Porrets 1990 (Burgundy), or another full-bodied Pinot Noir.

BLACKBERRY SAUCE In a 2-quart saucepan, melt the butter. Add the shallots, bay leaf, and ½ pint of the blackberries. Sweat over low heat for 3 minutes. Add the water, cassis, currant jelly, and stock. Simmer over medium heat for 30 minutes or until the sauce is the consistency of a light syrup. Remove from the heat, add the thyme leaves and fresh pepper, and set aside, off the heat, for 10 minutes. When cool, strain the sauce. Reserve.

POLENTA In a 4-quart saucepan, melt the butter. Add 1 tablespoon of the olive oil, the garlic, and bay leaf, and sweat over low heat for 30 seconds. Add the water, milk, and cream, and bring to a simmer. Remove the bay leaf. Whisking constantly, slowly add the cornmeal in a steady stream. Simmer for 10 minutes, until the polenta begins to thicken. Whisk in the cheese and season with salt and cayenne pepper. Line a half sheet pan with plastic wrap and pour the polenta onto the pan. Cover the polenta with plastic wrap and flatten to a thickness of about ½ inch. Refrigerate for 1 hour, then remove and cut into 2-inch squares. Heat the remaining olive oil in a sauté pan and cook the squares of polenta until both sides are golden brown. Reserve and keep warm.

FOIE GRAS Season each slice of foie gras with salt and pepper. Heat a sauté pan over high heat and sear the foie gras for about 30 seconds on each side, or just until a brown crust forms. Remove the slices from the pan and blot on paper towels. Pour off excess fat from the pan and deglaze with ½ cup of the blackberry sauce. Stir this mixture back into the sauce, and gently add the remaining pint of blackberries.

SERVICE AND GARNISH Toss the greens in a mixing bowl with the olive oil, salt, and pepper. Place a small bouquet of dressed greens in the center of each of eight warmed serving plates. On top of the greens, place two squares of the crispy polenta. On top of the polenta place a slice of the country ham. On top of the ham, place a piece of seared foie gras. Spoon the sauce and the blackberries over the foie gras, and garnish with chives.

CHEF NOTES Country ham is a salt-cured and dried ham made throughout the southern United States. The best hams are made from peanut-fed pigs.

millionaire's salad of wilted greens with foie gras, lobster, and papaya

YIELD: 4 APPETIZER SERVINGS

Because of the high price of foie gras, it is often used in conjunction with other luxury items, such as truffles or Sauternes. Jasper White pairs lobster with foie gras to create a rich appetizer that belies its origins as a salad. Although Jasper, a New England chef, is known for his seafood preparations, foie gras is a staple on his menus. He believes that when diners eat seafood, they are more inclined to splurge on indulgences such as foie gras and dessert.

LOBSTER

¼   cup coarse salt

1   chicken lobsters, about 1 pound each

SALAD

⅓   cup peanut oil

Black pepper, freshly ground

½   small red onion, about 2 ounces, thinly sliced

3   tablespoons aged sherry vinegar

Zest of 1 lemon, cut into thin strands

2   sprigs fresh basil, leaves only, chopped

Coarse salt

FOIE GRAS

8   ounces foie gras, cut into 4 slices about ½-inch thick

Coarse salt

Black pepper, freshly ground

GARNISH

½   pound mixed hearty lettuces, such as frisée, radicchio, mizuna, and/or endive, washed and dried

1   large, ripe papaya, peeled, seeded, and cut into 1-inch cubes

WINE RECOMMENDATION

Pedro Domecq Amontillado Jerez 51-1a Non-Vintage (Spain),
or another chilled sherry, either amontillado or fino.

LOBSTER Fill a 10- or 12-quart pot with water about two-thirds full. Add the salt and bring the water to a rolling boil. With your hand on the carapace, or central part of the body, place the lobsters in the pot and cook, uncovered, for exactly 3½ minutes. Using a pair of tongs, remove the lobsters from the pot and allow them to cool to room temperature. Remove the meat from the claws and knuckles, keeping the meat as intact as possible. Break the carcass off the tail and reserve for another purpose. Using a sharp knife or cleaver, split the tail in half lengthwise and remove the meat. Remove the dark "vein." Cut each half-tail in half again. Cover and refrigerate.

SALAD Set a 12-inch sauté pan over medium heat and add the peanut oil. Lightly season the lobster pieces with pepper and add to the hot oil along with the red onion. Cook the lobster and the onion for about 3 minutes, turning and moving the lobster pieces with tongs so they cook evenly. Remove the lobster to a plate and let it sit while you finish the salad. Leave the onions in the pan and remove the pan from the heat. Add the vinegar, lemon zest, and basil; season with salt and pepper. Also add any liquid that accumulates on the plate with the lobster meat. Set aside, leaving the dressing in the pan.

FOIE GRAS Score the slices of foie gras and season with salt and pepper. Place the slices directly into a hot, dry 10-inch sauté pan. Sear for about 30 seconds on each side, until a nice brown crust has formed. Remove the foie gras immediately and keep warm. Reserve the fat.

SERVICE AND GARNISH Return the 12-inch sauté pan with the dressing to the heat. Add the mixed lettuces to the pan. Using a pair of tongs, toss the lettuce over the heat until the greens are slightly warmed, but not cooked, about 1 minute of continuous tossing. When the greens are warm, lift them out of the pan and divide evenly among four serving plates. Work very quickly. Place the foie gras on top of the salad and lean the lobster claw meat against it. Garnish the salad with the remaining chunks of lobster and the ripe papaya. Spoon the remaining dressing over the salad and sprinkle with a few drops of the foie gras fat.

learning to cook with marion cunningham

author

Cookbook author and beginning-cook's-best-friend Marion Cunningham, whose previous books include the complete revision of *The Fannie Farmer Cookbook* as well as *The Fannie Farmer Baking Book*, *The Supper Book*, *The Breakfast Book*, and *Cooking with Children*.

why she wrote it

"I have become increasingly aware in recent years of the fact that very few people are really cooking at home. There are all kinds of reasons given — lack of time, other demands at the family dinner hour, anxiety about wasting ingredients not eaten up, the ease of eating in a restaurant, the lure of take-out foods. But the main reason nobody's in the kitchen, I began to suspect, was that people today are uneasy about cooking. They don't enjoy it, and many actually fear it. And that is very troubling to me, because I feel they are missing one of the greatest pleasures of life."

why it made our list

No complicated ingredients, no elaborate techniques — this is a book of basics, and they're presented in a way so calm, comforting, and complete that even the most skittish newcomer to the kitchen will be lulled into competency. In good no-nonsense style, Cunningham answers questions, suggests shortcuts, and provides beginners with a solid collection of recipes that are easy to prepare and easy to enjoy. And lest more experienced cooks turn away, we'll report that the recipes are so good, they're well worth going back to basics for.

specifics

304 pages, 150 recipes, 110 color photographs.
chapters Appetizers/Odds & Ends › Soup for Supper › A Bowlful of Salad › Easy Fish › Thank Goodness for Chicken › Meaty Main Meals › Meals Without Meat › Good Vegetables › Breakfast Can Be Supper, Too › Extras That Make a Meal › Here Comes Dessert
$29.95. Published by Alfred A. Knopf.

from the book

"**I often hear this complaint from home cooks: 'I don't mind cooking but I hate the mess afterwards.' But that's just a result of poor planning — of leaving everything to the end, letting the mess pile up, and allowing food to harden on your utensils so that everything is difficult to get clean. When I was teaching children how to cook, the first lesson they learned was: 'Wash your hands and fill a big friendly bowl with sudsy hot water.' Well, the lesson wasn't just for children. I wouldn't be without that bowl of sudsy water in my sink. It's so simple. As you are going along, just drop every utensil and pot you've used into that bowl. Then, when everything has soaked a few minutes, wash it up, rinse, and let drain while you continue your cooking.**"

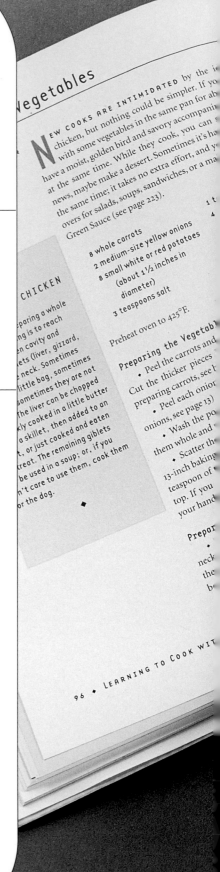

If there is a
pull or cut it off and dis
Hold the chicken under
and out. Shake off excess water and pat
Sprinkle the remaining 1½ teaspoons of
pepper over the outside of the chicken, rubbing them a
Set the chicken, the breast side facing up, on top of some
vegetables, with the remaining ones surrounding the bird.
Insert a dial-type (not instant-read) thermometer into the breast,
taking care that the rod of the thermometer does not touch any bones.

Roasting the Chicken

Put the chicken in the center of the oven and set the timer for 30
minutes.
When the timer rings, remove the pan from the oven and, using a
large spoon, turn over the vegetables that surround the chicken. Don't
bother with the vegetables under the chicken.
Return the pan to the oven and set the timer for 30 more minutes.
After 30 minutes, take the chicken out of the oven to check for
doneness. Insert the tip of a small paring knife   e meat of the
thigh where it attaches to the body. If the juice   are pink, if
the chicken needs to continue cooking for   tes. If
the juices are clear, it is done. The me   w a
temperature of 170°F to 180°F when

Carving the Chicken

Carve the chicken a
p
Scoop the ve
platter. Remove
Arrange
pan juices
mary

**REMOVING THE FAT
FROM A ROASTING PAN**

Remove your roast and vegetables
to a serving platter. Tilt the pan
they were cooked in and spoon off
and discard some of the shiny,
ear fat floating on the surface;
n also use a bulb baster to
You won't get every bit
dan't worry about
he good pan juices
d vegetables.

ck pepper
or 1 tablespoon
emary
cken, about
unds

osswise into 1½-inch-long pieces,
thwise as well (for full details on cutting
).
o quarters (for full details on cutting

r cold water to get rid of any dirt. Leave

ots, and potatoes on the bottom of a 9-by-
pan. *Sprinkle* 1½ teaspoons of the salt and ½
ver them, and lay 2 sprigs of the rosemary on
ried rosemary, put 1 tablespoon in the palm of
e it over the vegetables.

hicken
which consist of the liver, gizzard, and heart, plus the
in a package inside the cavity of the chicken, between
re them and discard or refrigerate them to use later (se
Cleaning the Chicken).

N CUNNINGHAM

LEARNING TO COOK
WITH
MARION CUNNINGHAM

AUTHOR OF THE FANNIE FARMER COOKBOOK

raised waffles

ABOUT 8 WAFFLES

Everyone who has eaten these waffles says they are simply the best. If you are serving them for breakfast, the batter, which is made with yeast, should be mixed the night before you want to bake them. If you want to have them for supper, make the batter in the morning. They are crisp on the outside and tender on the inside—you really have to make them to know how good they are. Incidentally, do not buy a Belgian waffle iron. The crevices are too deep and the waffles won't have the same delicacy.

½   **cup warm water**

1   **package dry yeast**

½   **cup (1 stick) butter, cut in 8 pieces**

2   **cups milk**

1   **teaspoon salt**

1   **teaspoon sugar**

2   **cups all-purpose white flour**

2 eggs

¼   **teaspoon baking soda**

Warm maple syrup

SPECIAL EQUIPMENT

a waffle iron

MAKING THE BATTER AHEAD OF TIME

> Put the warm water in a large mixing bowl. Sprinkle the yeast over the water. Leave it alone for 5 minutes to allow the yeast to dissolve.

> Melt the butter slowly in a small saucepan. Add the milk and stir until just warm, but not hot.

> Add the warm butter and milk, along with the salt, sugar, and flour, to the yeast mixture, and beat with a wire whisk or hand rotary beater until smooth.

> Cover the bowl with plastic wrap and let the batter stand overnight (or from breakfast until supper time) at room temperature. It will bubble up and then subside.

FINISHING THE WAFFLES

› Just before cooking the waffles, crack the eggs into the bowl of batter, then add baking soda and beat until smooth. The batter will be very thin.

› Turn the waffle iron on and, when warm, grease both sides with nonstick cooking spray, butter, or oil. Close the lid and wait until the waffle iron is very hot. Pour about ½ to ¾ cup of batter into it. Close the lid.

› After a few minutes, check to see if the waffle is done. Lift the top of the waffle iron up carefully—you don't want to tear the waffle—and open it just enough so you can peek at the edge of the waffle. It should appear golden brown. If it is still pale, close the top and bake another minute or two.

SERVING THE WAFFLES

› When the first waffle is done, lift the top of the waffle iron and gently pry out the waffle with a fork. Serve hot with a pitcher of warm maple syrup.

› While the first round of waffles are being eaten, make a second batch.

› If you don't use up all the batter, it will keep well for several days in the refrigerator.

LEFTOVER WAFFLE BATTER

Even if you have only a little waffle batter left over, don't throw it away. Put it in the refrigerator in a covered jar and one morning when you feel like a few pancakes for breakfast, you'll find you have a treasure ready and waiting. Just give the jar a shake, ladle spoonfuls of batter into a hot, greased skillet and cook them just as you would pancakes. Eat them with butter and warm maple syrup—I can assure you they'll be wonderful.

roast chicken with vegetables

SERVES FOUR

New cooks are intimidated by the idea of roasting a chicken, but nothing could be simpler. If you roast the chicken with some vegetables in the same pan for about an hour, you will have a moist, golden bird and savory accompaniments—all ready to eat at the same time. While they cook, you can set the table, watch the news, maybe make a dessert. Sometimes it's handy to roast 2 chickens at the same time; it takes no extra effort, and you will have plenty of leftovers for salads, soups, and sandwiches.

8   **whole carrots**

2   **medium-size yellow onions**

8   **small white or red potatoes (about 1½ inches in diameter)**

3   **teaspoons salt**

1   **teaspoon black pepper**

4   **sprigs fresh or 1 tablespoon dried rosemary**

1   **whole chicken, about 3½ pounds**

Preheat oven to 425°F.

PREPARING THE VEGETABLES

> Peel the carrots and cut them crosswise into 1½-inch-long pieces. Cut the thicker pieces in half lengthwise as well (for full details on preparing carrots, see page 248).

> Peel each onion and cut into quarters (for full details on cutting onions, see page 249).

> Wash the potatoes under cold water to get rid of any dirt. Leave them whole and unpeeled.

> Scatter the carrots, onions, and potatoes on the bottom of a 9-by-13-inch baking or roasting pan. Sprinkle 1½ teaspoons of the salt and ½ teaspoon of the pepper over them, and lay 2 sprigs of the rosemary on top. If you are using dried rosemary, put 1 tablespoon in the palm of your hand and crumble it over the vegetables.

PREPARING THE CHICKEN

> The giblets, which consist of the liver, gizzard, and heart, plus the neck, are usually in a package inside the cavity of the chicken, between the legs. Remove them and discard or refrigerate them to use later (see Cleaning the Chicken, page 248).

› If there is a pale-yellow chunk of fat on either side of the cavity, pull or cut it off and discard.

› Hold the chicken under cold running water and rinse it inside and out. Shake off excess water and pat dry with paper towels.

› Sprinkle the remaining 1½ teaspoons of salt and ½ teaspoon of pepper over the outside of the chicken, rubbing them all over the skin.

› Set the chicken, the breast side facing up, on top of some of the vegetables, with the remaining ones surrounding the bird.

› Insert a dial-type (not instant-read) thermometer into the breast, taking care that the rod of the thermometer does not touch any bones.

ROASTING THE CHICKEN

› Put the chicken in the center of the oven and set the timer for 30 minutes.

› When the timer rings, remove the pan from the oven and, using a large spoon, turn over the vegetables that surround the chicken. Don't bother with the vegetables under the chicken.

› Return the pan to the oven and set the timer for 30 more minutes.

› After 30 minutes, take the chicken out of the oven to check for doneness. Insert the tip of a small paring knife into the meat of the thigh where it attaches to the body. If the juices that run out are pink, the chicken needs to continue cooking for another 10 to 15 minutes. If the juices are clear, it is done. The meat thermometer should show a temperature of 170°F to 180°F when the chicken is done.

CARVING THE CHICKEN

› Carve the chicken according to the instructions on the opposite page.

› Scoop the vegetables out of the roasting pan and onto a serving platter. Remove the fat from the pan juices (see page 248).

› Arrange the cut chicken pieces on top of vegetables, spoon some pan juices over the chicken and vegetables, scatter the 2 remaining rosemary sprigs on top, and bring the dish to the table for serving.

HOW TO CARVE A CHICKEN

Carving a chicken is a simple process that takes a little patience; it gets easier each time you do it. If your chicken truly is cooked enough, it should be easy to remove the meat. It's not a delicate process, though, so don't be shy about manhandling the chicken a bit. Wait until it has cooled just enough for you to handle it comfortably.

Set the chicken breast side up. Pull the leg and thigh back to expose the joint that attaches it to the body (have a little patience; wiggling the thigh section and pulling it away from the body with your hands helps). 1) Use a sharp paring knife to probe for the socket and cut through it, separating the leg and thigh from the carcass.

Repeat with the other leg and thigh.

2) Use the knife to cut through the joint that connects the leg to the thigh.

3) Pull off the wings by gently twisting them away from the carcass. You may need the aid of your knife to separate the wings fully.

The breastbone runs along the top center of the chicken carcass. Feel for it with your fingers. Make a 3-inch-long slit along both sides of the breastbone. 4) Dig your fingers into one of the slits and peel the entire half of the breast meat off the carcass. Do the same to remove the breast meat on the other side. Slice each half of breast meat crosswise, making 5 or 6 slices per breast half.

Pick or cut off whatever meat remains on the carcass. Arrange the legs, thighs, wings, and meat on a platter and serve.

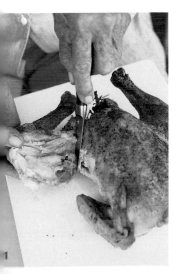
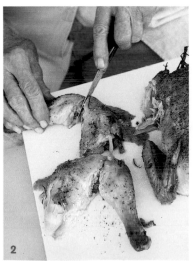

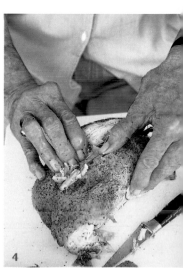

CLEANING THE CHICKEN

The first step in preparing a whole chicken for roasting is to reach inside the chicken cavity and remove the giblets (liver, gizzard, heart) and the neck. Sometimes they are in a little bag, sometimes loose, and sometimes they are not included. The liver can be chopped and quickly cooked in a little butter or oil in a skillet, then added to an omelet, or just cooked and eaten as a treat. The remaining giblets can be used in a soup; or, if you don't care to use them, cook them for the dog.

REMOVING THE FAT FROM A ROASTING PAN

Remove your roast and vegetables to a serving platter. Tilt the pan they were cooked in and spoon off and discard some of the shiny, clear fat floating on the surface; you can also use a bulb baster to suck it up. You won't get every bit of fat off, but don't worry about it. Now pour all the good pan juices onto the chicken and vegetables.

ABOUT CARROTS

Carrots are often used in soups and stews and surrounding chicken and meats as they roast. There they are simply peeled and cut into 1- or 2-inch chunks, and they always add flavor to whatever they touch.

Carrots keep well in the vegetable bin of the refrigerator and are handy to have around. Make sure that your carrots are still firm, not limp.

HOW TO PEEL, SLICE, AND CHOP AN ONION

TO PEEL   Using a paring knife, slice off the fuzzy brownish root end and the stem top of the onion and discard. 1) Peel off the papery outer brownish-yellow skin of the onion with your fingers or a paring knife, and discard.

TO SLICE AN ONION   2) Cut the onion in half from stem top to root end. Put the onion halves cut side down on a cutting board. 3) Cut slices crosswise from each half. The thickness will depend on how you plan to use it, but ⅛ inch thick is usually about right. As you slice, curl under the ends of the fingers of your hand holding the onion, so that you don't cut yourself; move your hand back on the onion after each slice.

TO CHOP AN ONION   Slice the onion in half from the stem top through the root end. Place each half flat side down on a cutting board. Holding a half firmly with one hand, make about 7 vertical slices into the onion, from the end to the root end, but don't slice completely through the root end (this will make it easier to slice). 4) Next, slice crosswise, letting the little pieces fall. Repeat with the remaining half of the onion.

almond butter cake

ONE 9-INCH ROUND CAKE

Almond butter cake is not to be taken lightly just because you can stir it together in about 3 minutes, pop it in the oven to bake, and serve it within an hour. It's truly a unique cake, because it doesn't rise very high and it comes out moist, sticky, and chewy, like a cookie. It also keeps twice as long as any conventional cake.

THE CAKE BATTER

¾ **cup butter (1½ sticks)**

1½ **cups sugar**

2 **large eggs**

½ **teaspoon salt**

1½ **teaspoons almond extract**

1 **teaspoon vanilla extract**

1½ **cups all-purpose white flour**

2 **teaspoons soft butter or nonstick cooking spray**
   (for greasing the cake pan)

TOPPING

1 tablespoon sugar

4 ounces sliced almonds (¾ cup)

Preheat oven to 350°F.

MEASURING AND MIXING THE INGREDIENTS

› Melt the butter in a small saucepan over medium-low heat, stirring regularly. Pour the melted butter and 1½ cups of sugar into a large bowl and stir until smooth.

Crack the eggs right into the same bowl and mix until the batter is creamy and all one color. Add the salt, almond extract, vanilla extract, and flour and stir briskly until the batter is smooth.

THE LAST STEP BEFORE BAKING

› Grease the bottom and sides of a 9-inch round cake pan with butter or nonstick cooking spray. Using a rubber spatula, scrape the batter from the bowl into the greased cake pan. Spread it evenly in the pan. Sprinkle the tablespoon of sugar, then the sliced almonds, over the top of the batter.

BAKING AND SERVING THE CAKE

› Put the pan on the middle rack of the oven and set the timer for 35 minutes. When it rings, check to see if the cake is done. It should be light brown on top, and when you insert a toothpick in the center, it should have a few sticky crumbs adhering to it. If the cake is not browned enough and the toothpick comes out too wet, put the cake back in the oven and check it again in another 10 minutes.

› When the cake is done, remove it from the oven and let it cool on a heatproof counter for at least 30 minutes.

› Cut the cake into small wedges and serve with fresh fruit. This cake will stay fresh for about a week and will freeze indefinitely. Wrap it tightly in foil, or in a plastic bag you can seal with a zip or a tie.

STORING NUTS

Whenever you have leftover nuts, freeze them in a plastic bag closed tightly. They will keep indefinitely in the freezer.

the wisdom of the chinese kitchen

author

Grace Young, recipe developer for *The Best of China* and *The Best of Thailand*, with help from her mother, her grandmother, and her extended Cantonese family.

why she wrote it

"For me, the principles that govern Chinese cooking and nutrition are far more intriguing than the Western notions of nutrition, with its focus on cholesterol, vitamins, minerals, fiber, carbohydrates, protein, and fats in the diet. It is a cuisine based on opposites, the yin-yang principles of cooking. This philosophy is so instinctively ingrained in my family that it was hard for them to articulate it verbally. I recognized that if I didn't begin questioning my parents, grandmother, aunts, and uncles, the wisdom of their diet and the lore of our culinary heritage would be irretrievably lost."

why it made our list

Part recipe collection, part memory album, this is a book that you can curl up with as well as cook from. Young's tales of her family's traditions, techniques, and beliefs about food are fascinating to read, and they also enhance our appreciation of the authenticity of the recipes, which range from everyday dishes to celebratory specialties to foods with healing properties. Don't skip over the headnotes; they're especially important because almost all have essential information about the ingredients or method, as well as interesting background on the dish. An altogether thorough and thoughtful effort.

specifics

282 pages, 151 recipes, 22 color photographs, 35 black-and-white photographs.

chapters The Meaning of Rice › The Breath of a Wok › The Art of Steaming › Shreds of Ginger like Blades of Grass › Going to Market with Mama › Cooking as a Meditation › The Good Omen of a Fighting Fish › New Year's Foods and Traditions › A Day Lived as if in China › Dutiful Daughter Returns Home › Cooking as a Healing Art › Baba's Mama's *Dong Quai* and Restorative Foods

$27.50. Published by Pocket Books.

from the book

"**The Chinese consider a strong appetite for rice to be a sign of good health and fortune. It's common for wives and mothers to brag of their husband's or children's ability to eat three or four bowls of rice at a sitting. Baba, like many Cantonese men, will insist that he does not feel right until he has eaten rice. Cooks are happy to see their guests *teem fan*, that is, get another helping of rice. It indicates that their vegetable dishes, cooked with a little meat, poultry, fish, or tofu, must be delicious enough to inspire such an appetite.**"

Sugar Ginger Chicken

my parents' oldest friends, Lady Ivy Fung, taugh
nese village recipe. You can use more or less ginge
The traditional technique for cooking this is to
ken in an extra-large wok, cover it with the lid, an
e down the sides of the pan. Some of the marinad
ade quickly. It is also easier to use a 14-inch skille
wok. Because the chicken and ginger finish cooki
the lid is finally removed, the room becomes f
thentic method is to chop up the chicken, but w
breast halves can also be cooked, in which case
by 5 to 10 minutes. I have experimented with
lated sugar in place of the rock sugar; the res

unds mixed chicken
arts, on the bone
cup Homemade Chicken
Broth (page 234)
tablespoons black soy sauce
2 ounces rock sugar, about
¼ cup
2 teaspoons vegetable oil
1½ cups sliced ginger, about
6 ounces
½ teaspoon salt

With a meat cleaver, c
inch pieces, or disjoin
In a small saucepan,
sauce, and rock suga
until the sugar is co
Heat a 14-inch sk
oil and ginger, a
minute.
Bring the ginge
and carefully
skillet. Cook
medium an
a metal spa
or until c
through.
kle the c
down t
ered, c
low, a
Serve

Serv

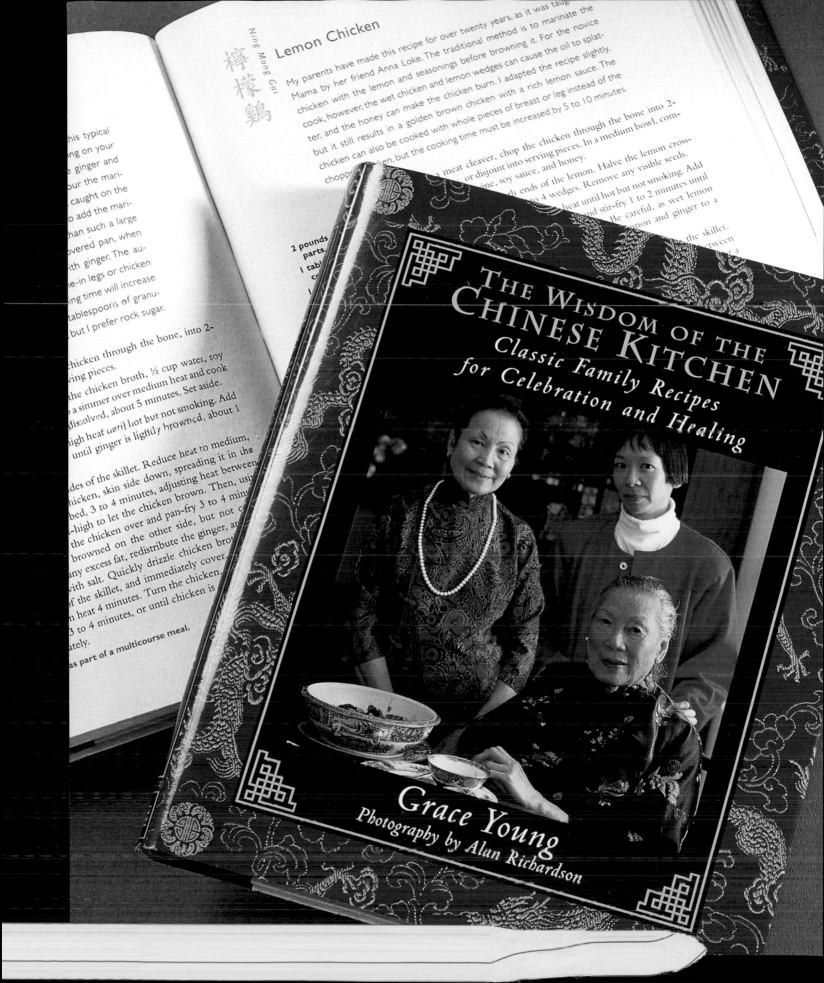

scallion cakes

MAKES 4 SCALLION CAKES

SERVES 6 TO 8 AS PART OF A MULTICOURSE LUNCH

I first tasted scallion cakes at Henry Chung's Hunan Restaurant on Kearny Street in San Francisco. I think I was about eleven years old as I sat on a stool at the counter and watched these curious rounds of dough being fried until golden brown and fragrant with scallion flavor. As I devoured the delicious, crisp cakes, Mama looked on, pleased that I loved them, for she had grown up eating them as a favorite street snack in China. This was the first Hunan restaurant I'd ever eaten in and, until then, our diet had been strictly Cantonese food.

Be careful when frying these cakes, as the oil will splatter, especially when you press a cake in its center. Any uncooked dough can be placed in a plastic container, refrigerated, and cooked the following day. If you do make them ahead, redust the dough lightly with flour to absorb any moisture from refrigeration, and allow the dough to sit at room temperature briefly so that it is not ice-cold when fried.

2	cups all-purpose flour, plus additional flour for kneading
¾	teaspoon sugar
2	teaspoons sesame oil
1¼	plus ½ teaspoon salt
⅓	cup finely minced scallions
⅔	cup vegetable oil

In a medium bowl, combine flour and sugar. Stir in ⅔ cup boiling water, mixing flour and water just until flour absorbs all the water. Gradually stir in enough cold water (¼ to ⅓ cup) so that a dough is formed and pulls away from the sides of the bowl. The dough should not be sticky.

Remove dough from the bowl and knead on a lightly dusted board with floured hands 3 to 5 minutes, or until the dough is smooth and elastic, adding more flour if necessary. Lightly cover with a dampened cloth and allow to rest for 1 hour.

Redust surface and hands with flour, and knead again for a few minutes or until smooth. Divide the dough into 4 equal pieces. As you work, always cover any unused dough with a lightly damp cloth. Using a floured rolling pin, roll each section into a 7-inch round. Lightly brush each round with sesame oil. Evenly sprinkle 1¼ teaspoons salt and scallions on each round, and then tightly roll each round into a fat rope. Tightly coil each rope, pinching the end of the rope into the dough to seal. Cover with a lightly damp cloth and allow to rest 15 to 20 minutes. Redust surface with flour, and using a floured rolling pin, roll each coiled bun into 7-inch rounds.

In a 14-inch flat-bottomed wok or skillet, heat vegetable oil over medium-high heat until oil is hot but not smoking. Carefully add one scallion round and fry 1 to 2 minutes, until golden. Carefully turn cake over and fry 30 seconds to 1 minute, or until golden brown. As the cake fries, lightly press the center with a metal spatula to make sure center is cooked. Transfer each cake to a plate lined with several thicknesses of paper towels. Continue frying the remaining scallion rounds one at a time. Sprinkle with remaining ½ teaspoon salt. Set oil aside to cool before discarding. Cut cakes into 6 to 8 wedges and serve immediately.

lemon chicken

SERVES 4 TO 6 AS PART OF A MULTICOURSE MEAL

My parents have made this recipe for over twenty years, as it was taught to Mama by her friend Anna Loke. The traditional method is to marinate the chicken with the lemon and seasonings before browning it. For the novice cook, however, the wet chicken and lemon wedges can cause the oil to splatter, and the honey can make the chicken burn. I adapted the recipe slightly, but it still results in a golden brown chicken with a rich lemon sauce. The chicken can also be cooked with whole pieces of breast or leg instead of the chopped chicken, but the cooking time must be increased by 5 to 10 minutes.

2	pounds mixed chicken parts, on the bone
1	tablespoon Shao Hsing rice cooking wine
1	tablespoon thin soy sauce
1	tablespoon honey
1	lemon
1	tablespoon vegetable oil
3	slices ginger
½	teaspoon salt

With a meat cleaver, chop the chicken through the bone into 2-inch pieces, or disjoint into serving pieces. In a medium bowl, combine the rice wine, soy sauce, and honey.

Shave ⅛ inch off both ends of the lemon. Halve the lemon crosswise and cut each half into 4 wedges. Remove any visible seeds.

Heat a 14-inch skillet over high heat until hot but not smoking. Add the oil, lemon wedges, and ginger, and stir-fry 1 to 2 minutes until lemon and ginger are lightly browned. Be careful, as wet lemon wedges will cause oil to splatter. Transfer lemon and ginger to a plate.

Carefully add chicken, skin side down, spreading it in the skillet. Cook undisturbed for 3 to 4 minutes, adjusting heat between medium and medium-high, as the chicken browns. Then, using a metal spatula, turn chicken over and pan-fry 3 to 4 minutes, or until chicken is browned on the other side, but not cooked through. Pour off any excess fat. Sprinkle on salt, rice wine mixture, browned lemon, and ginger slices. Cover and simmer on medium heat 3 to 4 minutes. Turn the chicken, reduce heat to low, and simmer 3 to 4 minutes, or until chicken is cooked through. Serve immediately.

FRESH VEGETABLES

1. Long beans, light green	**12.** Chinese eggplant	**23.** Mung bean sprouts
2. Long beans, dark green	**13.** Water chestnuts	**24.** Chestnuts
3. Flowering garlic chives	**14.** Ginger	**25.** Watercress
4. Chinese chives	**15.** Water spinach	**26.** Green turnip
5. Yellow chives	**16.** Chinese broccoli	**27.** Chinese turnip
6. Young bok choy	**17.** Broad-leaf mustard greens	**28.** Chayote
7. Winter melon	**18.** Scallion	**29.** Snow pea shoots
8. Taro root	**19.** Snow peas	**30.** Lemongrass
9. Luffa	**20.** Fuzzy melon	**31.** Lotus root
10. Cilantro	**21.** Napa cabbage	
11. Bitter melon	**22.** Soybean sprouts	

1. Sweet rice

2. Long grain rice

3. Expensive Chinese dried mushrooms

4. Inexpensive Chinese dried mushrooms

5. Dried chestnuts

6. Black moss

7. Salted turnip, *teem choy poe*

8. Salted turnip, *chung choy zack*

9. Brown candy

10. Rock sugar

11. Dried shrimp

12. Sichuan peppercorns

13. Dried scallops

14. Dried oysters

15. Sheet dried bean curd

16. Stick dried bean curd

17. Rice flour

18. Glutinous rice flour

19. Wheat starch

20. Tapioca starch

21. Water chestnut flour

22. Cellophane noodles

23. Rice vermicelli

24. Shark's fin

25. Black vinegar

26. Red rice vinegar

27. Sweetened black vinegar

28. Thin soy sauce

29. Black soy sauce

30. Hoisin sauce

31. Plum sauce

32. Chili garlic sauce

33. XO sauce

34. Chinese dried black beans

35. Sesame oil

36. Oyster flavored sauce

37. Shao Hsing rice cooking wine

38. Ground bean sauce

39. Wet bean curd (white)

40. Wet bean curd (red)

1998
best of the best
winners

CHEF'S COOKBOOKS

› *Alfred Portale's Gotham Bar and Grill Cookbook* by Alfred Portale (Villard Books)

› *American Brasserie: 180 Simple, Robust Recipes Inspired by the Rustic Foods of France, Italy, and America* by Rick Tramonto and Gale Gand with Julia Moskin (Macmillan USA)

› *Cooking with Too Hot Tamales* by Mary Sue Milliken and Susan Feniger with Helene Siegel (William Morrow and Company, Inc.)

› *Death by Chocolate Cookies* by Marcel Desaulniers (Simon & Schuster)

› *Emeril's Creole Christmas* by Emeril Lagasse with Marcelle Bienvenu (William Morrow and Company, Inc.)

› *The Food of Campanile* by Mark Peel and Nancy Silverton (Villard Books)

› *Matthew Kenney's Mediterranean Cooking: Great Flavors for the American Kitchen* by Matthew Kenney and Sam Gugino (Chronicle Books)

› *The New Making of a Cook: The Art, Techniques, and Science of Good Cooking* by Madeleine Kamman (William Morrow and Company, Inc.)

› *Pierre Franey Cooks with His Friends: With Recipes from Top Chefs in France, Spain, Italy, Switzerland, Germany, Belgium & the Netherlands* by Pierre Franey with Claudia Franey Jensen (Artisan)

ITALIAN AND MEDITERRANEAN COOKING

› *Flavors of Puglia: Traditional Recipes from the Heel of Italy's Boot* by Nancy Harmon Jenkins (Broadway Books)

› *The Food and Flavors of Haute Provence* by Georgeanne Brennan (Chronicle Books)

› *A Fresh Taste of Italy: 250 Authentic Recipes, Undiscovered Dishes, and New Flavors for Every Day* by Michele Scicolone (Broadway Books)

> *In Nonna's Kitchen: Recipes and Traditions from Italy's Grandmothers* by Carol Field (HarperCollins Publishers, Inc.)

> *Invitation to Mediterranean Cooking: 150 Vegetarian and Seafood Recipes* by Claudia Roden (Rizzoli International Publications, Inc.)

> *Kitchen Conversations: Robust Recipes and Lessons in Flavor from One of America's Most Innovative Chefs* by Joyce Goldstein (William Morrow and Company, Inc.)

> **BEST BOOK OF THE YEAR**
Marcella Cucina by Marcella Hazan (HarperCollins Publishers, Inc.)

BEST-SELLERS

> *The Good Housekeeping Step-by-Step Cookbook* edited by Susan Westmoreland (Hearst Books)

> *The Joy of Cooking* by Irma S. Rombauer, Marion Rombauer Becker, and Ethan Becker (Scribner)

> *Mr. Food® Cool Cravings: Easy Chilled and Frozen Desserts* by Art Ginsberg (William Morrow and Company, Inc.)

> *Naomi's Home Companion: A Treasury of Favorite Recipes, Food for Thought, and Kitchen Wit and Wisdom* by Naomi Judd (GT Publishing Corporation)

> *Sheila Lukins U.S.A. Cookbook* by Sheila Lukins (Workman Publishing)

> *Sweetie Pie: The Richard Simmons Private Collection of Dazzling Desserts* by Richard Simmons (GT Publishing Corporation)

VEGETARIAN AND HEALTHY COOKING

> *The Chinese Way: Healthy Low-Fat Cooking from China's Regions* by Eileen Yin-Fei Lo (Macmillian USA)

> *Martha Stewart's Healthy Quick Cook: Four Seasons of Great Menus to Make Every Day,* by Martha Stewart (Clarkson N. Potter, Inc.)

> *Mollie Katzen's Vegetable Heaven: Over 200 Recipes for Uncommon Soups, Tasty Bites, Side-by-Side Dishes, and Too Many Desserts* by Mollie Katzen (Hyperion)

> *Vegetarian Cooking for Everyone* by Deborah Madison (Broadway Books)

1999
best of the best
winners

> *The American Century Cookbook* by Jean Anderson (Clarkson N. Potter, Inc.)

> *The Best Bread Ever: Great Homemade Bread Using Your Food Processor* by Charles Van Over with Priscilla Martel (Broadway Books)

> *Cookwise: The Hows and Whys of Successful Cooking* by Shirley O. Corriher (William Morrow and Company, Inc.)

> *Great Fish, Quick* by Leslie Revsin (Doubleday)

> *Latin American Cooking Across the U.S.A.* by Himilce Novas and Rosemary Silva (Alfred A. Knopf, Inc.)

> *New Recipes from Quilt Country: More Food & Folkways from the Amish & Mennonites* by Marcia Adams (Clarkson N. Potter, Inc.)

> *Quick from Scratch: Fish & Shellfish* edited by Judith Hill (Food & Wine Books)

> *Stews, Bogs & Burgoos: Recipes from the Great American Stewpot* by James Villas (William Morrow and Company, Inc.)

> *What You Knead* by Mary Ann Esposito (William Morrow and Company, Inc.)

RESTAURANT CHEFS

> *Bobby Flay's From My Kitchen to Your Table* by Bobby Flay and Joan Schwartz (Clarkson N. Potter Publishers)

> *The Cafe Cook Book: Italian Recipes from London's River Cafe* by Rose Gray and Ruth Rogers (Broadway Books)

> *Emeril's TV Dinners* by Emeril Lagasse with Marcelle Bienvenu and Felicia Willet (William Morrow and Company, Inc.)

> *The Figs Table: More than 100 Recipes for Pizzas, Pastas, Salads, and Desserts* by Todd English and Sally Sampson (Simon & Schuster)

> *Jean-Georges: Cooking at Home with a Four-Star Chef* by Jean-Georges Vongerichten and Mark Bittman (Broadway Books)

> *Le Bernardin Cookbook: Four-Star Simplicity* by Maguy Lecoze and Eric Ripert (Doubleday)

> *Lobster at Home* by Jasper White (Scribner)

> *Simple Menus for the Bento Box* by Ellen Greaves and Wayne Nish (William Morrow and Company, Inc.)

SPECIFIC CUISINES

› *Bugialli's Italy: Traditional Recipes from the Regions of Italy* by Giuliano Bugialli (William Morrow and Company, Inc.)

› *Flavors of Tuscany: Traditional Recipes from the Tuscan Countryside* by Nancy Harmon Jenkins (Broadway Books)

› *Lidia's Italian Table* by Lidia Matticchio Bastianich (William Morrow and Company, Inc.)

› **BEST BOOK OF THE YEAR**
Mediterranean Grains and Greens: A Book of Savory, Sun-Drenched Recipes by Paula Wolfert (HarperCollins Publishers, Inc.)

› *My Mexico: A Culinary Odyssey with More than 300 Recipes* by Diana Kennedy (Clarkson N. Potter Publishers)

› *Rao's Cookbook: Over 100 Years of Italian Home Cooking* by Frank Pellegrino (Random House, Inc.)

› *The Two Fat Ladies Ride Again* by Clarissa Dickson Wright and Jennifer Paterson (Clarkson N. Potter Publishers)

GENERAL INTEREST

› *The French Culinary Institute's Salute to Healthy Cooking: From America's Foremost French Chefs* by Alain Sailhac, Jacques Torres, Jacques Pépin, and André Soltner (Rodale Press, Inc.)

› *How to Cook Everything: Simple Recipes for Great Food* by Mark Bittman (Macmillian General Reference USA)

› *Jacques Pépin's Kitchen: Encore with Claudine* by Jacques Pépin (Bay Books and Tapes, Inc.)

› *Newman's Own Cookbook* by Paul Newman and A. E. Hotchner (Simon & Schuster)

› *The Perfect Recipe: Getting it Right Every Time—Making Our Favorite Dishes the Absolute Best They Can Be* by Pam Anderson (Houghton Mifflin Company)

› *Taste: One Palate's Journey Through the World's Greatest Dishes* by David Rosengarten (Random House, Inc.)

› *The Yellow Farmhouse Cookbook* by Christopher Kimball (Little, Brown and Company)

SPECIAL SUBJECTS

› *The Barbecue! Bible* by Steven Raichlen (Workman Publishing Company, Inc.)

› *Born to Grill: An American Celebration* by Cheryl Alters Jamison and Bill Jamison (The Harvard Common Press)

› *The Complete Meat Cookbook: A Juicy and Authoritative Guide to Selecting, Seasoning, and Cooking Today's Beef, Pork, Lamb, and Veal* by Bruce Aidells and Denis Kelly (Houghton Mifflin Company)

› *Quick from Scratch: Herbs & Spices* edited by Judith Hill (Food & Wine Books)

› *Seductions of Rice: A Cookbook* by Jeffrey Alford and Naomi Duguid (Artisan)

› *Soup: A Way of Life* by Barbara Kafka (Artisan)

› *Vegetables* by James Peterson (William Morrow and Company, Inc.)

DESSERTS

› *Charlie Trotter's Desserts* by Charlie Trotter (Ten Speed Press)

› *Chocolate: From Simple Cookies to Extravagant Showstoppers* by Nick Malgieri (HarperCollins Publishers, Inc.)

› *Dessert Circus: Extraordinary Desserts You Can Make at Home* by Jacques Torres (William Morrow and Company, Inc.)

› *Desserts by Pierre Hermé* by Pierre Hermé and Dorie Greenspan (Little, Brown and Company)

› *My Mother's Southern Desserts* by James Villas with Martha Pearl Villas (William Morrow and Company, Inc.)

› *The Pie and Pastry Bible* by Rose Levy Beranbaum (Scribner)

credits & acknowledgments

restaurant cookbooks

PAGES 10 – 23

From *The French Laundry Cookbook* by Thomas Keller. Copyright © 1999 by Thomas Keller. Photographs copyright © 1999 by Deborah Jones. Used by permission of Artisan, a division of Workman Publishing, Inc.

PHOTOGRAPHS Deborah Jones
DESIGN LEVEL

PAGES 24 – 31

From *Chez Panisse Cafe Cookbook* by Alice Waters. Copyright © 1999 by Alice Waters. Illustrations copyright © 1999 by David Lance Goines. Reprinted by permission of HarperCollins Publishers, Inc.

ILLUSTRATIONS David Lance Goines
DESIGN David Lance Goines

PAGES 32 – 43

From *Blue Ginger: East Meets West Cooking with Ming Tsai* by Ming Tsai and Arthur Boehm. Copyright © 1999 by Ming Tsai. Photographs copyright © 1999 by Alan Richardson. Reprinted by permission of Clarkson N. Potter Publishers, a division of Random House, Inc.

PHOTOGRAPHS Alan Richardson
DESIGN Subtitle

PAGES 44 – 53

From *The Tra Vigne Cookbook: Seasons in the California Wine Country* by Michael Chiarello with Penelope Wisner. Copyright © 1999 by Michael Chiarello. Photographs copyright © 1999 by Karl Petzke. Used by permission of Chronicle Books.

PHOTOGRAPHS Karl Petzke
JACKET ILLUSTRATION Michael Mabry
DESIGN Michael Mabry Design

PAGES 54 – 61

Reprinted with the permission of Scribner, a division of Simon & Schuster, from *Daniel Boulud's Café Boulud Cookbook: French-American Recipes for the Home Cook* by Daniel Boulud and Dorie Greenspan. Copyright © 1999 by Daniel Boulud and Dorie Greenspan. Color photographs copyright © 1999 by Gentl & Hyers/Edge.

PHOTOGRAPHS Gentl & Hyers
DESIGN Britta Steinbrecht

PAGES 62 – 71

From *The Rose Pistola Cookbook: 140 Italian Recipes from San Francisco's Favorite North Beach Restaurant* by Reed Hearon and Peggy Knickerbocker. Copyright © 1999 by Reed Hearon and Peggy Knickerbocker. Black-and-white photographs copyright © 1999 by Henrik Kam. Color photographs copyright © 1999 by Laurie Smith. Used by permission of Broadway Books, a division of Random House, Inc.

PHOTOGRAPHS Henrik Kam (*black and white*), Laurie Smith (*color*)
BOOK DESIGN Pei Loi Koay
JACKET DESIGN Roberto de Vicq de Cumptich

books from tv cooks

PAGES 74 – 83

From *The Kitchen Sessions with Charlie Trotter* by Charlie Trotter. Copyright © 1999 by Charlie Trotter. Reprinted by permission of Ten Speed Press.
PHOTOGRAPHS Tim Turner
ILLUSTRATIONS
Matthias Merges and Mitchell Rice
DESIGN Three Communication Design, Chicago

PAGES 84 – 91

From *Every Day's a Party: Louisiana Recipes for Celebrating with Family and Friends* by Emeril Lagasse with Marcelle Bienvenu and Felicia Willet. Copyright © 1999 by Emeril Lagasse. Photographs copyright © 1999 by Philip Gould. Reprinted by permission of William Morrow and Company, Inc., a division of HarperCollins Publishers, Inc.
PHOTOGRAPHS Philip Gould
BOOK DESIGN Jill Armus
JACKET DESIGN Richard L. Aquan

PAGES 92– 101

From *Julia and Jacques Cooking at Home* by Julia Child and Jacques Pépin. Copyright © 1999 by A La Carte Communications. Photographs copyright

© 1999 by Christopher Hirsheimer. Reprinted by permission of Alfred A. Knopf, a division of Random House, Inc.
PHOTOGRAPHS Christopher Hirsheimer
JACKET DESIGN Carol Devine Carson

PAGES 102 – 107

From *Bobby Flay's Boy Meets Grill: With More Than 125 Bold New Recipes* by Bobby Flay and Joan Schwartz. Copyright © 1999 by Bobby Flay. Photographs copyright © 1999 by Tom Eckerle. Reprinted by permission of Hyperion.
PHOTOGRAPHS Tom Eckerle
BOOK DESIGN
Joel Avirom and Jason Snyder
JACKET DESIGN David Zachary Cohen

PAGES 108 – 115

From *Martha Stewart's Hors D'Oeuvres Handbook* by Martha Stewart with Susan Spungen. Copyright © 1999 by Martha Stewart Living Omnimedia, LLC. Photographs copyright © 1999 by Dana Gallagher. Reprinted by permission of Clarkson N. Potter Publishers, a division of Random House, Inc.
PHOTOGRAPHS Dana Gallagher
DESIGN Scot Schy

PAGES 116 – 121

From *B. Smith: Rituals and Celebrations* by Barbara Smith. Copyright © 1999 by Barbara Smith. Photographs copyright © 1999 by Mark Ferri. Reprinted by permission of Random House, Inc.
PHOTOGRAPHS Mark Ferri
BOOK DESIGN
Joel Avirom and Jason Snyder
JACKET DESIGN   Joel Avirom

dessert
books

more great books

PAGES 194 – 201

From *The Cook and The Gardener: A Year of Recipes and Writings from the French Countryside* by Amanda Hesser. Copyright © 1999 by Amanda Hesser. Illustrations copyright © 1999 by Kate Gridley. Used by permission of W. W. Norton & Company, Inc.

ILLUSTRATIONS Kate Gridley

BOOK DESIGN Susan McClellan

JACKET PHOTOGRAPHS Rita Maas

JACKET DESIGN Timothy Hsu

PAGES 202 – 215

From *Madhur Jaffrey's World Vegetarian: More than 650 Meatless Recipes from Around the Globe* by Madhur Jaffrey. Copyright © 1999 by Madhur Jaffrey. Reprinted by permission of Clarkson N. Potter Publishers, a division of Random House, Inc.

PHOTOGRAPHS Zubin Shroff

DESIGN Memo Productions

PAGES 216 – 223

From *Authentic Vietnamese Cooking: Food from a Family Table* by Corinne Trang. Copyright © 1999 by Corinne Trang. Photographs copyright © 1999 by Christopher Hirsheimer. Reprinted by permission of Simon & Schuster.

PHOTOGRAPHS Christopher Hirsheimer

DESIGN Toby Fox

PAGES 224 – 229

From *American Home Cooking: Over 300 Spirited Recipes Celebrating Our Rich Traditions of Home Cooking* by Cheryl Alters Jamison and Bill Jamison. Copyright © 1999 by Cheryl Alters Jamison and Bill Jamison. Used by permission of Broadway Books, a division of Random House, Inc.

PHOTOGRAPHS Ellen Silverman

BOOK DESIGN Vertigo Design

JACKET DESIGN Roberto de Vicq de Cumptich

PAGES 230 – 239

From *Foie Gras . . . A Passion* by Michael A. Ginor. Copyright © 1999 by Michael A. Ginor. Reprinted by permission of John Wiley & Sons, Inc.

PHOTOGRAPHS Gideon Lewin

PAGES 240 – 251

From *Learning to Cook with Marion Cunningham* by Marion Cunningham. Copyright © 1999 by Marion Cunningham. Photographs copyright © 1999 by Christopher Hirsheimer. Reprinted by permission of Alfred A. Knopf, a division of Random House, Inc.

PHOTOGRAPHS Christopher Hirsheimer

BOOK DESIGN Cassandra J. Pappas

JACKET DESIGN Carol Devine Carson

PAGES 252 – 259

From *The Wisdom of the Chinese Kitchen: Classic Family Recipes for Celebrating and Healing* by Grace Young. Copyright © 1999 by Grace Young. Photographs copyright © 1999 by Alan Richardson. Reprinted by permission of Pocket Books, a division of Simon & Schuster.

PHOTOGRAPHS Alan Richardson

BOOK DESIGN Vertigo Design

JACKET DESIGN Liz Trovato

guide to publishers

ALFRED A. KNOPF

(a division of Random House, Inc.)
201 East 50th Street
New York, NY 10022
(212) 751-2600
www.randomhouse.com

› *Learning to Cook with Marion Cunningham* by Marion Cunningham; ISBN 0-375-40118-0

› *Julia and Jacques Cooking at Home* by Julia Child and Jacques Pépin; ISBN 0-375-40431-7

ARTISAN

(a division of Workman Publishing, Inc.)
708 Broadway
New York, NY 10003
(212) 254-5900
www.workmanweb.com

› *The French Laundry Cookbook* by Thomas Keller; ISBN 1-57965-126-7

BROADWAY BOOKS

(a division of Random House, Inc.)
1540 Broadway
New York, NY 10036
(212) 354-6500
www.broadwaybooks.com

› *American Home Cooking: Over 300 Spirited Recipes Celebrating Our Rich Traditions of Home Cooking* by Cheryl Alters Jamison and Bill Jamison; ISBN 0-7679-0201-7

› *The Rose Pistola Cookbook: 140 Italian Recipes From San Francisco's Favorite North Beach Restaurant* by Reed Hearon and Peggy Knickerbocker; ISBN 0-7679-0250-5

› *Simply Sensational Desserts: 140 Classic Desserts for the Home Baker* by François Payard; ISBN 0-7679-0358-7

CHRONICLE BOOKS

85 Second Street
San Francisco, CA 94105
(415) 537-3730
www.chroniclebooks.com

› *The Tra Vigne Cookbook: Seasons in the California Wine Country* by Michael Chiarello with Penelope Wisner; ISBN 0-8118-1986-8

HYPERION

77 West 66th Street
New York, NY 10023
(212) 456-0100
www.hyperionbooks.com

› *Bobby Flay's Boy Meets Grill: With more than 125 Bold New Recipes* by Bobby Flay and Joan Schwartz; ISBN 0-7868-6490-7

JOHN WILEY & SONS, INC.

605 Third Avenue
New York, NY 10158
(212) 850-6011
www.wiley.com

› *Foie Gras . . . A Passion* by Michael A. Ginor; ISBN 0-471-29318-0

POCKET BOOKS

(A Division of Simon & Schuster)
1230 Avenue of the Americas
New York, NY 10020
(212) 698-7000
www.simonsays.com

› *The Wisdom of the Chinese Kitchen: Classic Family Recipes for Celebrations and Healing* by Grace Young; ISBN 0-684-84739-6

CLARKSON N. POTTER PUBLISHERS

(a division of Random House, Inc.)
201 East 50th Street
New York, NY 10022
(212) 751-2600
www.clarksonpotter.com

› *Blue Ginger: East Meets West Cooking with Ming Tsai* by Ming Tsai and Arthur Boehm; ISBN 0-609-60530-5

› *Madhur Jaffrey's World Vegetarian: More Than 650 Meatless Recipes from Around the Globe* by Madhur Jaffrey; ISBN 0-517-59632-6

› *Martha Stewart's Hor d'Oeuvres Handbook* by Martha Stewart; ISBN 0-609-60310-8

HARPERCOLLINS PUBLISHERS, INC.

10 East 53rd Street
New York, NY 10022
(212) 207-7000
www.harpercollins.com

› *Room for Dessert* by David Lebovitz; ISBN 0-06-019185-6

› *Chez Panisse Café Cookbook* by Alice Waters; ISBN 0-06-017583-4

RANDOM HOUSE, INC.

201 East 50th Street
New York, NY 10022
(212) 751-2600
www.atrandom.com

› *B. Smith: Rituals & Celebrations* by Barbara Smith; ISBN 0-375-50236-X

› *Spago Chocolate* by Mary Bergin and Judy Gethers; ISBN 0-679-44833-0

SCRIBNER

(a division of Simon & Schuster)
1230 Avenue of the Americas
New York, NY 10020
(212) 698-7000
www.simonsays.com

> *Daniel Boulud's Café Boulud
Cookbook: French-American Recipes for
the Home Cook* by Daniel Boulud and
Dorie Greenspan; ISBN 0-684-86343-X

SIMON & SCHUSTER

1230 Avenue of the Americas
New York, NY 10020
(212) 698-7000
www.simonsays.com

> *Authentic Vietnamese Cooking: Food
from a Family Table* by Corinne Trang;
ISBN 0-684-86444-4

TEN SPEED PRESS

P.O. Box 7123
Berkeley, CA 94707
(510) 559-1600
www.tenspeed.com

> *The Kitchen Sessions with Charlie
Trotter* by Charlie Trotter
ISBN 0-89815-997-0

W. W. NORTON & COMPANY, INC.

500 Fifth Avenue
New York, NY 10110
(212) 354-5500
www.wwnorton.com

> *The Cook and the Gardener: A Year
of Recipes and Writings from the
French Countryside* by Amanda Hesser;
ISBN 0-393-04668-0

WARNER BOOKS, INC.

1271 Avenue of the Americas
New York, NY 10020
(212) 522-7200
www.twbookmark.com

> *Alice Medrich's Cookies and Brownies*
by Alice Medrich; ISBN 0-446-52382-8

WILLIAM MORROW AND COMPANY, INC.

(a division of HarperCollins
Publishers, Inc.)
10 East 53rd Street
New York, NY 10022
(212) 207-7000
www.williammorrow.com

> *The Art of the Cake: Modern French
Baking and Decorating* by Bruce Healy
and Paul Bugat; ISBN 0-688-14199-4

> *Dessert Circus at Home: Fun, Fanciful,
and Easy-to-Make Desserts* by Jacques
Torres with Christina Wright and Kris
Kruid; ISBN 0-68-16607-5

> *Everyday's a Party: Louisiana Recipes
for Celebrating with Family and Friends*
by Emeril Lagasse with Marcelle
Bienvenu and Felicia Willett;
ISBN 0-688-16430-7

index

g

Julia's Caesar Salad, page 95, from Julia and Jacques Cooking at Home by Julia Child and Jacques Pépin. Photograph by Christopher Hirsheimer.